It All Started with a Trombone
~ The Hornman Memoirs ~

by Bill Nemoyten

It All Started with a Trombone

~ The Hornman Memoirs ~

by Bill Nemoyten

Edited by Jo Nemoyten

Introduction by Dr. Thom Ritter George

a foolish tree book
san francisco
2012

Published by foolish tree, 280 Granada Avenue #2, San Francisco, CA 94112.

info@foolishtree.com
foolishtree.com
thehornman.com

Cover and interior design by Jo Nemoyten.
Cover photos by Anne Mary Schaefer.
Interior photos by various family members and friends as well as several licensed under the public domain.

ISBN-13: 978-0615731438 (foolish tree)
ISBN-10: 0615731430

Table of Contents

Table of Images

Introduction

Bill Nemoyten's memoirs, *It All Started with a Trombone*, is a mosaic of stories, some personal, some professional, and some philosophical. Those who know Bill will be pleased that his writing style reflects his manner of speaking, dispensing with any stiff formalities. He is open to discussing the low points of his life as well as the high points, of which there are many.

Nemoyten gives us loving portraits of his family members, friends, and teachers. One of his great successes in life is his ability to stay in touch with people over many years. For example, he has a good idea of what happened to members of the dance bands he played with during his high school and college years. It is not unusual for him to track down old friends and visit them.

For much of his career, Bill was a band director. The reader of *It All Started with a Trombone* might be surprised to see how many of his band students, people he taught more than fifty years ago, he still knows today. Bill's stories about his students say something about teaching itself; the greatest reward in teaching is changing people's lives and possibilities.

Bill Nemoyten is fundamentally a musician. His writings tell of his early excitement with music, his involvement with the trombone, his teachers, and the groups in which he played. His musical tastes are broad, embracing both the classical and popular repertoires. For special occasions, he has done a bit of composing, and he has taken pleasure in working with major artists such as mezzo-soprano Marilyn Horne and pianist Victor Borge.

Starting as a soda jerk at the age of twelve, Bill has worked his entire life, but he was never a slave to a particular job. After teaching music at various schools starting in 1951, he became manager of the Akron Symphony Orchestra Association in 1968. With his growing interest in Arts Councils, Bill arrived a year later in Quincy, Illinois as Executive Director of the Quincy Society of Fine Arts, where I had the pleasure of working with him. Although he did an outstanding job in Quincy, he did not stay there long. By the summer of 1972, he had moved to California to become Executive Director of the San Mateo County Arts Council.

In September 1978, Bill Nemoyten became Administrator of Peninsula Temple Beth El in San Mateo. This appointment was right for Bill who has a deep, life-long commitment to Jewish faith and culture. After six years at Temple Beth El, he started his own business, BACP Brokers, Inc., and at age fifty-nine, he returned to teaching public school music, this time in San Leandro, California.

Since he retired, he has hardly given up music! He has continued by working with an orchestra, with bands, and developing "The Hornman Show."

His various jobs and interests have been the core around which his adventures have been built. Unlike many who desperately cling to the known fixtures of their lives, Bill embraces change and is open to following new developments when they arise.

No one can read *It All Started with a Trombone* without noticing Bill Nemoyten's strong sense of humor which sometimes moves into the ribald. His story, "The Audition," remains perhaps the funniest series of calamities ever experienced by a player. Bill's version is only matched by Paul Statsky's description to Bill and I right after the incident occurred in the 1970s.

I have one memory of Bill that perhaps best sums up the spirit of the man and his stories. He played the father in the Quincy Community Little Theater production of "The Fantasticks." It proved to be a role designed for him: he was a father, he could sing, he could even dance a bit, and he had a keen sense of humor. This venture was a big success and a perfect reflection of his unquenchable thirst for new experiences among the arts he loves.

Thom Ritter George
Appleton, Wisconsin
September 23, 2012

Ritter with Bill at an event in Quincy in the early 1970s

Ritter in 2004

Acknowledgments

This project would not have been possible without the encouragement, prodding, inspiration, patience and incredible talent and expertise of my daughter Jo Nemoyten. She is one of those extraordinary humans who always seem to be up to succeeding at whatever she tackles. Jo believed this book was possible from the very beginning and then convinced me that I must write it. She edited the manuscript and designed the format with great care and love. And as to all the parental grief she gave me and her mother Sally those many years ago, "Jo, all is forgiven!"

Since the largest part of this book is a memoir, it seems appropriate to acknowledge those individuals who had a great deal to do with shaping who I am as a person and to those who smoothed my life's road. The following are listed more or less chronologically.

My first wife, Sally, who supported and encouraged me in making many life changing decisions and gave our family a depth of love that a quarter of a century after her death continues to enrich our lives.

Mark Nemoyten, David Nemoyten, Susan Nemoyten Cortez, our other children who have helped me immeasurably to grow as a person and have encouraged me in this writing endeavor while continuing to challenge me to be a wise and understanding father.

Ralph Katz, my Patrick Henry Junior High band teacher who got me off to a good start playing the trombone.

Merritt Dittert, Cleveland Orchestra trombonist and my private teacher who developed my playing technique.

Joe Lanese, my Glenville High School band director who provided me with the model of what a fine teacher could and should be.

F. Karl Grossman, Western Reserve University music professor, who taught me how to be a conductor and did it with so much of the love and joy of music.

Amos Wesler, band and orchestra teacher at John Adams High School and my gruff practice teaching mentor who gave me an incredible amount of conducting experience.

Bill Gregg, my friend, and superintendent of the Boston Northampton School District, who didn't just hire me, but supported all of my efforts and helped me build a top notch music program.

Ralph Gillman and John Mayhew, Superintendent and Assistant Superintendent of the Summit County Schools, respectively, who put me into the position to move to a new and higher professional level.

Eleanora Buchla Kubinyi, friend, dancer, choreographer, director and an extraordinary artist who taught me so much about the inter-relationship of the arts that enriched my life personally and professionally.

George Irwin, the man I have described as "an eccentric millionaire philanthropist" who put me into a sphere of influence I never would have dreamt was possible.

I am proud and honored to have had the Introduction to this book written by my friend, the American composer Thom Ritter George. While his name, like most contemporary composers, is not known to the general public, it is well known to many musicians in America and elsewhere in the world. Dr. George has composed more than 350 works, many of which have been published and recorded. His compositions cover a vast array of musical offerings for orchestra, concert band, chorus, soloists, and small ensembles. We met in 1971 when he became the conductor/composer in residence with the Quincy (Illinois) Symphony and I was the orchestra manager.

To Barbara, my loving wife and travel partner for twenty five years of unforgettable adventures across America and abroad. She has opened my mind to new ideas and ways of thinking and has been an incredible "roadie" to the Hornman.

To my grandchildren Forest Walz, Aaron Nemoyten, Sarah Nemoyten, Angela Cortez and Jeremy Cortez who have given me the immeasurable pleasure of being a grandfather and for whom I have the hope this book will, in time, become an important part of their heritage.

Editor's Acknowledgements

I would like to thank my dad for trusting me with this material and allowing me to publish his work. Editing this book has made me understand and appreciate him and be prouder of him than I could ever imagine. His life is an illustration of what one person can do to enrich the lives of everyone around them when they live by their talent and passion. And although we haven't always seen eye to eye, I never doubted his love and have always known he would be there for me if I needed him, which I have on many occasions.

Special thanks go to Hope Hart Petrie for jumping in and finding all the things I couldn't any more after looking at this for so long. Her insightful comments and eagle eye copyediting were extremely valuable.

Thanks to Anne Mary Schaefer for her eleventh hour professional photo session, her amazing expertise in getting just the right shot and her ever present laughter.

Thanks to all of my friends and family. I've collected some really good ones and I am grateful every day for that.

And speaking of a good one, my eternal love and thanks go to my husband, Ian Carruthers, for supporting me in every way possible in making this book a reality without going *too* crazy. A little craziness helps!

Preface

These stories describe in some detail, my truly surprising life. I've chronicled as best as I can the journey from my beginnings to where I am now and how the path has twisted and turned in ways I could never have imagined.

I was born in 1928, a year before the crash that brought on the Great Depression of the 1930s. I am an only child (or so I thought!) and a first generation American, raised in an orthodox Jewish family in a predominantly Jewish neighborhood in Cleveland, Ohio.

I grew up around many first cousins. Most of them were very successful in accounting, business or medicine and almost all of them stayed in Cleveland. I chose music and that led me on a very different path. Although I have worked at and enjoyed other endeavors, music has always been central in my life as a teacher and as a performer.

There was a time when I thought that I would teach in the same Ohio school system until I retired. But one fateful morning I decided to attend a meeting of the Akron Musician's Union's Board of Directors and what happened that day led to a series of events that changed everything for me and my family. I credit whatever success I have had in all of my subsequent challenges to the fine education I received in the Cleveland Public Schools and at Adelbert College of Western Reserve University (now Case Western) and the experience I gained as a school band director for seventeen years.

I became a symphony orchestra manager and worked with world famous artists. Next, I became the executive director of America's oldest community arts council and studied Arts Administration at Harvard University. That led to a presidency of the National Assembly of Local Arts Agencies, and a reception at the White House. I was the first director of the San Mateo County Arts Council and later became a synagogue administrator. I ran a cemetery brokerage and owned a diet restaurant. I taught arts administration and finally before retiring, returned to music teaching for five more years. Then in retirement, I developed the Hornman Show which I am still performing in my eighties.

My hope in writing this book is that the reader will find the stories entertaining and in some cases educational as it will give younger people a glimpse of what my world was like way back in the 1930s and beyond.

Bill Nemoyten
Hayward, CA
2012

Growing Up

Baby Billy in 1929

School Days

PART 1: Parkwood Elementary plus six weeks at Hazeldale

While I strongly suspect that I learned quite a lot between kindergarten and the sixth grade, most of the specific memories I have were not about reading, writing and arithmetic. Instead, I remember many small and large incidents that were somehow significant to me as a child. We lived near East 105th Street and the school was on East 110th and then two blocks further. Until I got my bicycle, I walked to school every day in all kinds of weather. And believe me—Cleveland has all kinds of weather, from below freezing and deep snows in February to sweltering humid days in the summer.

Parkwood Elementary was built in the 1890s. The red brick building looked pretty old and shabby, and like many buildings in Cleveland, the brick had darkened from exposure to the smoke in that industrial city. The school had four floors. There was a basement with the steam heat boiler, hot water heater and such, two floors of classrooms and an auditorium on the top floor.

My earliest memory goes back to the first day of kindergarten. I met Larry Braun, who at five was far more advanced than I in shoelace tying and helped me learn the trick to it. Larry and I remained close friends for the next seventy-three years.

One of my favorite activities in kindergarten was playing in the rhythm band, especially if I got to play a drum or anything that made more noise than a triangle, an instrument that I thought was kind of dumb.

I recall how we progressed from handling crayons to big fat pencils and finally to pens. We had to buy our own pens, pen points, the strange smelling pen wipers and blotters and learned the Spenserian handwriting technique, drawing circles, ovals and straight lines until we had become skilled scribes.

The playground was a fun place, but things could get a little raucous at times. A classmate named Arthur Bregman was a hyper

Billy carrying his cousin Irving (Ergie) at Euclid Beach in Cleveland

kid. He was the kind of boy who moved about as if he had springs on his shoes. One day I was talking to another student when someone ran into my back and nearly knocked me down. I turned around to discover it was good old Arthur Bregman. I was so angry that without thinking of the possible consequences I hauled off and socked him in the jaw. After all, that's what they did all the time in the movies! I must have hit him pretty hard since what he did next was haul off and sock me right back. That ended the fight because we were both in pain and crying. After Parkwood days I lost track of Arthur but I saw him in Cleveland a few years ago. I was surprised to discover that he was a second cousin to my wife Barbara who I met in California, but who was born in Cleveland. Arthur, in his seventies, no longer had springs in his shoes, or even a spring in his step for that matter. I related the story about our brief fisticuffs to him but he had no memory of it!

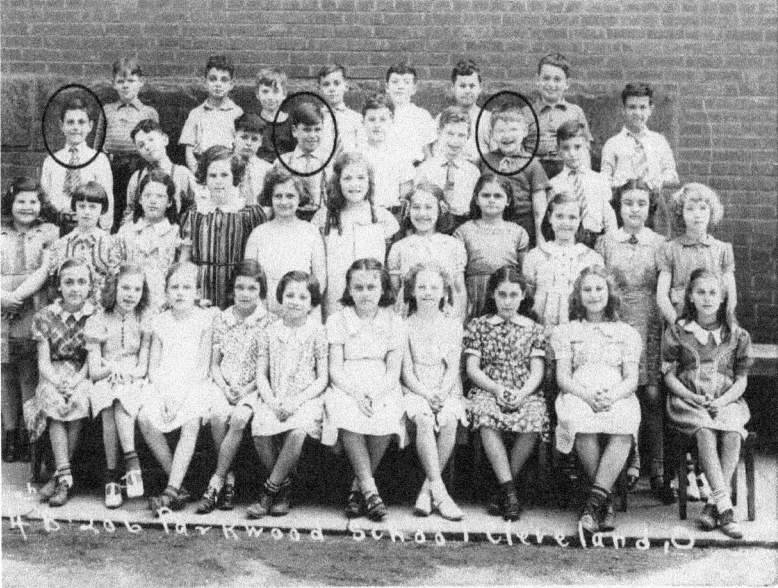

Fourth Grade at Parkwood School
Larry Braun circled on the left, Billy on the right, and in the center ring? Arthur Bregman!

One favorite activity was the annual school paper drive. Yes, all the way back in the 1930s we were into recycling! Prizes were awarded to the homeroom that could collect the most paper. The competition was keen. I was probably in the fifth grade when I recall finding lots of paper and piling a huge load on my trusty red wagon. I arrived just a few minutes before the judging was to take place and proudly remember some kids shouting, "Here comes Billy with his red wagon and a big load of paper!" It turned out to be just enough to win the contest and I was a hero for a day.

In the sixth grade I took piano class lessons. We were first given cardboard keyboards that could be placed on our desks. After drilling on them for a while we actually got to play the piano. I guess I did alright because I was invited to participate in a piano recital. The teacher put me together with Martin Spencer. I remember him and his name because he was one of the two black students in our class. We were to play a piece for four hands at the piano. We nervously sat down on the bench. I played two measures, then Martin played two measures, then we played together. We came to the first ending and the repeat sign. I remembered to repeat and we went back to the beginning. We played through the section again. Then, when we came to the first ending, I must have been really enjoying myself because I played it again and so we had to go back to the beginning once more. This repeating over and over again went on and on for a while until Martin kicked me under the piano bench and I finally remembered how to take the second ending. Needless to say we ended our somewhat repetitious performance to thunderous applause.

Euclid Beach May 30, 1937
Aunt Pearl kneeling with cousin Phillip and baby Allan, Shirley (Mom) standing and Billy waving (during separation)

Sometime in the fourth or fifth grade my parents separated for six weeks. My mother and I moved out of the house on Olivet Avenue and moved in with my Aunt Pearl and Uncle Meyer and their two sons Philip and Allan on Eddy Road. I had to go to a different school called Hazeldale. I have great memories of that school. I sometimes wonder if the teachers were told to be particularly nice to me because of the circumstances under which I was there. I was a shy, chubby kid who wore glasses and had hair that was stiff and unruly, but they treated me with such warmth that I carried that feeling from them for the rest of my life. On the very first day the music teacher welcomed me and asked me if I liked to sing. When I said yes, I don't even think she waited to hear me, but invited me to join the school choir, something that Parkwood didn't even have.

Singing in that choir was a sheer delight. How could I not have been entranced when our soprano voices sang the poetic words of "Deep Purple?"

> *When the deep purple falls over sleepy garden walls and the stars begin to twinkle in the sky-*

> *In the mist of a memory you wander back to me breathing my name with a sigh...*

My other favorite was the musical setting to Joyce Kilmer's famous poem "Trees."

> *I think that I shall never see a poem lovely as a tree.*

A tree whose hungry mouth is prest against the earth's sweet flowing breast;

A tree that looks at God all day and lifts her leafy arms to pray;

A tree that may in summer wear a nest of robins in her hair;

Upon whose bosom snow has lain; who intimately lives with rain.

Poems are made by fools like me, but only God can make a tree.

There was one other Hazeldale activity that I enjoyed immensely. At 3:30, when the bell rang to end the day, somewhere in the school where everyone could hear it, a piano would play the march called "The Caisson Song" and we all marched out of the building to that music. Remember?

Over hill, over dale, we will hit the dusty trail, as the Caissons go rolling along!

I had mixed emotions when my mother decided we had to move back to Olivet Avenue. But I soon overcame my disappointment about having to leave Hazeldale when I was selected to appear in a school play based on the children's story, "Rumplestiltskin." I was cast as the miller. To this day, I have no idea what part the miller played in "Rumplestiltskin."

PART 2: Patrick Henry Junior High

Patrick Henry Junior High was built in 1922 and still looked fairly new when I went there. It was a very large school where students from several elementary schools were enrolled. We were assigned to classes based on our I.Q. scores. The top group was called "Major Work." Below that were sections one through about seven. I was placed in section one. Quite often we had classes combined with the Major Work geniuses. And geniuses are what some of them seemed to be to me. The kids in the top sections were given the more academically challenging courses while the ones in the lower sections were directed more toward trade school types of courses.

About Arthur Goodman

I recall one particular event when we had an English class together with the "geniuses." There was a boy named Arthur Goodman in the Major Work class. He was a strange kid—awkward and shy. He had a funny high voice and appeared to be somewhat effeminate. Arthur was teased mercilessly by some of the boys. I don't remember having teased him myself, but I do remember making unkind remarks about him to some of the other guys, just so I would fit in. That all changed for me when Mrs. Ganzenmueller, our excellent and wise English teacher, chose to read a story to the class that Arthur had written. What I remember is that the story was brilliant and very moving and that I had a new respect for this odd kid. I learned that inside that strange exterior, there was a fine, sensitive, articulate young man who I would never again tease or make fun of just to be one of the guys. After graduating I lost track of Arthur. Then, in my seventies, while visiting my oldest friend, Larry Braun at the Montefiore nursing home in Cleveland, I found out that Arthur Goodman was also a patient there. Arthur had gained a lot of weight since I had seen him last, but he had also gained a lot of life experience. I always thought he was the kind of very bright kid that would perhaps become a famous scientist, but Arthur surprised me again. He had spent his life as a social worker. When he told of the work he had done and the causes he had fought for, he became very animated and excited. I was astounded to learn that this social misfit as a boy had spent a wonderfully productive life helping others who had problems fitting into society themselves.

Sicnarf Nitniap and Nivram Oripahs

I made many new friends at PH (what we always called Patrick Henry) with some of the boys from other elementary schools. We often would bring our lunches and eat together. When the weather permitted, we would eat outside on the grounds and then go for an exploring hike down in a culvert below the school. One of our favorite things to do was to climb down into and walk through a huge corrugated iron storm sewer. That sounds dangerous, but we never had a problem. It was our special place to go and we perhaps enjoyed the secrecy and the remote possibility of danger.

We got into the habit of calling each other by our names pronounced in reverse. I still remember and love pronouncing the names of Francis Paintin which was Sicnarf Nitniap and Marvin Shapiro, Nivram Oripahs. I, of course, was Mailliw Netyomen. Many of my closest friends were in the band or orchestra. Francis was a skinny kid with a big protruding Adam's apple and practically no chin. He played the cornet. Marvin was a very tall pimply faced boy who played the violin. Francis became a very successful attorney who practiced law in Washington, D.C. and Marvin became a pharmacist in Cleveland.

Shop Class

In those days, all the boys were required to take Shop Class and all the girls to take Home Economics. The shop teacher, Mr. Melquist was a tough and demanding teacher and a good one. We learned how to work with wood and then later with metal. Mr. Melquist taught us how to safely handle tools and how to prevent electric shocks when we made our own lamps and were taught to make so-called "Underwriter's" knots with the lamp wires. I made a very nice lamp and a toy sail boat, each out of a block of wood and also fashioned a pancake flipper out of steel and aluminum.

A couple of my shop classmates were Ernie and his cousin Howie. One day in shop the cousins had an intense argument. Howie got so angry he grabbed a can of mahogany stain and poured it on Ernie's head. Mr. Melquist was not amused, but the rest of the class sure was. Ernie was a red head for a while and for many months you could still see the traces of the stain around the rims of his glasses. I lost track of Howie many years ago, but Ernie and I remained friends. His family was fairly wealthy and sent him to private schools. He eventually moved to San Francisco. Dr. Ernest Rosenbaum became a highly respected Oncologist and author with his wife, of books and pamphlets about the care of cancer patients. He was the doctor of Herb Cain, the famous San Francisco Chronicle writer. Ironically Ernest, my old friend

7th Grade at Patrick Henry
Top row circled: left to right, Larry, Ernie and Howie, under Howie, Bill

the Oncologist, died from cancer.

The Zephyrs

While at Patrick Henry, Larry Braun and I formed a club together at the urging of his older brother Howard who had belonged to a very popular school social club called the Zephyrs. Howard's group had all graduated from Glenville High School and the club was no more, but he wanted his brother to have the same great experiences that he had going through Junior and Senior High.

So we formed the Zephyrs Juniors and later, when we got to high school, dropped the Juniors from our name. We met at each other's houses on Friday nights, elected officers, collected dues and held business meetings according to "Robert's Rules of Order." I didn't realize it at the time, but it was excellent training that came in handy many times in the future when I would serve on various boards. The snacks provided by the host were usually pretzels and/or potato chips and the preferred drink was Dad's Old Fashioned Root Beer in the big brown bottles. We tried to end the meetings as fast as we could, because on most Fridays we would visit a meeting of a girl's club somewhere in the neighborhood.

This was a time when girls wore saddle shoes, pleated skirts, and, if they could afford it, angora sweaters. But the other feature of the time that we especially appreciated was that under the sweaters they wore very pointy bras. There were often heated discussions about which of the girls had the pointiest.

We Zephyrs had our own specially designed maroon and white sweaters with a big Z inscribed on them and gold plated Zephyr lapel pins. We even had a secret handshake and our own whistle signal. In

The Zephyrs and their girlfriends

addition to the meetings, we sponsored roller skating parties, went on hay rides and had our own basketball team. One night, I remember having gotten a hold of two pairs of boxing gloves. We went into someone's attic and tried to find out who was the best fighter in the club by beating each others' brains out. It wasn't me.

We aspired to become one of the most popular clubs, but were lacking the most important ingredient—athletes. Instead, we had many of the class brains, who would be called nerds today. At one time we had ten members. There was Arthur Baum, Bernie Rich, Eddy Silver, Herbie Seaman, Eugene Chadwick, Stan Katz, Ernie Rosenbaum, Stan Goldberg, Larry Braun and yours truly. As far as I know, the only surviving members are Eddy and myself. As long as one of us is alive, the memory of the Zephyrs will survive!

PART 3: Glenville High School Athletics

"Tar Blood, Whack Thud! Tar Blood, Whack Thud!" That was the strange but most popular cheer at football and basketball games at old Glenville High where the school colors were, oddly enough, red and black. The cheerleaders would get that going and everyone stamped their feet on the floor or the bleachers of the ancient gymnasium until the whole place shook violently. Our football team usually wasn't very good. The only games we were sure to have a chance of winning was with John Hay High which had an enrollment of about 700 girls and 300 boys. I went out for football in the tenth grade and though I survived the toughest part of the training in Cleveland's hot and humid August, I came to an important understanding of my athletic prowess and lack thereof. I reasoned that I would be a much greater asset to the red and black as the best and loudest trombone player in the marching band rather than one of the worst football players who warmed the bench for the whole season.

I loved to go to athletic events in addition to marching in the band at football games I attended many of the track meets and most of the basketball games. Glenville High was about seventy percent Jewish at that time and most of the families, like ours, were Orthodox. So when there was an important Jewish holiday the school was practically empty.

Prejudice against Jews was still rampant in some parts of Cleveland at that time. I remember a game with East High where there was a lot of tension and threats were made. I left immediately after, walking rapidly down to a side street to get the East 105th streetcar home. I learned the next day that several students had been beaten up by East High gangs including a friend who lost several teeth in the encounter. Our team had beaten East High that night. We had a good basketball team and nearly all of the members were Jewish. They were Perry Silverstein, Phil Kazan, Izzy Orloff, Jason Rosenberg, Al Stern and the one gentile, Eddie Langowkski, who at six feet, two inches was the tallest on the team.

The Teachers

My favorite teacher was Mr. Hartinger, the history teacher. Not only was he inspirational, but he was also very entertaining. He would walk up and down the aisles lecturing and suddenly whip completely around, point his finger at me and say things like, "Mr. Nemoyten looks unusually alert today. Mr. Nemoyten, are you alert today? If so, can you give us an account of the landing of the pilgrims?" He also liked to linger on words that felt good on the tongue to pronounce like "Tutuila."

Then there was Miss Winship, a woman who was born in the wrong century. She was from the Victorian era. We may have learned something of value in her class but all I can remember is her warning the girls not to ever walk up or down a fire escape because the boys could see up their dresses. She also warned them about the reflection off of shiny patent leather shoes.

Mr. Civiletto was the head football coach and our gym teacher. One of his favorite games for us involved the use of a huge medicine ball he called "Blood and Guts." The class was divided into two teams of about twenty each. The ball was thrown up in the middle by the coach and the object was to take the ball and get it past the opposing team doing whatever you needed to do to get it to the other side of the gym. There were few rules and no protective equipment. The fact that no one was ever killed playing "Blood and Guts" was a minor miracle.

When it came to gymnastics I was incredibly bad. I couldn't do a diving roll. I couldn't chin. I couldn't climb a rope. I couldn't manage the pommel horse. I couldn't do the rings. But there was one thing I could do that some of the other guys couldn't manage. I could stand on my head. As a result, some of my buddies started calling me "The Flipper."

Our gym class must have been one of the only ones in existence where it was possible to leave class weighing more than you did when you got there. Glenville High was situated on a city street. We had no such thing as an athletic field or track. Often on days when the weather was decent, Coach Civiletto told us to go outside and run around the block. It wasn't a race, so you could take as much time as you wanted to take as long as you got back before the period ended. When we knew that was to be the activity we would rush back into the dressing room, get some money and stuff it into our gym shorts. We would then run the two blocks to East 105th Street and head directly to Perkels Delicatessen where you could get a nice fat kosher corned beef, pastrami or tongue sandwich on fresh Jewish rye or perhaps buy a nice hunk of marble style sweet and nutritious Halvah.

We had some pretty old teachers on the staff and sometimes they were a bit forgetful. There was Mr. Kimber Persing, the chemistry teacher. One day he lit a Bunsen burner and when he extinguished the flame, forgot to turn the gas off. The class and Mr. Persing were beginning to succumb to the gas but one of the students was alert enough to realize what was happening, opened the window and turned the burner off just in time.

Mr. Grey, the physics teacher was another old man. He was demonstrating the power of an electro magnet by having it lift a very heavy piece of equipment high above the work table. Instead of lowering it slowly and carefully, he said, "And so you see the power of the electro magnet!" He then absent mindedly threw the switch, cutting off the power to the magnetic field. The heavy steel object came crashing down and made a huge hole in the work table!

It sounds like we had some pretty weird teachers at Glenville. But actually, it was a great school with high academic standards, always ranking very well in statewide tests. In addition to the academic subjects there was a great music department with a fine band, orchestra and choir. I belonged to all three. The drama department put on excellent plays and there was a radio club that produced dramatic radio shows that were presented on the P.A. system. There was a well run student council and I was the elected representative from my homeroom.

Changing Times

In the 1950s the neighborhood changed and many upwardly mobile Jewish families moved to Cleveland Heights and other eastern suburbs. As they left, upwardly mobile African American families moved into the neighborhood. The synagogues became churches and the kosher butcher shops were no more. Glenville High was, by the 1960s, a very old building and was torn down and replaced with a new Glenville High several blocks away. Over the years it had many distinguished graduates, but probably the two best known were Jerry Siegel and Joe Schuster. They got their start working on the Glenville Torch school newspaper and teamed up to create the world's greatest fictional superhero, Superman!

Working and Soda Jerking

Franklin's Ice Cream Store and Factory was located at 110th and Superior Avenue, a five-minute ride from our house on my Roadmaster bicycle. That bike remains, in my memory, the best present my parents ever gave me. It was a surprise I found waiting in our backyard upon my return from two great weeks at Camp Baker. It had fat, white side-walled balloon tires, a built-in horn, a carrier over the rear wheel and a big round headlight mounted on the front fender.

Money was tight in our family and I wasn't getting much of an allowance so I needed to find some work. A year earlier I had decided I would make my fortune selling "Liberty" and "Physical Culture" magazines door to door. But after selling three or four subscriptions, I ran out of neighbors and friends and quickly lost interest in the publishing business. The rejection was too hard to take. But now I had my Roadmaster and Franklin's was always looking for eager young sales representatives. So, at age eleven, I became involved in my second business venture.

In those days there were very few laws prohibiting kids from working. I was outfitted with a small but very heavy steel chest, a supply of dry ice and five dozen two ounce paper cups of vanilla ice cream, most covered with chocolate syrup and a few, maybe a dozen, with strawberry syrup. I attached the chest to the carrier on the back of my trusty bike. It took a while to get used to balancing the heavy load on the rear tire, but I soon got the knack and off I went again to make my fortune in the world of business.

After a week or two of sold out inventories and perfect weather (a rarity in Cleveland—even in the summer), I ran into competition and ninety-degree temperatures for several days running. Late on those scorching afternoons my supply of dry ice dwindled and my tiny ice cream sundaes became more like thin milk shakes and were unsalable. There was nothing to do but eat or drink my potential profits after setting aside a few of the less soft cups for my parents. If any dry ice was left at day's end, I dropped it into a cup or bowl of water to boyishly watch with fascination the smoky vapor rise from the churning bubbles.

Though my two ventures into the world of business were less than distinguished, I must have felt a welling up of confidence derived from my growing experience in the work force. When a friend told me he heard that Ostend Drug was looking for a soda jerk, I headed straight there after school. By that time I was a chubby, bespectacled 12-year-old with a generous crop of adolescent pimples and hard to manage brown hair held down with greasy, smelly red pomade or Brylcreme—"A little dab'll do ya!"

Somehow I managed to favorably impress Mr. Shapiro, the pharmacist and owner, who was a tall heavy-set man who moved and spoke in his own slow, deliberate rhythm. He had a quiet, confidential way about him—as if he were letting me in on well-kept secrets. He was also a good and patient teacher. He paid me twenty-five cents an hour, taught me how to work the big ornate National cash register, how to make change, how he wanted his dishes washed, how to wait on customers and, of course, "sodajerkology."

Bill with his mother, Shirley
Age 9

We began with ice cream cones and quickly moved on to sundaes, banana splits, milk shakes and malts, and chocolate phosphates. We only had "cake" cones—no sugar cones. Waffle cones were not to be developed by modern science for several more years. The scooping technique was easy enough to learn except when the ice cream was very hard. When it was, I had to be careful not to break the cone. Like many adolescent boys, my coordination wasn't terrific, so I crushed many a cone in the first two weeks, often having to set aside the remains to eat them later when there were no customers around.

Ostend was a small drug store with a small soda fountain—only six stools adjacent to a marble topped counter. We only had three or four flavors of ice cream; vanilla, chocolate, strawberry and occasionally butter pecan or "Parkerhouse" made up of vanilla ice cream with bits of maraschino cherries.

Something we had in those days that is rarely offered today is the classic ice cream soda, the preparation of which is all but a lost art. Here's how I remember the process:

- Take a tall heavy soda glass.
- Put in a few generous squirts or ladles of chocolate, strawberry or pineapple syrup.
- Add a dollop of ice cream and mix it with the syrup using a long handled spoon.
- Tip the glass slightly as you add soda water, slowly blending the mixture.
- When it's about two thirds full add two scoops of ice cream.
- Top off with whipped cream and a maraschino cherry.

It is delicious, cooling and very filling.

There was an old man who trudged into the drug store almost every afternoon. He would sag down on a stool, dig into his pocket and pull out two pennies, plopping them down on the counter. He would always say the same thing in his low gravelly voice,

"Gimme a gless seltza."

I filled his glass with plain soda water. He drank it slowly, loudly burped once or twice, and got up and left. We never had a conversation.

Thinking of him reminds me that, as all drug stores in those days, we had a small menu of drinks designed to "relieve people of gas" or "settle their stomach." Apparently, some people had an urgent need to do so immediately, or particularly enjoyed doing it in public where they might garner a few words of sympathy along with their fountain concoction. The aids of choice were Bromo Seltzer and Alka Seltzer. As the soda jerk, my assignment was to get one of the large tablets from the counter dispenser, drop it into a large glass and fill the glass with water while stirring the loudly fizzing tablet with a tall spoon. I then shoved the glass into the person's hand before it overflowed with bubbles encouraging the client to drink it all down at once. I prepared a second glass of clear water to wash down and out the bitter unpleasant taste. The other choice, less frequently called for, and even more foul tasting, came from the odd looking bottles of Citrate of Magnesia, a drink I considered one step below castor oil on my personal "horrible tasting stuff" scale.

I worked at Ostend through the end of the school year and on into the summer.

My next job was at Times Square Drug where my pay went up another ten cents an hour but the work was twice as hard. Times Square Drug was at the corner of East 105th Street and Superior Avenue. It was just three blocks from our house at one of the busiest intersections on the east side of Cleveland. Street cars stopped on all four corners. There were several stores near the corner and two movie theaters. There was the Liberty Theater, where I usually went on Saturday afternoons and the Manhattan, which in the thirties presented live Yiddish Theater that my parents attended a few times. Customers flowed in and out of Times Square Drug all day and on into the night.

The store was owned by the three Levy brothers. This was during World War II and the oldest brother Stan, who was a pharmacist, had been drafted into the army. Before Stan was drafted he and the youngest brother Harold, had split the staffing of the pharmacy from 7:00 a.m. to midnight, six days a week. The middle brother Sam was not a pharmacist. He managed the other parts of the store and mostly served as the cashier at the cigarette counter. Now Harold alone was left to fill all the prescriptions seventeen hours a day.

My duties, which were part-time after school and on weekends, were to tend to the soda fountain, haul cases of "pop" up from the basement, restock the merchandise, and sweep the floors. The work was hard and continuous, but I enjoyed the lively environment. On weekends I worked until the store closed at midnight. Often the last two people there were Harold and I. We became friendly enough to use those quiet times to talk about our personal lives. I was fourteen at the time and Harold was about thirty. Working all those hours had taken a toll on him. He was thin and pale. During the months I worked in the store he appeared frailer each day. He even came to work when he was sick with a cold. I asked why he didn't hire a pharmacist to cover some of the hours. He told me that because of the war there were simply none available. I felt compelled to tell him that I was worried about him and that I felt strongly that he had to find some way to take it a little easier. But he dismissed me by reminding me that he had to keep the business going so his brother Stan would have a job when he got out of the service. Also, he was concerned about his customers who needed their medicines.

Then, one day when I came to work there was a sign on the door. It simply read "Store Closed, Death in the Family." I immediately thought that they had received one of those terrible telegrams sent out by the War Department that began, "We regret to inform you..." and that Stan Levy, the soldier, had been killed in action. But I was wrong. It wasn't Stan. Harold had suffered a massive heart attack and had died the previous night shortly after we had closed the store together. People forget that, in addition to the hundreds of thousands of soldiers, sailors and marines that lost their lives during that terrible war, there was also a tremendous toll on those who toiled on the home front. I didn't return to work at Times Square Drug and was very saddened by my experience there. The store reopened several weeks later under new management. It would be a long time before I would even stop in to buy anything.

In the meantime, my pal Eddy Silver was working at Orville Drug. He was making forty-five cents an hour and told me that Mr. Davidson, the owner/pharmacist was looking for an experienced soda jerk who would get the same pay. I applied and had a new job. Orville was a neighborhood store. It was more spacious than the other two where I had worked, but nowhere as busy as Times Square Drug.

Mr. Davidson was a man of medium height in his mid-forties. He had wavy blond hair and wore thick-lensed glasses that exaggerated the size of his eyes. He ran a tight ship. The store had to be kept sparklingly clean to satisfy him. He also had devised ways to save money. The one I was particularly involved with was the making of our own chocolate and simple syrups.

There was a trap door in the pharmacist's room that led to very steep steps into the basement where the syrups were made. Mr. Davidson instructed me on how to mix the sugar and chocolate powder into a large cauldron of boiling water to make chocolate syrup, and how to make the simple syrup that was mixed with strawberry and other fruit toppings for sundaes and sodas. The odors emanating from the mixtures were overwhelmingly delicious! After the mixture had cooled, it was poured into thick heavy glass gallon jugs and brought up to the soda fountain area.

The basement was also used to store a lot of merchandise, some piled precariously high. On one occasion after I had finished making the syrups, I headed up the steep ladder with my two heavy jugs, one in each hand. As I neared the top where I would have to push the trap door open, I brushed against a towering stack of very large Kotex boxes. They swayed for a moment and then the whole stack leaned over stopping against my right elbow.

I was trapped! I couldn't move. If I did, the boxes would tumble all over the basement. I couldn't put the jugs down because there was no place to put them. The syrup jugs were getting heavier by the moment. I had no free hand to open the trap door. In addition to the predicament I was in, I was embarrassed about being trapped by a wall of Kotex. I yelled as loudly as I could, but couldn't be heard. The only rescue possible was that Mr. Davidson might wonder what was taking me so long. Naturally, just at that time, I heard a lot of footsteps overhead, meaning the store was busy. I was beginning to sweat profusely but was determined not to move until help came, which it did about fifteen very long minutes later when I was liberated from my load and awkward situation by a very amused Mr. Davidson.

That summer I started to smoke cigarettes. Remember that in those days it seemed like everyone smoked. Movie stars smoked a lot in movies. Athletes smoked. My mother and some of my aunts and uncles smoked. So why not me? But I think the main reason I took up smoking in addition to trying to look more grown-up, was that I could actually get cigarettes at a time when they were in short supply for the general public. But what did I smoke? You couldn't get the popular brands like Lucky Strike, Camels, Chesterfields, Pall Malls or even Kools. I smoked English Ovals and Lord Salisbury's. Fortunately, I discovered that I would almost always get a sore throat after smoking, something I didn't enjoy. I quit a few months later and smoked a few cigars and a pipe years later, but thankfully never really developed the cigarette habit.

There is one other incident that occurred one hot steamy summer night in Cleveland at Orville Drug that I will share. Eddy Silver and I were both working that evening when about eight o'clock a young man came rushing into the store. His face was flushed and red and he was disheveled with the tail of his shirt hanging out of his pants. He excitedly approached Eddy who was behind the soda fountain. He took a close look at Eddy, who although he was my age, had a sort of baby face. The man said to Eddy, "Never mind, you're too young."

He then rushed over to me and said, "Can you sell me some rubbers? Quick! Hurry up! She's in the car!" (In those days people commonly called condoms either prophylactics or rubbers.)

As he reached into his pocket for some money, I called out for Mr. Davidson in a very tremulous voice because I was so embarrassed, saying to the now very agitated stranger, "Sorry. They are back there with the pharmacist. You'll have to ask him."

He darted over to Mr. Davidson who, assessing the situation, quickly filled the night's most urgent prescription and served another satisfied customer.

I worked on and off for Mr. Davidson for about two and a half years where I learned a lot about business and even more about life.

The Yeshiva

When I was ten, my parents enrolled me in the orthodox Jewish school known as the Yeshiva. I had gone to a conservative Jewish Sunday school the previous two or three years in a large building on East 105th Street. It was known as the Jewish Center, a grand edifice that included a large ornate synagogue, an auditorium, many classrooms, and offices. It may even have had a gymnasium. It was a bright and airy place with both girl and boy students and many women teachers. I mention this because the contrast with my new school was dramatic.

The Yeshiva was housed in a pair of connected very old, run-down two-story town houses. The classrooms, made out of former bedrooms, were small and cramped. The students were all boys and the only teacher I remember was Rebbe Zaninsky. A Rebbe is not the same as an ordained Rabbi, but is nevertheless a highly respected Jewish scholar.

I very quickly learned that this school was on a whole different plain. One of our first instructions was that we were to always wear yarlmukes in class. That was to be expected, but what wasn't expected was the requirement that we all buy and wear "Tzitzit." They are small prayer shawls that are worn over your undershirt and under you shirt. If you have seen the musical "Fiddler on the Roof," you will likely remember Tevye wearing something that had fringes hanging down below his coat. They were Tzitzit, but much larger than ours. Their purpose was for one to always be prepared to pray. And pray we did. We were taught the prayer for putting on our tzitzit, for getting up in the morning and going to bed at night, to say before meals and for a myriad of other occasions. There was also the prayer thanking God for making us male. There was no such prayer for females. Early on we were to be indoctrinated into the idea that we were superior to women.

Rebbe Zaninski, a burly man with a brown beard, was a great believer in the benefits of corporal punishment, which he practiced with gusto. Talking out of place or in any way showing disrespect was rewarded with an energetic slap in the face. If one dropped a prayer book on the floor and failed to kiss it after picking it up, one might expect either the slap or a whack across the knuckles with Zaninski's ruler. After we purchased our tzitzit, he would inspect us to be certain we were wearing them. We had to reach down under our shirts and pull out the fringes so he could see them. I recall walking a block or two out of my way in order to avoid the possibility of encountering the Rebbe on the street if I wasn't wearing my tzitzit.

He taught us to read Hebrew, but the emphasis was on speed rather than knowledge. That was so that as soon as possible we might be able to go to the synagogue and daven (which means to pray) with the mostly old men who attended the services. The Rebbe told us what we were supposed to do and not to do, but never welcomed any discussion about why those things applied to our lives. Of course, as children, we accepted that that was the way things were supposed to be.

My cousin, Don Singer, a year older than I, also attended the Yeshiva. Don was a very energetic and unruly kid. Some of the family would describe him as "wild" and would attribute that to the fact that his father died suddenly when Don was just six years old. He had no father to discipline him. In addition, Don became a stammerer after the tragedy of his father's death. At the Yeshiva, he was a bit of a holy terror. He was always getting into trouble with Rebbe Zaninski, who was constantly punishing him with slaps with his hand and whacks with his ruler. Finally, Don told his mother he didn't want to go to the Yeshiva anymore. After much prodding he confessed to her about being hit by the Rebbe. His mother, my aunt Libby, much to her credit said, "If the teacher is hitting you, you don't have to go to that school anymore!"

I continued at the Yeshiva for a couple of years until it was time for me to prepare for my Bar Mitzvah. At that time I was turned over to a special tutor who taught me by rote to chant my assigned Torah portion, and what is call the Haftorah portion and the blessings that preceded them. I also was taught to deliver my speech in both English and Yiddish, much to the delight of my parents. Although my 13th birthday was on November 23rd, because the Hebrew calendar was used, my Bar Mitzvah took place on Saturday morning, December 6, 1941. Unlike today, when many of my relatives have elaborate Bar Mitzvah or Bat Mitzvah receptions for their sons and daughters in large hotel ballrooms or party rooms, my parents held the reception the next day, December 7, 1941 on the second floor of our modest two bedroom, one bath home. The food, which was of course kosher, was prepared by my mother and her sisters.

Early that morning we were listening to the radio, as we often did to get the news. Suddenly the regular program was interrupted with a special announcement. The Japanese had attacked Pearl Harbor. Our reception went on, but everyone crowded around the radio and stayed there most of the day. We heard President Roosevelt's famous "…a day which will live in infamy!" speech. A cheer went up from our family and guests when the president said we had declared war not only on the Empire of Japan, but also on the other Axis Powers, Germany and Italy. Jews had been pressing hard for America to enter the war because of the sinister news that had been coming from Germany and those references to the places called "concentration camps." Now, at last, we would bring our country's mighty power to bear against fascism. I believe that on some level we understood what great changes this would bring about in all our lives.

There is a surprising addition to this story. It occurred sometime around the year 2000. I had landed at the Cleveland Hopkins Airport. My cousin Violet Sternfeld had made arrangements for me to be picked up by the Mach

Schnell cab company which was owned and run by Orthodox Jews. The name means "hurry up" in Yiddish. I sat up in the front seat with the bearded driver who was wearing an ornate yarmulke on his balding head. I made conversation with him during the forty-five-minute trip by telling him that though I had flown in from California, I was originally from Cleveland and had grown up in the old Jewish neighborhood along East 105th Street. Seeing that he was an Orthodox Jew I couldn't resist the temptation to tell him that I once attended the old Yeshiva and that I even remembered the name of my very strict teacher, Rebbe Zaninski, even though it was over sixty long years ago. The driver then astounded me when he said, "You were taught by Rebbe Zaninski? He's my uncle!"

Bill with Chaim Singer who was his maternal grandfather

I could hardly believe my ears. Was the man still alive? Before I could ask the question, it was answered by the cab driver asking me if I would like to talk to the Rebbe, as he pulled out his cell phone and dialed before I could respond. Seeing it was already in process, I said, "Sure, OK." I was about seventy-two at that time and I suddenly remembered that the Rebbe was a pretty young man in 1938, perhaps twenty-four, so he would now be eighty-four. The driver handed me the phone after saying a few words to his uncle. I could hardly believe that I was speaking with this brusque relic of my distant past. Naturally, he didn't remember me. But then I thought of my one great connection to the Orthodox community and told him my grandfather was the sopher, Chaim Singer. (A sopher is a scribe who hand prints holy works.)

He responded immediately, "Your grandfather was Chaim Singer? Oh yes, I remember him well! He was a great man!" And then it occurred to me that sixty years ago he knew I was Chaim Singer's grandson and as such, he expected me to become another great Jewish scholar. I must have been a disappointment to him.

I doubt that Rebbe Zaninsky had been taught or experienced anything of good pedagogy. He, no doubt, was emulating the way his teachers treated him and then just passing it on to the next unfortunate generation.

The house Bill grew up in
on Olivet Avenue in Cleveland, Ohio

Memories from a Lifetime Ago

A lifetime ago,
A hot summer,
the steaming sidewalks of Cleveland in July:
Sitting by the window hoping for a breeze,
The humid air choking energy and ambition,
The pollen calling the asthma to attack.
The weak electric fan doesn't help.

No sleep tonight, only sweating and dreaming
Of a new place, a different place,
Any place, but this place.

Here's how it was during the third decade
Of our century on Olivet, Hampden and Tacoma Avenues,
And a million avenues in a thousand cities.

The milkman's wagon pulled by a horse
Delivering milk in sturdy bottles
With paper lids pushed out in a the winter freeze.

The iceman giving samples in summer
Before climbing the stairs, balancing his burden
on a muscled and leather covered shoulder.

Five of us upstairs.
Six of them downstairs.
Two bedrooms upstairs.
Two bedrooms downstairs.
One bathroom upstairs.
One bathroom downstairs.
Somehow, we managed.

A coal bin in the darkness of the basement,
A furnace hungry for bituminous
Demanding to be fed night and day.

Mom's reddened hands at the wash tub, the wash board,
and the hand powered ringer, the smell of
Brown Fels Naptha soap lingered.

Escaping to "Radio World"
Adventure and comedy,
Melodrama and mystery,
The beloved Indians playing the hated Yankees,
The news and gossip from Walter Winchell, Gabriel Heater and H.V.
Kaltenborne.
Jack Armstrong, the Lone Ranger
and "I Love a Mystery"
Jack Benny, Fred Allen, Eddie Cantor
Scared to death on stormy nights when my folks were away and
hiding under the covers listening to sinister voices
on "Inner Sanctum" and "Suspense!"

Being quarantined for measles, mumps and Chicken Pox with the red
warning sign on our house.
Mom and dad worried, me feeling rotten
With a high fever, sore throat, shivers, foul tasting cures
And Dr. Gittleson coming to our house to save me every time.
Mom tucking me in tight and cozy after the mustard plaster
And the menthol vapors of Vicks Vaporub.

Growing up in a kosher home:
Separate dishes, pots and pans, spoons, forks and knives
For milk and meat.
Separate dishes, pots and pans, spoons, forks and knives
For Passover.

On the menu; blintzes, kishke, knishes and gefilte fishes,
Chopped liver, corned beef, pastrami and salami.
No can eat pork or shrimp except in a Chinese restaurant.

Going with mom to Leiser's poultry market where
She selects a chicken, turkey, goose or capon
And Leiser kills and koshers it.
The old women singe and pluck out the feathers
And the awful smells linger in your hair.

The schnorrer Rabbinical students ringing our bell asking
For money to spend

All their time studying the Talmud and mom,
Always strapped for cash, never turning them down.

The Liberty Theater on Saturday afternoon.
Ten precious cents for a grade B movie,
The "March of Time" news
And the next episode of "Flash Gordon."
Sometimes if you're lucky, Yo Yo demonstrations included.

Wednesday nights at the Liberty they gave green
"Depression" glass or had bank night when you
Could win a fortune: $25.00; a week's wages for Dad.

It was a different time, a different place.
With some good stuff and some bad stuff,
But an OK life!

A green Depression glass from the Liberty Theater
Jo still has a set of six.

First Love

I was thirteen-and-a-half and in love with Frances Kovacs. I'd seen a lot of movies about people in love by that time and I was pretty sure I knew how you were supposed to feel when the "love bug" bit you. I was constantly thinking about Frances, her lovely face, and those two cute pigtails she wore so becomingly.

Frances was in some of my classes at Patrick Henry Junior High and every time I saw her in a classroom, a study hall or walking in the halls my heart skipped a beat or two and I got this funny little twinge in the pit of my tummy.

I don't know whether my malady showed to other people or not. I don't remember revealing my condition to any of my friends, but I did give a few hints to my cousin Annette, who lived on our street and was a good friend of Frances. If I heard that Frances was going to visit Annette I would find some excuse to pop in for a visit. I recall my excitement at the prospect of seeing Frances in my cousin's house where it almost felt as though I was all alone with her. Not only was Frances beautiful, but she was also very intelligent and was in the class they called "Major Work"— what is called "Advanced Placement" today.

I was extremely shy and self-conscious about my appearance. I was chubby, wore glasses and had an abundant crop of adolescent pimples. For a long time I yearned for Frances from afar. A year or two passed and my pimples had all but disappeared. I had

Bill as a teenager

grown taller and had become a busy musician, playing in several different big dance bands, all of which boosted my confidence. I also had spending money from my soda jerk job and from playing for dances. I was fifteen and it was time to ask a girl on a date. Did I dare ask Frances? Would I be too devastated if she turned me down? Could I get the nerve up? I spoke to my confidant, Cousin Annette. She encouraged me, so I phoned Frances and nervously asked her for a date on the coming Saturday night. There was a long silence at the other end of the line and then finally the words I had dreamt about for so long, "When will you be here?"

Saturday couldn't possibly come too soon. I took a bath, shined my shoes, put on my most up to date outfit, made sure I had some Sen Sen to protect against bad breath and took the streetcar to Frances' house. Of course, I had to come in and meet her parents before we could leave.

We walked to the Ritz Theater which was just a block or two away. Then we had a sundae at a nearby drug store soda fountain.

It was a rare balmy, beautiful evening in Cleveland as we walked slowly back to Frances' house and I began to wonder if there was any chance that I might get a good night kiss. I walked slower and slower as we drew closer and closer to her house, not wanting the magical evening to end. We climbed the stairs to her porch. She moved to her door, turned around and said, "Good night." Then she paused for a moment, gazing at me as though she sensed how much her kiss would mean. She leaned her face into mine. We kissed. Her lips were full, soft and very warm. She turned to the door and was gone.

I floated down the street, my body feeling like I could easily levitate. Frances had kissed me. How could life be better?

Seduction Breakthrough

You may think you know where this story is going, but I bet you'll be wrong!

Let's begin late in the summer of 1948. I was four months short of my 20th birthday, had completed my freshman college year and had found a tough, but good paying job for the summer. I was making ninety-nine cents an hour (equivalent to about eighteen dollars an hour today) spending my summer "vacation" as a laborer for the Cleveland Electric Illuminating Company. I was digging ditches, breaking up pavement with a jack hammer, pushing around wheel barrows full of wet cement and sometimes just standing and leaning on my shovel, waiting to be told what to do next.

I worked with a motley crew of company regulars, laborers and college kids like me. The summer was hot, humid and sweaty, the language rough and four-letter-word-laced; "f*$!'n" this and "mf#*!@'n" that. The conversation was macho stuff about wildly exaggerated exploits. After a while I learned to tell tales with the best of them!

The first weeks were hard on my body. My soft musician's hands bled and my back ached but by August I acquired hard calluses, my flab had turned to muscle and my aching back was a dim memory. I was tanned and as fit as I would ever be in my life. On top of all that I had the raging hormones of a young man, testosterone and energy to burn and the mounting sexual frustration of my celibate summer.

One fateful afternoon in mid-August I ran into Shirley Rollins. Shirley had been a trumpet player in the Glenville High band with me. She graduated one semester later and I hadn't seen her for a year and a half. She was a good musician, not particularly attractive and had an almost boyish manner in high school. I had thought of her as "just one of the guys."

What happened? How had this transformation taken place? Suddenly she was attractive, animated, friendly and, in fact, downright charming and flirty! We talked about our lives since high school and as we parted she said, "My mom and dad have a cottage at Mentor-on-the-Lake. Would you like to come up next weekend? We could go swimming and play some tennis, if you like."

I said, "Yes, of course. I'd love to."

I was excited all week thinking of the coming weekend and fantasizing about what might happen with this new Shirley who acted as though she were up for anything!

Friday finally rolled around. I took off from work early, threw my stuff in a bag and drove to the small town on Lake Erie. After meeting her parents we went down to the beach on that sunny afternoon. We swam and fooled around in the water, and to my delight, made lots of physical contact.

We had a late dinner at the cottage with her parents and sat around and talked until 11:00. It was time to go to bed and I wondered what the sleeping arrangements would be.

Shirley said, "There's only one bedroom in the main cottage, so you and I will be sleeping in the guest house out back."

What was that? Had she said *you and I will be sleeping in the guest house out back?* Yes, that's what she said alright.

What was going on here? I couldn't believe my luck! The prospects for an exciting evening were exploding in my head! We said goodnight to her mom and dad and walked back in the dark to a small older building. Shirley showed me where the tiny bathroom was located and said I was to sleep in the screened-in porch area. She would be in a small adjoining bedroom that had no door—only a flimsy curtain.

I washed, undressed quickly, and slipped into bed in a nervous and excited state. I lay there listening to the sounds she made as she prepared for bed, my mind and imagination running wild. The light in her room remained on. Was that some kind of a signal? The evening was warm and sultry with the fragrance of peonies. The crickets were in full voice and there was no way I was going to be able to fall asleep.

So I started a conversation in my head...

Shirley?

Yes?

I had a good time today.

Me too.

I don't think I can fall asleep. Could we...uh...talk for a while? (long pause)

Yes, I guess so.

I got up, walked to her room and drew aside the curtain. My bare feet felt the roughness of the scratchy ancient wooden floor. She was sitting up on a rusty old metal framed bed wearing a slightly revealing silky nightgown. A brightly lit lamp with a shade that looked like it had come from Woolworth's sat on a chair next to the bed. She smiled at me, a knowing smile, as if she knew how I wasn't really taking all this in stride, though I tried to act "cool" (an expression not actually used in those days).

There being no chair in sight, I stood awkwardly at the foot of the bed, then asked if it would be alright if I sat down. She hesitated for a moment and then said okay. I sat, my pulse beating hard enough to feel in my throat. We talked some more about the day. Shirley told me that her bike was broken. The chain had come off. I moved closer to her by about a foot and said,

"Tell me where the tools are and I'll fix it for you."

She told me where to find them and I inched a little closer. We talked some more. I got up and sat down again closer to her. I could feel the heat of her body. As I reached out for her hand there was suddenly an earsplitting BANG!! It sounded like someone had fired a shotgun into the room. We were both momentarily stunned by the sound and then, to my horror, I realized what had happened. The bed was no longer parallel to the floor. The two thin metal bed legs at the foot of the bed had explosively broken through the ancient rotting floor boards and the bed now sat at a twenty-degree angle.

I said, "Oh, my God! Look what happened! Shirley, if you'll get up out of bed, I'll see if I can pull the legs out and set it down straight in another place."

But she just sat there with a disgusted look on her face and said, "No, never mind, just go!"

"But I can fix it, please let me fix it," I pleaded. "How are you going to sleep on that angle?"

She answered, "I'll be alright. Just go back to bed."

I left her room and returned to my bed, knowing there would be no sleep that night. I was a basket case of emotions; guilt, embarrassment and frustration were running neck and neck and neck!

As the sleepless night wore on, I made a decision. I'd get up at first light, get dressed, fix Shirley's bike as promised, write her a short note and head for home. And that's exactly what I did.

I had intended to call Shirley a few weeks later, but the third week of school, I met Sally, the woman I would fall in love with and marry three years later. I didn't see Shirley Rollins again until thirty-nine years later at our fortieth Glenville High School class reunion. There she was with her husband and some other classmates. Shirley was a heavy smoker. The years had not been kind to her. She had aged more than most of the women there.

She introduced me to her husband and invited me to join them.

I said, "Do you remember the last time we met?"

She answered, "I'm not sure, tell me about it."

I then related this whole story to her and to those within earshot.

After I finished, she looked at me curiously for a moment and said, "You know, Bill, I don't remember any of that!"

Terror on the Playground

This was a harrowing experience that showed me just what I might expect as part of being a teacher in the poorer schools. It happened when I was twenty and had just finished my sophomore year of college. Summer vacation was coming up and it was time to look for a job. I had finally gotten it through my thick head that I must check out the various bulletin boards on the campus. There it was, *maybe* just what I was looking for. The Cleveland Public Schools were looking for summer playground supervisors. I called the number and quickly filled out the application when it arrived. I received a letter the first week in June asking me to show up at the Board's downtown office for orientation and assignment.

I wasn't happy with my assignment. It was in a low income, blue collar, tough neighborhood on Cleveland's south side. The playground was a big ugly black-topped schoolyard behind a dingy old smoke-stained brick school building of 1920s' vintage. There were a few rusty pieces of playground equipment. Its main asset was the black-topped space where all kinds of games could be played. I had a co-worker named Peggy Klein. She was a large and exceptionally strong young woman both physically and in her demeanor. Peggy was a college senior and a physical education major. She knew a lot about all sorts of games and she took charge of the balls and other equipment assigned to us.

We worked well together and the only problem we had was with a group of six or seven high school boys who hung out in the school yard at various times—smoking, acting rowdy and playing baseball on the playground. That was prohibited because of the danger to the smaller children from the hardball they used. Peggy and I kept warning them and trying to stop them and usually succeeding. We had gotten to know some of the boys and learned that their leader was a kid named Frankie who was in reform school but would be getting out pretty soon. There were some ominous warnings that things would be different once Frankie was around.

As I arrived to go on duty on one of those unbearably hot and humid August afternoons in Cleveland, I spotted a new boy with the gang. He looked a little like a young Mickey Rooney, only a lot taller and with a sullen and vaguely dangerous manner about him. He was the notorious Frankie and was batting a baseball while some small kids were trying to play games in the same area. The situation was obviously dangerous.

At that moment I was the only adult on the playground. Peggy hadn't arrived yet and the school custodian, who sometimes helped out with the neighborhood kids, wasn't around either. I was thinking about what I could do to stop the game when my opportunity came rolling right up to me in the form of a scuffed old hardball that Frankie had hit in my direction. Staring down at that ball on the dusty old black top, I knew what the implications of my choice in that moment would be. If I ignored the ball and walked away, I would be derelict in my duty to protect the younger kids and I might just as well quit my job. If I picked it up, it was likely that I would enrage the gang of boys and could be inviting serious trouble. Then, of course, there was also the matter of my own self-respect.

There really was no choice. I scooped the ball up and walked quickly to the door leading to the basement where we kept the equipment locked up. My heart raced and I had a sinking feeling in the pit of my stomach as I wondered what the guys out there would do to me for taking their ball. I ran down the steps into the school basement, threw the ball into the equipment locker and locked the door. I heard shouting at the top of the stairs. My pulse quickened and then started to race like a Harley Davidson going at full bore. The sound of the boys led by Frankie came thundering down into the cramped, dingy basement room. They were all yelling that they wanted their ball as they crowded in around me.

Frankie leveled an icy gaze at me and said, "You better give us our ball right now."

I said, "Sorry, it's locked up. You guys were warned about playing ball on the playground. I'm just doing my job."

One of the other boys said, "We don't give a shit about your job. Just give us our ball."

As they closed in on me I could smell the stench of their sweating bodies. I began to wonder if any of them had a weapon. I feared for my life. Would there be a story about my murder in the paper tomorrow? I tried to hide my anxiety and keep my voice steady as I turned to face Frankie and said, "You know Frankie, since you just got out you can't afford to get into trouble again, can you?" He didn't answer, but took a step back.

During my life, up to this point, I had been pretty lucky. I had been in some very sticky and dangerous situations a few times but somehow always got out of them unscathed. I was heavier than any of the boys at about 205 pounds, but there were six of them, ages sixteen to eighteen, and only one of me. I knew that I really wasn't much of a fighter, always preferring to use my brains and negotiate. In this case, the only way to negotiate would have been to surrender the ball which I knew I couldn't do.

I could feel myself sweating profusely as the heat of the day and tension in the basement was building. I was, by that time, convinced that I was about to be beaten up by that gang of hoodlums unless a miracle occurred. Maybe Peggy or the custodian would show up. They wouldn't want witnesses. Then I noticed that all the boys seemed to be waiting for Frankie or someone else to land the first punch. As they began to talk to each other instead of me, I sensed the right moment. My "fight or flight" charge of adrenalin kicked in. I burst through the group, and ran up the stairs, flung the door open, and ran to another part of the building faster than I had ever moved in my life. I found the pay telephone and immediately called the police.

The gang knew that that was what I would do. They had no desire to get involved with the police—especially Frankie, who had the most to lose. Much to my relief, the gang stayed away long enough for the playground program to end for the summer, a week later. Except for that incident, I had enjoyed the job and applied again the next summer, specifying that I wanted a different playground!

My Mom, the Oldest Shirley

The Singer family must have liked the name Shirley. They named four of their women Shirley and my mother was the first. Her maiden name in Yiddish was Sura Basha Zynger. She was born in a little shtetl (village) in Poland on a date she later chose because she had no official birth certificate. October 1, 1905 was easy to recall and it seemed to put her in the right chronological order in relation to her three brothers, Israel, Harry and Nathan and her three sisters, Jenny, Pearl, and Mildred.

She had very little, if any education in Poland. Her family immigrated to America in 1921, landing at Ellis Island along with millions of others from Europe escaping poverty, prejudice and pogroms. The family settled in Cleveland where the two older brothers, Israel and Harry had already established themselves. They moved into a neighborhood that was predominantly Jewish along East 105th Street, mostly between Superior Avenue and St. Clair Avenue.

East 105th was a street of kosher butcher shops and poultry markets, synagogues, and bakeries where you could buy challah, rye bread, bagels and bialys. There were kosher delis with sour pickles and schmaltz herrings right out of the barrel and the halvah was cut directly off of a big sweet wheel of the confection.

My mother married Jacob Nemoyten in 1926 when she was twenty-one years old. I learned from her sisters that her family didn't like my father, who was thirty-four. They tried to dissuade her from the marriage. I theorize that she was concerned about becoming an old maid if she didn't accept Jacob. He was nice looking, a good dancer and ran his own tobacco business. He owned a car and a truck. What could go wrong?

Shirley as a young woman

In my earliest years I wasn't aware of how unhappy my mother was in her marriage. But by the time I was ten I began to think that my parents would be better off apart. They were very unhappy but wouldn't consider a divorce, which was rare in those days. Perhaps because her marriage was a constant battle, my mother became the peace maker of her large extended family of brothers, sisters, aunts, uncles and cousins. She was especially distressed about her two younger sisters who lived up and down in a two family house but didn't talk to each other for several years. She always remained on good terms with everyone and never gave up on her mission of getting her sisters to make peace with one another, finally succeeding one day, at least temporarily.

Shirley on her wedding day

When I was very young, Mom was Mom, and that was always good enough, but as the years rolled by I began to think of her in heroic terms. One Saturday afternoon when some of my cousins and I had gone to see the matinee movie followed by the *Flash Gordon* serial at the Liberty Theater, my mother was tending to my four-year-old cousin, Irving, who everyone called Ergie. He had been a sickly child and was very frail. As my mother and he were crossing the street, a drunken driver crashed through the red light and was bearing down on them. My mother saw the car coming and had just enough time to throw little Ergie out of harm's way. Ergie hit the curb and sustained a broken nose and my mother was struck by the car. Miraculously she survived with no broken bones, but was hospitalized for some time with several other injuries. There was no doubt in anyone's mind that her action had saved Ergie's life.

Mother could not read English and she was ashamed of that. So she enrolled in night school and studied very diligently. The goal was to be able to pass the test to become a U.S. Citizen. The day she passed that test in 1938 was one of the proudest days of her life.

During World War II, Mom worked in a defense plant doing assembly work. All of the employees in her unit were women except for Leon, the foreman, who was a black man and a very nice person. She related this story to us. It was the last day before Christmas and the employees were having a holiday party. There was food and drink and a lot of hilarity and everyone was going around kissing everyone else—that is, everyone except for Leon, who was sitting by himself in a corner of the room. My mom felt that Leon, who had treated everyone with kindness and respect, was being unfairly slighted because of his color. So she did what was extremely courageous in those days, and to the shock of everyone, including Leon, planted a kiss on him.

My parents fought constantly. When I was in my teens I again urged her to seek a divorce but she was determined to wait until I grew up. Finally, when I was in college she started divorce proceedings. But a civil divorce alone would not serve her purposes. She was an orthodox Jew and had had an orthodox wedding. Therefore she would need an orthodox divorce which is called a "Get." The orthodox Jewish divorce was created centuries ago in a patriarchal society. A woman seeking a divorce has to appear before a panel of rabbis and tell them the reason she is doing so. It is usually a humiliating experience. My mother knew what it would be like and perhaps that was another reason she dreaded it for so many years. She would also be the first person in her family to be divorced. But she finally found the courage to go through with it. And in the long run, it turned out well both for her and my father.

Shirley, Bill and Jacob
August, 1941, Bill ~ Age 12

Although my mother had been in America for a number of years, was interested in improving her education, and appreciated the many scientific advances that were taking place, some of the superstitions she brought from the old world were still a part of her. One was that you should not step over a small child because that will prevent him or her from growing. The only way to correct this is to step back again.

Another—my mother refused to sew a button on my clothes if I was wearing them. She insisted that I must take the clothes off. But if the situation was really urgent and I couldn't do that, she told me I must chew on a cracker or something else while she was sewing. I never knew the reason when I was a child but learned later that the only time that sewing should be done while you are wearing something is when you are sewn into your death shroud. Chewing the cracker was a message to the angel of death that since you were eating you must still be alive!

Often, whenever learning that a person had something good happen to them, she would use the Yiddish expression "ken eine hora," which is a way of invoking a power to keep the "evil eye" away.

About a year and a half after the divorce, my mother told me that she had met a man who was a recent widower and he had an eleven-year-old son. The man's name was Max Robinson. She told me that he wasn't very good looking, but that he was a good, kind and generous man who had asked her to marry him and be a step-mother to his son, Kenny. She asked me if it would be OK. Of course, I said yes, realizing that her old world way of thinking was still a part of her. She now thought of me as the man of the house to whom she would have to go for permission to marry.

Max was wonderful to my mother, and, incidentally, had two other brothers who also lived in their house and for whom my mother cooked and cleaned. But they all treated her with affection and respect and eventually both brothers, Nate and Carl, married and left the house. Kenny grew up, went to Ohio State University, married and moved to Miami. My wife and kids loved my mother and Max, and we visited their home frequently. A favorite time was the annual Passover Seder when my mother would prepare the dinner for as many as twenty people.

Shirley, Kenny and Max Robinson

Those were happy days but they ended when, in his sixties, Max had a terrible crippling stroke. He made a partial recovery but was never the same again. He tried to drive, but one day, after crashing through the garage door, reluctantly admitted that his driving days were over. My mother, also in her sixties, had never driven, always depending on the men in her life. With Max disabled, she felt she had no choice and was determined to learn to drive—whatever it took. Her goal was to be able to visit her sisters and friends, all of whom lived within a few miles of her home, and to be able to go shopping as needed. She took lessons but had three or four minor accidents, including one with our oldest daughter in the car. Mom failed her first two driving tests. But she wouldn't give up and eventually was issued a license.

It was a beautiful day in New York in 1973. I had just arrived and checked into my hotel. I went to my room, put a few things away and then did something I had never done before or since. Immediately after checking into the hotel, for a reason I cannot explain, I went down to the front desk and asked if there were any messages for me. I was told that there was an urgent call from Cleveland. My mother had had a very serious stroke. I took the next plane out of New York. After she had recovered a bit, I took her to California and she lived in our home. Her horrible stroke was one where she had a lot of pain and her mind was partially affected, but she was well aware of how miserable she was. She was not happy in our home or in any of the other places she lived in the rest of her life until her death in 1980.

Despite growing up in a home where my parents argued nearly every day of my life, I feel that I was not damaged by the experience because my parents always made me aware that I was loved and cherished by both of them. My mother was always there for me, a very nurturing person who was loved and respected by all of the people who knew her. I was blessed to have such a mother. She died in Cleveland on August 21, 1980.

Uncle Hy, My Manhood Mentor

Hyman, or "Hy" as he was known to all of us, was a member of a family that was friends with my family as far back as I can remember. I always thought of him as if he was my uncle, but I always just called him Hy.

The Gottlobers lived near us in Cleveland in the 1930s. Hy's father, Alex, was an artist and a sign painter, and so was Hy. The sign painting provided an adequate but not substantial living standard for both of them.

After his disastrous first marriage broke up, Hy became a border in our house. That was during the Great Depression and taking in borders was a way that many families survived the bad times. A year after he moved in, he asked if it would be OK if his son Lou joined him as a boarder in our house. Lou had been living with his grandparents. I was delighted. Lou was two years my junior. We were both only children and loved the idea of having at least "pretend" brothers.

Hy Gottlober
The signature reads "Affectionately, Hy"

Hy had "lady killer" movie star good looks that made you think of actors like George Raft and other gangster types. His dark hair was always neatly slicked back and his meticulously groomed mustache was pencil thin. He was a "sharp dresser" and always wore newly shined shoes. And his voice and personality fit well with his appearance. When he entered a room he was the center of attention and although he could be very pleasant, somehow he projected a sense of danger.

Hy had a strong influence on me, mainly because my own father, Jacob, was so completely different. Hy said whatever was on his mind, never filtering to suit his audience. It is sad but true that although I never questioned my father's love for me, I realized he was not well respected as a role model. So Hy was the one I looked to as a teacher of "manly things." He had a spirit of adventure about him. He had traveled and "been around" and had lived through experiences I could only dream about.

Hy did things like take me fishing for the first time in Lake Erie, and on a day when there were rough seas. As a teenager I have vivid memories of him guiding me toward manhood. He presented me with a gift of a shaving mug, a brush, shaving soap, a razor and a supply of blades. Then he instructed me in the fine art of shaving. And when I was older, he did essential things like teach me how to concoct a perfect dry martini.

But a very unpleasant experience occurred with Hy when I was

36

seventeen and had learned to drive. He asked me to help him out with his Hudson Terraplane sedan. It needed repair and he had borrowed a car to push it to the mechanic's garage. He didn't tell me what was wrong with the car and apparently there was one thing wrong that he didn't even know about. In those days none of us could afford AAA membership and towing services and you would often see cars pushing other cars.

I was to drive the Terraplane while he pushed me down Lee Road in Cleveland Heights, a heavily traveled street. When I approached a traffic signal that had just turned red, I stepped on the brake. The pedal went down to the floor without resistance and my stomach felt like it was following close behind. I kept right on going toward the cars waiting at the signal, swerved to the right around them and made a sharp left turn in front of the lead car, careening almost on two wheels, and headed for the grass on the right side that was at the edge of a park. I finally remembered to pull on the hand brake and eventually slowed to a stop without hitting anything. I was scared to death and told Hy what he could do with that car in very graphic terms!

To support himself, Hy seemed able at any time to go down the street and convince any merchant that he needed a sign or two. Then, wherever he lived, he would bring in the materials, construct the sign and paint it perfectly with what looked like a minimum of effort. He told me a story about one time when he was living in an apartment house with his second wife, Mary. He was painting a large sign on the second floor landing for a local poultry market. While he was painting, several children kept running up and down the hall disturbing him. He yelled at them and threatened bodily harm, but to no avail. Finally, he completed the sign and proudly asked Mary to take a look at it. When she came out into the hall she immediately burst out laughing. The sign said *Special Sale this Weekend, Children 29 Cents a Pound!*

Hy's younger brother Abe was a psychotherapist who lived in a grand home in Bel Air, California. At a certain point in his life, Hy was constantly migrating back and forth from Cleveland to California every six months or so. I never quite understood why he did that but learned the reason later which also explained some other aspects of his behavior.

One of the two things I learned after his death was that Hy never paid any income tax! Somehow he had managed his entire life to avoid the IRS. He always insisted on payments in cash and though he had a social security number he was very discriminating in his use of it. By moving back and forth across the country he made it even less likely he would be found out. Not paying any taxes also explained why he was able to get along on so little money. While I don't approve of what he did, there is a part of me that admires his cleverness in pulling off what many people only dream about.

The other thing I found out about long after he died and when I, myself was sixty-two years old was that Hy Gottlober was not merely a friend of the family or my uncle. He was also my half-brother!

Jo with her Uncle Hy and Aunt Mary
Hy is painting a landscape in the front yard of the house in Peninsula, Ohio.

Uncle Phil, My Gentleman Mentor

Phil Balaban was my Aunt Bess's husband and Aunt Bess was my father's sister. In the 1930s, she and Phil lived downstairs in our two-family house on Olivet Avenue with their daughters, Beatrice and Linda, and my grandparents, Morris and Sonia.

Uncle Phil worked at the Post Office selling U.S. Postal Savings Bonds and sorting mail. Though he only had an eighth grade education, he was the first person who came into my life who I would think of as a "highly educated person." Uncle Phil grew up in an orphan home and was sent out to work when he was thirteen. But somehow he was able to educate himself. He was very well read and knowledgeable in a wide variety of subjects. About five foot eight, he had a slightly stocky build and a large and friendly face. His voice was pleasant and his speech had a vaguely northeastern accent.

Young Aunt Bess and Uncle Phil Balaban looking very film noir

When I look back on those days when I was about ten and he began to take a great deal of interest in mentoring me, it now occurs to me that there were two reasons for that interest. First, he had two lovely daughters but no sons, and second, he wanted to help me develop in ways that he felt my father wasn't able to.

One day Uncle Phil asked if I would like to learn to play ping pong. Shortly after I said yes, he bought a table, set it up in our attic and began to teach me the game. Not only was he a good player but he was an excellent, patient instructor. After a year or two at it, I began to give him the kind of competition he was looking for. But my victories were few and far between. Most memorable was the time he took me to see a professional table tennis tournament which was a real eye opener and inspiration.

Aunt Bess, Cousin Bea and Uncle Phil

After a while he thought I was ready for tennis and I agreed. Uncle Phil gave me his old tennis racket and a tube of balls and off we went to the clay courts at Rockefeller Park. I began to learn another sport which I enjoyed immensely for many years to come.

Uncle Phil was the first adult that I knew who had a personal library. He had several bookcases filled with classics and books on a wide variety of subjects. He encouraged me to read and loaned me books. He also taught me to play chess, another game in which he was very skilled.

Around 1940, Uncle Phil, who was still struggling to make a living, decided to move his family to Detroit where his brothers had a thriving office supply business. I missed him, my Aunt Bess, and my cousins, but I had greatly benefited from the many gifts given to me by my special uncle at the most opportune time of my life.

In Detroit things only got slightly better financially. He was low man in the office supply business and his brothers turned out to be less generous than one might expect. Being a creative person, Uncle Phil took to inventing in his spare time. He invented a lint remover and label holder for notebook binders among other things, but never made any money on them.

His expenses must have been very high because my Aunt Bess had a lot of psychological problems. She could not bear to be alone at any time and had many phobias, like not being able to get into an elevator. Uncle Phil was very devoted to Bess and his love for her was so strong that it never wavered. I saw her for the last time on a visit to Detroit many years later when I was an adult. She was a victim of Parkinson's disease. Her body had shriveled up and she was this silent little person lying in a fetal position in her bed as Uncle Phil spoke to her tenderly.

Bill, Forest and Phil in Santa Cruz getting ready to go on their adventure

A year or two later, shortly after she died, I phoned my condolences and urged Uncle Phil, who was by that time in his late seventies, to come out to our home in Foster City, California to visit us when he felt he was ready. I knew that for years he had been unable to leave Aunt Bess's side and wasn't able to travel at all. To my delight, he accepted my invitation and I made plans for a very special treat for him. It was summer and my eight-year-old grandson Forest could come along.

So I planned for the three of us to drive to Disneyland. My wife, Sally, couldn't get away from her job and she gave us her blessing.

As we headed down Route 10, Uncle Phil was enchanted by the varied California landscape as we passed through San Jose, farmlands, vineyards and the coastal mountains. As we neared San Luis Obispo I decided it would be fun to show my companions the Madonna Inn, one of America's most unique hotels.

We were wandering through the gift shop when I asked Forest if he needed to use the bathroom because I knew he would enjoy a very novel feature of the men's room. The urinal is a trough in front of a wall of rocks that jut out from the surface of the wall. When you step in front of it, an electronic eye turns on a huge waterfall that comes cascading over the rocks into the trough. Forest got so excited that he kept stepping up to and away from the urinal in order to get the waterfall going on and off. Suddenly he took off toward the gift shop, looking for Uncle Phil. When he reached him he said, "Uncle Phil, you've got to go to the bathroom!"

Uncle Phil replied, "But I don't need to go to the bathroom."

Forest insisted. "Yes you do, Uncle Phil!" And with that, he grabbed Phil's hand and practically dragged him to the men's room. I was waiting for them when they came out and I enjoyed the broad grin on both their faces.

The next stop was Disneyland. I took Forest on some of the more vigorous rides like the "Matterhorn" and Uncle Phil, who had been having some heart problems, mostly just watched us. When we came to the "Mine Train" I thought it would be a rather mild ride and asked Uncle Phil if he would like to try it. He said OK and I

Uncle Phil and Forest at the Madonna Inn

boarded one train while Uncle Phil and Forest boarded the one after mine. I was surprised at how fast the train was moving and pretty soon it was careening up and down and taking sharp turns at a breakneck speed. I became very worried about what might be going on with Uncle Phil in that train behind me because of his heart condition. When the ride ended, I stood on the platform nervously awaiting the next train. When they arrived, I asked Uncle Phil if he was OK. He grinned at me and said, "That was pretty exciting. Don't worry! I'll take a nitroglycerin pill and I'll be just fine."

We had a marvelous time and headed home the next day. As we drove north on Route 280 toward evening, it was one of those enchanted times when fingers of fog come cascading down over the coastal mountains as the sun is setting, creating an otherworldly vision. All three of us were transfixed by the sight.

On the last evening of his visit we went to an upscale gourmet northern Italian style restaurant. Uncle Phil's idea of good Italian food was pretty limited. As we placed our orders Uncle Phil looked the menu over carefully and said, "I don't see spaghetti and meatballs on the menu." He was clearly flabbergasted that an Italian restaurant didn't have his favorite Italian dish. Apparently, he had never heard of pesto sauce or northern Italian style cooking. Nevertheless, it was an enjoyable evening for the whole family with lots of fun and fine dining.

The next morning as I took him to the airport he thanked me repeatedly for my hospitality and we said goodbye for what would turn out to be the very last time. After he returned to Detroit I received a call from his daughter Beatrice telling me how her dad continually raved about his visit to California, saying it was the best time he had ever had in his life. Fifteen months after Aunt Bess died, Uncle Phil passed away. My memories of him will always be precious to me. He was my mentor, my teacher, my role model, and my friend.

All About Sally

Sally Ann Fisher was born on March 31, 1930 in Cleveland, Ohio. We were married on January 28, 1951. And Sally died from breast cancer on September 18, 1985 in San Mateo, California.

Sally's Childhood and Family

Her parents were Joseph Fisher, a businessman, and Norma Mahrer Fisher, a retired teacher who had graduated from Cleveland Normal School. They had married later than most people did in those days. Norma was close to 40 when Sally, their only child, was born.

Sally - Age 1 ½

As a small child, Sally lived in Cleveland Heights. Her parents were Reform Jews and Sally was consecrated at Rabbi Barnet Brickner's temple on Euclid Avenue. In those days Jews often referred to the temple or synagogue to which they belonged by the name of their rabbi. The two largest, most influential Reform temples in Cleveland in the 1930s were led by Rabbi Brickner and by Rabbi Abba Hillel Silver, who was one of the most famous rabbis in America.

The story related to me about Joe Fisher was that he had been working faithfully for a clothing store as a salesman for many years. But in the early years of the Great Depression, the owner of the business abruptly fired him in order to give his own son a job. Joe learned a hard lesson; that working for yourself is the only way you can have job security. Somehow he was able to scrape together enough money to buy a "dry goods and ready to wear" store

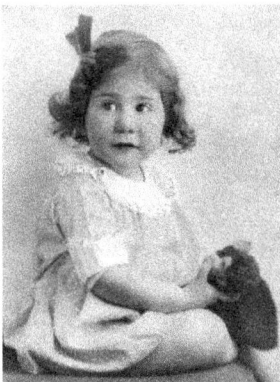

Sally - Age 2 ½

on Main Street in the small town of Clyde, Ohio. I suspect, but have no proof, that some of the money came from Norma's two brothers. Joe actually purchased the entire three story building. He named the store *Fisher's*. It was located in the very center of the small downtown. Joe, Norma and Sally, when they first moved to Clyde, lived for a while with a wonderful woman named Gertude Shell on Maple Street. They lived in two other houses before moving into an apartment they had built on the second floor over their store. When Joe's sister Lillian Kabb was widowed, she came to live with them as well. All four of them worked in the store. One day, on a visit, when I expressed my curiosity about what was on the third floor, Sally took me up to the mysterious room. She put the key into the ancient lock and we opened the big

Sally - Age 3 ½

creaking old door. I was amazed to discover that the third floor had, many years before, been a ballroom, certainly the only one in town. There was a stage and a well-worn dusty old dance floor. If you gave your imagination free rein, you could imagine a time, so very long ago, when the room was filled with waltzing dancers, or even perhaps shaking the whole building doing the "Lindy Hop." I'm certain the Fisher family had no interest in restoring the ancient, run down ballroom. If they did, they would lose their place to sleep!

The Fishers were the only Jewish family in Clyde. Since they ran a business they were particularly sensitive about being model citizens in every way possible. They taught Sally that her behavior must at all times be beyond reproach and that was a powerful influence toward making her the person she became. There was a small Jewish congregation in Fremont, the next town to the west. The Fishers joined it for a while, but gave it up because Joe said they hurried through Shabbat services in order to get to their card games. Joe Fisher wasn't that interested in cards!

Sally - Age 9

A famous book of short stories by Sherwood Anderson entitled "Winesburg, Ohio" was actually written about the people of Clyde, where he was a writer for the Clyde Enterprise newspaper and lived for part of his life. According to Wikipedia, Anderson's writing influenced Hemingway, Faulkner, Steinbeck, Salinger and Fitzgerald, among others. Sally often pointed out places to me that were referred to in the famous book. The most memorable was the day she introduced me to old Mr. Hurd, the grocer. His store was a few doors down Main Street. She told me that Mr. Hurd had stolen away Sherwood Anderson's sweetheart.

Sally's oldest and closest Clyde friend, Emily Sayles Brown, who still lives in her family's old home on Buckeye Street, shared some stories about Sally with me. Emily was the high school class valedictorian. She told me that Sally graduated third in the class and the two of them acted in school plays together, played four hands at the piano duets and competed in "Prince of Peace" speech contests. Sally wrote articles that ran in the town newspaper, the "Clyde Enterprise," and as a senior was awarded the "Citizenship" certificate.

One of Emily's most revealing stories concerned a boy named Benner

Merrick. Benner, it seems, was a rebellious kid. He smoked and was a sort of free spirit who spoke his mind without restriction. Emily implied that Benner often said what other students were thinking but were afraid to say. He was perhaps the least popular kid in school and had few friends. But Emily remembered that Sally surprised her and perhaps shocked the other students when she "went on a sort of date" with Benner by sitting with him at a basketball game. I don't know her reason for doing that, but it seems like it took a girl with a very special strength of character to do something that was frowned upon by her peer group. It was also part of her character for Sally to seek out the goodness in a person.

SALLY FISHER   EMILY SAYLES VALEDICTORIAN

Sally and Emily class pictures
1948 Clyde High School

Emily and Sally in 1975

When I mentioned Sherwood Anderson and "Winesburg, Ohio" to Emily she told me that she was sure one of the stories in the book concerned her grandmother. It was about a couple who had fallen in love. The boy had given the girl a beautiful gold ring as a token of his love for her, but shortly afterward left Clyde to seek his fortune out west. He met another woman there and married her, leaving Emily's grandmother with that gold ring and a broken heart.

Norma Fisher had two brothers, Harvey and Herbert Mahrer. I don't remember ever being told what Harvey did for a living, only that during World War II he was in charge of the rationing program for the city of Cleveland Heights. During the war everyone was issued a ration book that regulated the amount of items they could buy such as meat, gasoline, butter and cigarettes. To be selected for such a prestigious position, one would have to have been a highly respected member of the community. Although I don't remember much about his wife, I know he

Harvey, Herbert and Norma Mahrer

had two children, Sue and Herb. Sue married Al Strom, a very talented furniture designer. They had a son, Peter. Sue died in her forties, a victim of cancer. Herb Mahrer owned a gas station. He married Charlotte and they had

Harvey J. Mahrer

four children. They moved to Florida and then we lost track of them. I recently located one of their sons, David Mahrer, and learned that his father had established an auto parts business and that Herb and Charlotte are now deceased. Their children live in Lake Worth, Florida. I was surprised to learn that Herb never talked about his first cousin Sally to his children.

Norma's other brother was Dr. Herbert Mahrer. Dr. Mahrer founded the radiology department at Cleveland's Mount Sinai Hospital. There was a fine portrait of him in the radiology department waiting room. I wonder what was done with it when the hospital was torn down several years ago. Dr. Mahrer married Florence, who had been a nurse, but not until they were both in their sixties. After his death, Florence moved to Florida. When I wrote her about Sally's death she reminded me about the many other members of the family who had succumbed to cancer.

Dr. Herbert Mahrer

Norma Fisher had several other relatives named Steiner. There was Uncle Theo, Aunt Flora and Aunt Min. Aunt Clara, who had been a single woman school teacher, died a short time before Sally and I were married. We were surprised to receive a letter inviting us, along with Sally's other cousins, to attend a reading of her will. Aunt Clara lived frugally and invested her savings in "Blue Chip" stocks. We learned that Sally was to receive about $9,000 in stocks issued by companies like General Motors and Standard Oil. That was more than what I was making in two years at the time and helped us raise our standard of living somewhat.

Joe Fisher's sister Lillian had a son who was killed in World War II. That son, whose name I never knew, had a son named Kenneth Kabb, an attorney practicing in Cleveland. Lillian had another son named Bob who we visited from time to time. Bob was married to Hortense. They had a son named Eldon, who as far as I know, still lives in the Cleveland area. The only other relatives of Sally who are still living that I know of are Lois Levy Greenberg, who is in a retirement home in Chicago and Dr. John Moses, of Lincoln, Massachusetts who I last spoke to in 2008.

Courting

The first time I saw Sally was at the Hillel House on Bellflower Road on the campus of Western Reserve University. It was September of 1948. Rosh Hashanah services were being conducted by the Hillel director, Rabbi Stephen Sherman. Sally was wearing a grey dress that was modestly appropriate for the occasion. I was immediately attracted by her pretty face

Sally and Bill on an early date

and her shapely figure. She was seated between her parents, and directly in front of me. She was someone new and—I guessed correctly—an incoming freshman at Flora Stone Mather College. I hoped to meet her, but her parents were hovering and there was no opportunity that day. Rabbi Sherman announced that the Hillel Choir would be meeting later that week and invited students who like to sing to come to the rehearsal. When the announcement was made I noticed that the mysterious new girl said something to her mother, who nodded. I made a mental note to attend that choir rehearsal, thinking that she might be there.

I could hardly wait for the rehearsal to see if I guessed correctly—that the new girl would be there. Yes. She was there. And I wasted no time in introducing myself before we began singing. She was a soprano with a very sweet voice and we both enjoyed the rehearsal. Afterwards, I asked her if I could walk her back to her dormitory. It was called Smith House and consisted of a large old home on Euclid Avenue and an annex connected by a closed in bridge from one building to the other on the second floor. Sally lived in the annex. Over the next three years I was to visit Smith House many times. I got to know Mrs. Ackerman, the kindly old house mother, and many of the girls in the dorm. It got to the point where, when I was seen coming up the walk, someone would automatically call Sally.

After a few visits and having lunch together once or twice, I asked her out. It was a double date with my oldest friend, Larry Braun, and his wife of two years, Natalie. They picked us up in their small coupe and we were jammed into the tiny back seat. We went to the Keith's 105th Theatre and saw "The Red Shoes," a great ballet-centered film starring the famous ballerina, Moira Shearer. Today it's considered a classic. After that we went on many dates. One I particularly remember was for a Halloween party at the farm owned by the college. The announcement said there would be dancing, refreshments

Going to a formal dance in 1950

and a costume contest. We decided to do something fairly simple and threw together a couple of hobo outfits. Sally looked funny and adorable. When we got to the party we discovered that we were the only people there who had made any kind of real effort to be costumed. We felt embarrassed until the awarding of prizes began. Since there was no real competition we were given all the prizes! We received two dinners at the Golden Bowl Restaurant in Little Italy, a case of Coca Cola and some gift certificates at local stores. While getting to know Sally, I became more and more fascinated with her background, which was so different from mine. She came from a small town and I was a "big city" kid. When Christmas vacation came I wanted to drive to Clyde to visit her and see what her town looked like. My mother was opposed to it because my 1938 Hudson wasn't very reliable and neither was the northern Ohio weather. But I insisted and went anyway. Sally introduced me to her family and some of her old high school friends.

After vacation we continued to date from time to time. But Sally was dating other guys as well. One of them was Paul Gayman, a fine young man who I knew from Glenville High. Paul was a dwarf! Sally was just over five feet tall and Paul was a full head shorter. I admired her for the fact that she didn't care what other people might think. She liked Paul for the kind of person he was and that's all that mattered to her. She was also dating Ralph Blumenthal, a violinist, who also frequented Hillel House. After Sally and I had been dating for a year, I asked her to "go steady" with me. By that time we had become "love birds" and could be seen walking together on campus holding hands. When I told Ralph Blumenthal that Sally and I were going steady, he didn't believe me and went to Sally to ask her if it was really true. I think he was quite crushed.

During the summer Sally worked in the store in Clyde and I always had one or more jobs in addition to playing in dance bands. We corresponded by mail and I looked forward with great anticipation to receiving her letters which got increasingly more affectionate over the next couple of years. But my favorite thing to do was to take a bus to Clyde to visit her in person. The family set me up to sleep on the sofa which was very comfortable. I loved walking the streets of Clyde with her and meeting Sally's many friends. One summer there was a big carnival on Main Street right in front of the Fisher's store. I recall with delight looking out of the second floor window, waving at the people as they rode by on the Ferris Wheel. Then there was the old Clyde Library with the engraved names of famous authors and poets like Longfellow and Thoreau adorning the entrance. Whenever I see Meredith Wilson's *The Music Man*, I always picture the Clyde Library as the model for the place where "Marian, the librarian" might have worked.

So, what did our parents think? I believe that, although Joe and Norma were always kind and courteous to me, they were disappointed. They had sent their daughter to a fine private university that graduated people in professions like medicine, dentistry, business, law and science. Instead of connecting with one of them she went for a music teacher! There is no doubt in my mind that Norma just plain thought I wasn't good enough for her daughter. My mother Shirley had some misgivings as well. Sally's parents were Reform Jews. They didn't keep a kosher home and were different in many ways from all of our family and friends. But Sally's sweetness and warmth eventually won her over just as she won over everyone who knew her. Norma realized that Sally and I were very much in love and I believe she came to understand that I would always work hard to be a good husband and take care of her daughter.

Joe, Sally, Bill and Norma

We were married between semesters during my senior year and Sally's junior year. The wedding took place at a restaurant called Owen's Plantation on Euclid Avenue. Some of my fellow university music students provided the music and Rabbi Sherman of Hillel House, where we first met, presided. There was a memorable incident that took place that we actually have on film. When Sally leaned over to give our very special friend, Rabbi Sherman, a kiss, her veil caught fire! The Rabbi was very quick to see what happened and put it out. I guess I must have been in a "bridegroom haze" at the time.

It was January and in the middle of a typical Midwestern winter when we took off on our honeymoon at the Cleveland Greyhound bus station to Potawatomi Inn, in Angola, Indiana. It was a rustic lodge with warm and comforting fireplaces and I went skiing there for the first and only time in my life. From Indiana we took another bus to Detroit where we spent the rest of our honeymoon and I introduced Sally to Uncle Phil, Aunt Bess and my cousins Bea and Linda. When we returned, we moved in with my mother and continued our school work. Two weeks after our wedding, we received the terrible news that Joe Fisher had suffered a fatal heart attack. That would eventually necessitate Norma selling the store and moving to Florida to escape the harsh winters. Sally inherited her father's dark blue 1949 Dodge Meadowbrook.

On their honeymoon

Family Life

We started our family in 1952 with the birth of Jo Ann. She was followed by Mark Howard in 1955, then David Carl in 1958 followed by Susan Beth in 1960. All four were born at Cleveland's Mount Sinai Hospital and delivered by Dr. Joe Gross who took special care because of our blood types. I had Rh-positive blood and Sally's was Rh-negative. Luckily, we never had any complications.

The Nemoytens in 1960
Sally, Susan and Bill in back,
Mark, David and Jo in front

One thing about our relationship that I feel I must mention is that early on we agreed never to argue in front of our children. That was very important to me because I was brought up in a house where my parents fought nearly every day of my life.

Sally never finished her college work. She had been an education major and was preparing to teach elementary school. But that really was her mother's idea more than Sally's. If she had had her choice, she would have majored in theatre. Sally had enough college credit to qualify as a substitute and she did do some teaching over the years. But I believe if she truly had a burning desire to teach she would have found a way to earn her degree.

During our time in Quincy, Illinois, when Jo and Mark were deeply involved in their rebelliousness, I was having a difficult time handling the situation. But Sally was a rock. No matter how deeply hurt we both were by their words and their actions, Sally was always stalwart in expressing her unconditional love. When Jo invited us to visit the commune where she was living, I couldn't bring myself to do it. But Sally did.

When we moved to California, Sally got a job working at Raychem

Family at Jo's 60th Birthday Party
From left: David, Sue, Bill, Jo and Mark

Corporation as a secretary. She was well liked and respected by her co-workers and was contributing to our income. But there were times when I became aware that she somehow felt unfulfilled. She was a woman of the age that had missed out on the Women's Liberation movement. I know she wanted to feel like a liberated woman but her background and up-bringing pre-dated that new era. She felt most comfortable on the stage where she could, for a few hours, take on a new persona.

We always loved one another but as with most couples, we had our ups and downs over the years—that turned out to be thirty-four in all. One fateful day in 1982, Sally went to see our physician, Dr. John Sadie, about a cold that had been hanging on too long. As a matter of routine with women of her age, he gave her a breast exam and discovered a lump. After it proved to be malignant, Sally had a lumpectomy followed by radiation and chemotherapy.

For a time we were very optimistic because it seemed like she was in full remission, but I'll never forget that terrible night in bed when she wept and turned to me saying, "Bill, I'm scared." She must have sensed that the disease had returned and indeed it had—and with a vengeance. It had spread to her bones and then to her liver. When there seemed to be nothing effective in stopping the advance of the disease, she tried an extreme vegan diet. When that didn't help I consulted with my old boyhood friend from Cleveland, Dr. Ernest Rosenbaum, who was one of San Francisco's most respected oncologists. Ernie arranged for Sally to have tests and a consultation with the doctors at the University of California at San Francisco Medical School. There was nothing more they could do.

Realizing that the end wasn't far off, she gathered her emotions and told me, "Bill, I love you and you are a good person. After I'm gone I want you to find yourself a new wife." It was very hard to listen to those words, but not as hard as it was for her to speak them.

I asked Sally if there was anything that she always wanted to do, but never thought she would ever get around to doing. She surprised me when she said, "I always wondered what it would be like to go up in a balloon." A week later we headed for Yountville at 6:00 a.m. for her balloon ride. We waited while they inflated the balloons and then a very excited Sally climbed into the basket with three or four others. I watched and filmed her as she floated away. We followed her in a van and picked her up after the surprisingly smooth landing. Sally told me how much she enjoyed the ride and especially how much of it was quiet and peaceful.

A few weeks later her condition worsened, her disease-damaged liver caused her pain and the doctor told us to take her to Mills Hospital. Another awful memory was when we entered the room she was assigned to. It was a private room, but small and rather bare. Sally looked around for a moment or two. Then, with a sense of hopelessness, she uttered the words I'll never forget, "You mean, this is it?"

Her funeral was held at Peninsula Temple Beth El and the large sanctuary was nearly filled. In addition to our family, there were the members of our Chavurah, the Temple Sisterhood, Brotherhood and Fifty Plus Club and some former co-workers of hers from Raychem. I'll never forget how much I appreciated my cousins, Drs. Philip and Allan Lerner coming from Cleveland to represent my many Cleveland cousins. Sally is buried next to our friends Harvey and Lillian Veprin in the Jewish section of Skylawn Memorial Park, a cemetery that I was involved in establishing when I was the Temple Beth El administrator. I own the grave site next to hers.

Sally Anne Fisher Nemoyten
1930 – 1985

Touching the Holocaust

Recent stories in the news about Catholic Bishop Richard Williamson, a Holocaust denier, and the rantings of Iran's Ahmadinejad have stimulated my memory concerning elements of the Holocaust that have touched me personally. I recall the time during World War II when we first heard the sinister stories about places called concentration camps set up by the Nazis. Then more sinister rumors surfaced about terrible things happening at those camps. It wasn't until Germany was defeated and the Allies reached the camps that the world became aware of the horror that was to be named the Holocaust.

After the war was over, sometime late in 1945, survivors from the death camps began arriving in the United States. We learned that some of my mother's cousins were among them. I have a very large extended family in the Cleveland area—a family that has always been generous in taking care of its own members. When the first of the refugees arrived, my parents were asked to house him temporarily until the family could arrange to get him a job and permanent housing.

My parents agreed and I was quite excited and curious about what he would be like. At last the day came and he arrived. His name was Moshe Prengler. I was in my late teens and although he wasn't more than two or three years older than I, he appeared to be in his early thirties. He was cadaverously thin and had bad teeth which made him look even older. There was something of the wild animal in him. He was nervous and high strung. His eyes were constantly darting about the room. At the dinner table he hunched over his plate as if protecting it and had very crude table manners. It took a while for him to get over the habit of sneaking slices of bread into his pockets. We all participated in gently trying to calm him and normalize his behavior.

Moshe spoke Yiddish and Polish. I tried to communicate with him using the little Yiddish I knew, but he was much more interested in learning to speak English. After several weeks he went to work in my Uncle Dave's food market and Americanized his name to Martin. While he continued to work for my uncle and tried to live as a normal American citizen, Martin always appeared to function as a wounded person. His arm bore the concentration camp number tattoo that was a constant reminder of the horrors that he never spoke of but forever haunted his soul. Still, whenever he saw me, either at a family event like a wedding, Bar Mitzvah or funeral, or when I visited Uncle Dave's store, Martin gave me one of his broad, mostly toothless smiles and a warm greeting.

Martin worked for Uncle Dave for many years and while doing so, saved his money. I always had the strong suspicion that he was helping himself to some of the profits and learned recently from one of my cousins that that was probably true. Martin was not at all good looking and I don't think he would have been handsome even if he hadn't experienced the Holocaust. But eventually he got married to a remarkably unattractive woman and they had some children. I don't know how many because by that time we had moved out of the area and frankly, Martin and his family always seemed to function at the edges of the consciousness of my Cleveland relatives.

A long time passed…several years without seeing or hearing about Martin. Then one of my cousins filled me in. Apparently, he had managed to save up enough money to buy a small motel on the outer edges of downtown Cleveland, a depressed area where real estate prices were low. But Martin was in trouble with the police. In his effort to live the American dream of entrepreneurship, he took a shortcut. He reasoned that the best way to utilize the motel without having to invest money in remodeling it was to turn it into a brothel, and that's what he did.

Martin was not influenced by a society that harbored humane notions about the abhorrent practice of exploiting women for profit. Though he had become a much different person than that wild animal-like creature from the concentration camp, there was still a "dog eat dog" part of him left over from the camp that continued to direct his behavior. Investigating further, I found out that he served six months in a minimum security Ohio prison either for operating a house of prostitution or for tax evasion, or maybe both.

His oldest son took over the motel, got a loan, remodeled it and ran a legitimate business. I'm told he ran it quite well. After his prison time, Martin went on the straight and narrow. And although, on those few occasions when I saw him, he always greeted me with that almost toothless, broad smile, when I think of him, I always recall that frightened creature who had survived horrors beyond my comprehension.

In 1970 on a trip to Israel I visited Yad Vashem, the famous Museum that hauntingly displays the world's most complete record of the Holocaust. Many world leaders have toured the somber halls of Yad Vashem, being deeply affected by what they experienced, just as I was.

But, in a way, I was more deeply affected by my visit to the Museum of the Diaspora in Tel Aviv and by what I discovered there. It was a database with the records of where Jews lived before World War II. I found the name of the town where my mother was born, Losice, Poland. The database stated that, according to the poll tax, there were 4,200 Jews living there until 1942. In that year all 4,200 men, women and children were shipped to the Treblinka Concentration Camp. End of their story. My mother and her family came to America in 1920, landing by boat at Ellis Island. Had they not emigrated, they and all their relatives and friends would have perished and I would not be here to tell their story.

During my long life I have met many Jews with camp tattoos on their arms. In 1989, while traveling in Austria, I visited the notorious Mathausen

Concentration Camp. I saw for myself the gas chambers, the ovens and the photos of what took place there. The Holocaust story has been one of the best documented human tragedies in the history of the world. And yet, millions allow themselves to be duped by the Holocaust deniers who have learned to use the Nazi device of telling a lie over and over again until it is believed.

Life and Music

Glenville High School trombones
Bill is on the left, looking at the camera.

Trombone

I fell in love with the trombone when I was twelve. The year was 1940. My cousin Don played the tuba in the Patrick Henry Junior High band. His was an old tuba, all dented and beaten up, an aging warrior that had survived a generation of rough handling by ungainly pubescent youths. Don showed me how to make that buzzing sound with the mouthpiece and then he placed it on the tuba and let me blow into it. The instant the awful cow-like moan spilled from its depths, I was hooked on the idea of playing some kind of a horn.

It was September when I officially moved from Parkwood Elementary to enroll at Patrick Henry Junior High, the school we all called "PH." There was a war on in Europe. The faces in the newsreels at the Liberty Theater were Roosevelt, Chamberlain, Stalin and Hitler. Our family business had all but died in the years of the great depression that had started some ten years before and had continued for us. When I told my mom I wanted to play in the band she reminded me that I hadn't stuck with my piano lessons. She wasn't interested in throwing away any more very hard to find money on my musical education.

I must have pleaded my case eloquently. When school started in September she said it would be OK for me to sign up for beginning band lessons. The fact that the school would loan me an instrument and that the lessons were free helped a lot!

Our music teacher was Mr. Katz. He was Jewish like most of his students, but unlike most of the teachers. Mr. Katz played the violin. He had very dark wavy hair and a "five o'clock shadow" that never seemed to leave his face. He wore dark rimmed glasses and always dressed neatly. He was a good music teacher who really knew his stuff but sadly, in about five years he left the teaching profession to sell roofing material. It was something about having to support his family.

The band and orchestra room was located in what seemed to be a mysterious part of the building. First you had to find your way behind the stage of the school auditorium. Then a narrow staircase led up to the third floor area at the rear of the auditorium. It was hard to believe, as you started your long ascent, that there was such a wonderful world of music at the top of those stairs. I was amazed to learn that many kids went to PH for three years without a clue as to where the band room was located.

There were three small practice rooms off the main rehearsal room. Names of former students, various "artworks" and "insightful" comments adorned the dingy walls. From the practice room windows you could look out over the roof of the building and see for some distance, maybe two or three miles. That was the only place in the entire building that provided such a view of the neighborhood, my world.

One of the most intriguing features of the bandroom was a small and very odd looking door on the rear wall. It was about five feet tall and about thirty inches wide and always kept locked. You would have to stoop down to go through it. When I asked my cousin Don, he said it led to a secret passage over the stage. I remember day-dreaming, as a typical adolescent boy, of fantastic discoveries behind that locked door, like a tunnel that led to a wall on the other side of the girl's locker room with a big one-way mirror!

Mr. Katz looked at my lips and teeth and declared that I looked like a trombone player to him. I was certain he was right. He had a way of talking that made you believe him instantly. He went into the instrument storage room and brought out a very old, badly dented, gray/brown tarnished natural brass trombone. It looked like a poor skinny relative of my cousin Don's tuba. I was disappointed. It didn't shine.

That turned out to be a small part of what was wrong. The water key or what we called the "spit valve" leaked and the slide barely moved even after Mr. Katz cleaned it and drowned it in trombone oil. God, I loved the super refined petroleum smell of trombone oil. It was the perfume of my new world!

I took the trombone home that night, swinging the ancient raggedy case across the handlebars of my beloved red/orange Roadmaster bike. I was determined not only to learn to play it, but to find a way to make it a source of pride. I worked for hours with rags and polishes finally making the whole instrument gleam, only to find that in a few days it returned to its natural state of dull ugliness.

I made good progress through the great classics of beginning band instruments; "Mary Had A Little Lamb," "Twinkle, Twinkle, Little Star" and "Jingle Bells." I played well, despite the struggle with my nearly immovable slide. Soon I was the star of the beginning band class. It was the first time I could remember getting recognition for something I really loved doing. Mr. Katz said we were to practice at least half an hour every night. Many times I would practice for well over an hour until my father would "encourage" me to take a rest.

I began at a time when the trombone was as popular an instrument as it would ever be during the twentieth century. Two of the most famous band leaders of the day were trombonists, Tommy Dorsey and Glenn Miller. They were my idols. Dorsey played a gold plated King trombone that was made by the H.N. White Company in Cleveland, just a few miles from my home. I went to their beautiful factory showroom to buy oil and a mute. The room was crammed with gleaming gold lacquered brass and burnished silver trombones, trumpets, cornets, French horns, sousaphones, tubas and saxophones. The more expensive models like the "Silvertones" with their sterling silver bells, plated on the inside with twenty-four carat gold, were elaborately engraved.

The H. N. White Band Instrument catalogues were printed in lush colors filled with photos of the famous musicians who performed on their instruments. The showroom was bursting with all sorts of stimuli for a young aspiring musician, none more stimulating than the musicians who frequented the place to have their horns repaired, buy reeds or other supplies or try out a new horn or a mouthpiece. Occasionally a member of the Cleveland Orchestra would come in, or it might be a member of some big "name" dance band that was in town to play a one-nighter at the Aragon Ballroom. I just couldn't get enough of that musician talk and yearned to be part of that scene.

Speaking of "musician talk," this is a good place to give you a brief history of the trombone, my oldest friend.

Trombones, in the form of their ancestors called "sackbuts," have been around for over 500 years. The earliest clear evidence of a double slide instrument is in a fresco painting by Filipino Lippi in Rome dating from 1488. Sackbuts look like skinny relatives of the modern trombone and have a much smaller, thinner tone that could blend well with string instruments.

The trombone is the only brass instrument that has an unimpeded flow of air which makes for the purest tone quality. It has a scale of nearly three octaves and a dynamic range from an earsplitting quadruple forte to an almost inaudible triple pianissimo. The slide makes it possible to play perfectly in tune or to adjust to another instrument that is out of tune. It is one of the most difficult brass instruments to play because it requires a very good musical ear to be able to place the slide in precisely the right position. The other challenge is in developing the technique to play fast passages on an instrument where you must move the slide 20 or more inches while the players on all the other instruments are moving their fingers on the their keys less than an inch.

Trombones are amazingly versatile. They can be found in Dixieland jazz bands, ragtime orchestras, big dance bands, salsa bands, rock bands, symphony orchestras, marching bands, concert bands, brass quintets and brass choirs.

Trombonists have their heroes. The first great trombonist who became known to the American public was Arthur Pryor, who gained his fame as the trombone soloist with John Philip Sousa's famous band. He wrote and performed incredibly difficult solos, dazzling American and European audiences.

In addition to Dorsey and Miller there were and are many great jazz trombonists, some with colorful names. There was "Kid" Ory, Jack Teagarden, J.C. Higgenbotham, "Miff" Mole, J.J. Johnson, Kai Winding, Urbie Green and "Trummy" Young and one of my favorites, Bill Harris of the old Woody Herman band.

The great French composer and brilliant orchestrator Hector Berlioz wrote in his "Treatise on Instrumentation,"

> *"In my opinion the trombone is the true head of the wind instruments which I named the 'epic' one. It possesses nobility and grandeur to the highest degree; it has all the serious and powerful tones of sublime musical poetry, from religious, calm and imposing accents to savage orgiastic outbursts. Directed by the will of a master, the trombones can chant like a choir of priests, threaten utter gloomy sighs, a mournful lament or a bright hymn of glory. They can break forth into awe-inspiring cries and awaken the dead or doom the living with their fearful voice."*

My close friend Ernie Rosenbaum's cousin, Howie Newmarker, had an old silver plated York trombone that his parent's gave him permission to sell. I rode my bike to his house to inspect it. He wanted five dollars. I had some money in my account at the Cleveland Trust Bank, but seeing how important the trombone had become to me, my parents agreed to buy it for me. It didn't sound any better than my school horn, but it looked and worked a little better. And now I had the pride of ownership!

Playing an instrument in the band and later in the orchestra meant getting to know and be known by a whole new segment of the student body, and I was too soon learn, some of the brightest kids in the school. I had been a pretty shy child as a result of having to wear glasses beginning in the third grade and always being chubby. But now it seemed like my ability to make friends and gain a degree of respect improved as my playing improved. After a while, I began to understand that with musicians everywhere, respect comes with playing ability. Soon the other students sensed that I was an "up and coming" player, and increasingly, I was taken more seriously in the groups.

Two of my friends—Alan, a clarinet player and Stan, a cornet player, had been taking private lessons since the fourth grade and they went directly into the band in the seventh grade. I had a lot of catching up to do, but by the time I was in the eighth grade I began to get invitations to play in various dance bands. A friend, who learned that I played the trombone, asked me if I would like to join the Jewish War Veterans drum and bugle corps. I was given a bass bugle and had to learn the music by just listening to the other players. That was my first experience marching and playing at the same time and I enjoyed the challenge.

Morty Gold played the drums and had the overactive imagination of a fourteen-year-old about his possibilities in the music business. Though he was mostly talk and little action, I'll always remember him with fondness. He hired me for my very first paid playing engagement. We were to appear at the Elk's Lodge on Tuesday night at 8:00 p.m. I was to prepare the music to "There's a Hot Time in the Old Town Tonight" on the trombone. Morty played the bass drum. There were just the two of us. We each received five dollars for marching around the hall once leading a small parade of people campaigning for a club president candidate. It took about three minutes not counting travel time to and from the lodge and waiting for the program to begin. There was no stopping me after that!

Realizing how serious I was getting to be, my parents arranged for me to take some private lessons with a Mr. Schneider. I don't remember much about him except that he gave me a good foundation and lots of encouragement to build on. I had worked my way up to second chair in the junior high band and orchestra by the ninth grade and had a sense of the hierarchy of "trombonedom" not only at my school, but also at Glenville High and at John Adams High where several of my cousins went. Glenville had a super trombone player named Allan Kofsky and Adams had a virtuoso named Ernie Miller, both of whom, as well as most of the best players on the east side of Cleveland, studied with the principal trombonist of the Cleveland Orchestra, Mr. Dittert.

As I advanced further in my playing, my parents began to understand that something special was going on with me and my trombone. They arranged for me to audition for Mr. Dittert. After he heard me play he said he would accept me as a student, but that I would need a much better trombone if I expected to reach my potential. He had heard that there was a particularly good buy at the H.N. White Company.

It was a Saturday afternoon and a lot of musicians were around in the showroom when the salesman went into the back room and brought back the trombone that Mr. Dittert had recommended. He told us the owner's name was Del Dupuy and that he had bought the trombone a few months ago. Then he decided to enlist in the Marines rather than wait until he was drafted. It was 1942 and we were well into World War II. During the next three years, many of the best young trombone players would go off to war, some into combat and some into service bands. That eventually enabled me to get a lot of playing opportunities that I might not otherwise have had. But I dreamed of being old enough to join an army or navy band, or better yet, be able to enlist in the infantry and get a chance to kill Nazis.

The trombone, though used, looked brand new. It was a "Liberty Model" King 2B, gold lacquered, with a nickel silver slide. It was the same as Tommy Dorsey's except that his was gold plated! It came in a formfitting simulated alligator case and to me was the most gloriously beautiful trombone I had ever seen. I simply couldn't believe my parents would consider buying such a splendid and expensive instrument for me.

Del, the previous owner, had added one custom feature to his trombone. It had two balancer weights instead of the one that was standard on most trombones. Its purpose was to make it easier to hold the bell up when playing solos. The extra balancer gave my trombone a distinctive look, feel and appearance and, in a way, became my "trademark." I was to keep that instrument for the next twenty-two years and earn thousands of dollars on it. It cost my parents fifty-five dollars, a week's wages (or more) for my father, who was now working in a defense plant.

Playing my old trombone was like struggling to run while wearing huge heavy boots. With my new horn, not only could I run, I soon soared to the highest notes and zipped through the fastest passages with ease and artistry.

Mr. Dittert encouraged, prodded and challenged, always handing me assignments that seemed just beyond my reach. He had little patience when I came to a lesson unprepared. When I first began my studies with him he said he liked my tone quality, but I must learn to attack the notes correctly, so my first two years were mainly devoted to tonguing exercises. I began to think of Mr. Dittert as the trombone teacher whose name, when spelled out, sounded like a tonguing exercise: "M-E-R-R-I-T-T D-I-T-T-E-R-T." He taught in a rented studio room in an old house on Euclid Avenue known as the Hruby Conservatory of Music. Curiously, the room was cold and drafty in the winter and unpleasantly hot and stuffy in the summer, and especially bad when Dittert encouraged me to use a full and deep breath just after he passed gas!

The Hruby family was famous in Cleveland. Over a period of 20 or twenty or thirty years there were always two or three Hruby brothers in the Cleveland Orchestra, including Alois, trumpet, Bill, violin and percussion, and Frank, clarinet. There was always a Hruby or two around the Conservatory and often they had kind and encouraging words to say to me and the other students that they could hear so easily through the thin walls of the old building.

Dittert was unique. He had started the trombone at age twenty-six and by the time he was in his mid-thirties, he was a member of the Chicago Symphony under Fritz Reiner. His trombones (he had several!) were all huge compared to mine. He had an incredibly rich and solid sound and played with an elegant symphonic style. Yet, he appeared to be far more interested in his accomplishments as an amateur photographer than he was in being the principal trombonist in the Cleveland Orchestra under Erich Leinsdorf and later the bass trombonist for the great George Szell.

As an eager young music student I often went to the library to find and read books about the lives of the great composers. I studied the schedules of works programmed by the Cleveland Orchestra and came to my lessons full of questions about the up-coming concerts, great guest conductors and world renowned soloists. More often than not, Mr. Dittert would burst my bubble of enthusiasm with remarks about what a phony the guest conductor was or how bored he was with the pieces that were to be played.

He, and apparently the rest of the brass section, had little respect for the orchestra's assistant conductor, Dr. Rudolph Ringwall, who mainly conducted children's concerts and late Sunday afternoon programs known as "Twilight Concerts."

Once I noted with excitement that the orchestra was going to be playing Tchaikovsky's Fourth Symphony, which has a thrilling final movement with great brass parts. His response was "Oh, that old thing again? We (meaning the brass section) sit back there and sing, *Shove it up your ass, Dr. Ringwall* to the famous melody!" Talk about bursting your bubble!

I was to discover after some time that Dittert's attitude was not that unusual. There are many professional musicians who, after many years of repeatedly playing pieces in the standard repertoire, become jaded and bored with the music. The only antidote for that problem is having a conductor who will program new music, but the public keeps insisting on hearing the "old chestnuts." Nevertheless, Dittert as a performer and teacher maintained very high professional standards. He simply knew no other way to function.

As I began to play in orchestras as well as bands, I learned the extreme differences between the roles of the trombone in each of the groups. In a concert band the trombones are playing, on the average, about eighty percent of the time and the parts are fairly interesting a good deal of the time. In an orchestra, the trombones often are playing less than twenty percent of the time and in many compositions the parts are minimal, but when they do play they are very exposed and must be played with great care.

I spent the standard three years in junior high school, most of my time in the music room. I still find it hard to believe that we had a total of five band and orchestra teachers during those years. Ralph Katz moved up to Glenville High after I completed the seventh grade. He was followed by Mr. Gerkowski, also a fine teacher but with a tougher exterior than Mr. Katz. Next came Mr. Morovitsky. Though an excellent violinist, he had no real understanding of how to relate to us, was poorly organized and of a high strung nature. He didn't last the whole year. Next came Mr. Dobkowski, a fiery diminutive man with a sparkling personality and a good sense of humor. He finished out the year and was gone!

The fifth and last teacher was Joe Lanese. Joe was an inspiring teacher with loads of patience and high musical standards. He had the kind of warmth that evoked loyalty and even affection from his students. More than any other person, I was influenced to become a music teacher by him. I was fourteen at the time and he was twenty-eight.

By ninth grade, life had seemed to become one ongoing rehearsal with a few performances scattered here and there. I belonged to the high school band and orchestra and went to the practice rooms instead of study halls nearly every day. I practiced nightly when I wasn't going to a rehearsal or playing at a dance with one of three or four dance bands that I belonged to at different times.

One of my favorites was Bill Webster's band. Bill was a fascinating person. He was seventeen and went to University School, a private suburban high school. I had never known anyone who had gone to a private school. Bill played pretty good tenor sax, lived in Cleveland Heights and had his own car. He had enormous energy and a lot of charisma. I enjoyed the group of young musicians he had gathered. I was the youngest and least experienced, but Bill and the others gave me lots of encouragement.

One experience I remember with great fondness was the time after rehearsals in Bill's living room. There was a record player and we would listen to the latest recording by the famous big bands of the day. We listened to the great bands of Glenn Miller, Tommy Dorsey, Benny Goodman, Harry James, Artie Shaw, Woody Herman, Duke Ellington, Count Basie, Louie Armstrong and dozens of others. The guys talked about the kinds of music each band made and the quality of the jazz solos. Most everyone had a strong opinion and expressed it freely. I mostly listened and learned.

Harrowing Experiences

I had some harrowing band experiences in the brutal Cleveland winters. Bill Webster's band was scheduled to play a high school dance in the far eastern suburb, Willoughby. We were a fourteen-piece band but only had two cars available. Bill rented a cheap two-wheeled open trailer which was all we could afford. In a hard driving, face and hand numbing snowstorm, we loaded the drums, music stands, string bass and baritone sax along with me and one of the other younger members. They threw a big tarp over us and off we went in ten-degree weather during a blizzard. The trailer skidded from side to side on the icy streets. When we arrived forty minutes later it took an hour to thaw out my body and warm up my horn to playing temperature. Brass instruments play very flat when they are cold. I also have vivid memories of being left off on a lonely corner at 2:00 a.m. clutching my trombone and bag of mutes with gloved but frozen fingers in below zero weather, waiting for a bus for half an hour or more.

A favorite place to play was Foster's Ballroom on Euclid Avenue in East Cleveland. One night, trouble broke out at one of the many dances we played there. A group of rivals of those who were sponsoring the dance tried to ruin the evening. We had just launched into Glenn Miller's classic big band arrangement of "Little Brown Jug" when mysterious stuff came flying up to the stage. Somehow we managed to keep our concentration and finish the piece. We discovered that we'd been pelted with condoms filled with raw eggs, a waste of both perfectly good eggs and perfectly good condoms!

A "Ringer" in a Catholic School Dance Band

That band broke up when Bill Webster went off to college. Shortly afterward I received a phone call from, of all people, a member of the Catholic Cathedral Latin High School dance band. I think it was Kenny Kondas, a short, swarthy guy and terrific trumpet player. Kenny told me they had a really good band but their trombone player couldn't handle the high notes in the first trombone parts or play the solos. They'd heard about me from various high school musicians and he asked me if I would come and sit in at their next rehearsal. I had never been through the doors of a Catholic school and the only thing I knew about Cathedral Latin was that their football team clobbered my school, Glenville High, every year, even when they had their third string team on the field.

"Sit in" was, of course, the code word for audition. I passed the test and became the official "ringer" in the Cathedral Latin Dance Band. I was welcomed warmly by everyone and also got to know several of the priests. That experience was one of a great many to come in my lifetime, falling under the category of my trombone serving as a ticket to meeting new people, admittance to countless new places, and a great many new experiences.

Kenny Kondas Band
Bill is highlighted in lower right next to Kenny, standing with his trumpet.

Not only was I the only non-Catholic in the band, but I was Jewish and those were the days when prejudice was still rampant in some places. The very important lesson that I learned early on was that in the world of music the only thing that ever matters to real musicians is a person's talent and dedication to the music.

Among the musicians I worked with over the years, I found most to be very fine people who were easy and fun to work with. But there were those with inflated egos, some temperamental types, and a few that were just plain nasty. More often than not, the rest of the musicians were remarkably tolerant with these people, especially if they had exceptional talent, which was many times the case.

Here are some sketches of a few of the band members:

There was the aforementioned Kenny Kondas. Kenny was one of the best lead trumpet players I ever worked with. He was very rhythmically precise in his playing. He had an always ready smile, laughed a lot and appeared to be a happy guy. But several years later I looked him up on a trip to New York. We met on Times Square. I offered to buy him a drink. He said, "OK, but let me go in here first." He went into a restaurant and ordered a milk shake explaining to me that he needed to coat his stomach before drinking alcohol because he had an ulcer.

In addition to the pressure from his job, there was another reason for his condition that he shared with me. Directly across from his third floor apartment there was a beautiful woman who could be seen clearly undressing every night with her shades open and who often had sex in plain view of anyone who wanted to watch. Sadly, Ken, a bachelor, not particularly good looking and very shy, was apparently filled with sexual frustration—enough to cause his ulcer. I don't know if that was the cause, but I heard that tragically, Kenny died very young.

Jerry "Red" Burns was another trumpet player. Jerry was a large and husky guy. He had flaming red hair and a pleasant cordial way about him. He was one of the best jazz improvisers I had worked with. He had a great natural musical ear and seemed to pick up tunes and harmonies instantly, almost without any effort. He was seriously into the "Jazz Scene." So, emulating certain jazz greats, Jerry was hooked on some drugs, mainly "bennies," meaning Benzedrine.

Jim Hall, guitarist was, as far as I know, the only musician I played in big bands with in those early years who became a big name artist in the field of jazz. Jim went to the Cleveland Institute of Music and studied classical composition because in the 1950s very few conservatories offered guitar instruction. But Jim used the intricate composition knowledge he gained as a foundation for his unique and elegant jazz guitar stylings. He moved to Los Angeles and later to New York where he hooked up with some great jazz musicians. He has performed on recordings with such jazz giants as Ella Fitzgerald, Bill Evans, Art Farmer and Paul Desmond. No listing of the great jazz guitarists of the twentieth century would be complete without the name Jim Hall.

My son Mark was very impressed when I told him I had played in bands with the Jim, so when he was to appear at the Keystone in San Francisco's North Beach several years ago, we went there to catch the show with his great quartet. I hadn't seen Jim for at least thirty years and that was back in Cleveland. During the break we approached the stage. I looked up at him and all I said was "Jim."

He gazed at me for a moment with a puzzled expression, then, with a sunny smile of recognition, he pointed his finger at me and just said, "Trombone." We had a great reunion talking about the old days and the bands we played in half a lifetime ago. Jim Hall, now over eighty years old, is still performing.

Playing in Orchestras

I remember that my first orchestral trombone experience was with the student orchestra of the Cleveland Institute of Music when we performed Beethoven's First Symphony. I also played in our school orchestra and was selected to be the first trombonist in the Cleveland all-city high school orchestra where, among other selections, we performed Beethoven's Leonore Overture Number 3.

Later, while attending college, I played in the Cleveland Philharmonic, an excellent semi-pro orchestra not to be confused with the famous Cleveland Orchestra. The Philharmonic played many great orchestral standard works and gave me much orchestral experience, mainly benefiting from playing with excellent musicians.

The part about orchestra playing that I didn't enjoy was counting rests, especially during rehearsals. We would count as many as one hundred or more measures of rests, often at a very slow tempo such as; 1-2-3-4, 2-2-3-4, 3-2-3-4 continuing in the same pattern to perhaps 105-2-3-4, 106-2-3-4, lift our horns to make our entrance only to have the conductor stop just short by a measure and start again at the very beginning. In the middle of the rest counting, if you lost your concentration for a moment, you lost the count. Or you would look over to the person next to you who was also counting and discover that you were on measure ninety-five and they were on ninety-four! Neither of you knew who was correct, and on measure ninety-nine you were to make a confident double forte entrance that signaled the climax of the piece. It was at those moments, even though I absolutely adored the music, that I began to understand that symphony orchestra playing was not for me. I simply resented the precious time spent doing nothing but counting rests while others played their hearts out. I felt there was something better I could do with my life.

The War Years (1941-1945)

During the war years I played at war bond rallies and for various patriotic functions. My absolute favorite was playing at dances for soldiers and sailors and marines who were on leave at the so called "canteens." St. John's Canteen was located in downtown Cleveland in the elegant recreation hall of St. John's Cathedral, home of the Cleveland Catholic Diocese.

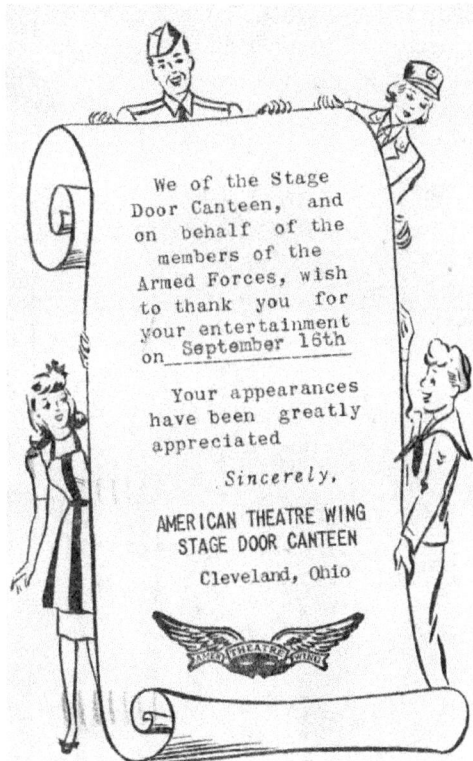

We of the Stage Door Canteen, and on behalf of the members of the Armed Forces, wish to thank you for your entertainment on September 16th

Your appearances have been greatly appreciated

Sincerely,

AMERICAN THEATRE WING STAGE DOOR CANTEEN

Cleveland, Ohio

Thank-you postcard to Bill for playing at the Stage Door Canteen in Cleveland

During the Christmas season the hall was decorated with colored twinkling lights and a huge splendidly adorned tree. A warm and welcoming fireplace greeted the servicemen on those frosty evenings. Lovely women volunteer hostesses greeted and danced with them. The band was always treated wonderfully and invited to enjoy whatever food was set out. There was something magical about the whole scene that still, after 60 sixty years, gives me a warm feeling!

We also performed at the "Stage Door Canteen." It was next to the Palace Theater, one of Cleveland's fine old movie palaces. During those days the big "name" bands would put on a show for about ninety minutes then volunteer their services and play for an hour at the canteen while the feature film was on at the theater. We would always arrive very early in order to hear the great bands for free and in order to mingle with their musicians as they were leaving for the next show at the Palace as we were setting up to continue the entertainment at the canteen.

Bill Nemoyten and His Band

In 1946, when I was a high school junior, I was elected to the Glenville High School student council as the representative from my homeroom. I enjoyed my first political experience and saw an interesting opportunity arise. The student council had some funds available and they wanted to sponsor some school dances during the year with live music, if possible. At the same time I took note of the fine group of musicians we had available at Glenville

Bill Nemoyten and his band

The GLENVILLE TORCH

Vol. XXVI—No. 14　　　GLENVILLE HIGH SCHOOL, Cleveland 8, O., March 1, 1946　　　Price 10 Cents

Proposed School Band To Play At All Student Council Affairs

Bill Nemoyten Leads Fourteen Piece Band; Council Appropriates Money for Orchestrations

A tentative plan for a council band has been proposed by Bill Nemoyten. The outline, which includes a band for all Student Council affairs, has been brought before this body. At the Council meeting on February 12, the project received a vote of confidence with only three representatives opposed. If such a project were to be established, the members would be giving service to the school, and at the same time, be receiving publicity and valuable band experience.

Although most of the plans are indefinite, Bill Nemoyten, who will probably be the leader, stated that "the band will contain approximately fourteen members, who have been handpicked, since no auditions were held."

As far as known, the fourteen will include: John Cloud, guitar; Orville Johnson, piano; Elliot Beskin, drummer; Bill Nemoyten and Al Weiner, trombones; Shirley Robbins, the only girl member of the troupe, with Stanley Goldberg and Chuck Vance will play the trumpet.

The "sax" will be played by Jimmy Griffith, Ronnie Rosenberg, Bill Stein, Dick Wengel, and Dick Webb. The vocalist will be Elliot Beskin, who will sing novelty numbers.

The Glenville High School Band

At a recent Student Council meeting, it was decided to make an oppropriation to the band for five orchestrations, so that the band might start practicing immediately. The five selections purchased were "Robin Hood," "Blue Flame," "Symphony," "Autumn Serenade," and "Along the Navajo Trail." The band will be permitted to keep all of the music that the Student Council provides.

According to Bill, they hope to be able to play their five pieces at the first Student Council affair. The group would like to practice in the Auditorium for two and a half hours during the week, but if this is impossible their second choice would be the Social Room.

If the band is successful in the opinion of the student body, it will continue to receive appropriations totaling $20.00 from the Council for necessary band equipment, such as front stands, mutes, sheet music, etc.

Later, if the band proves to be an aid to the success of the Student Council affairs, the addition of another vocalist will be considered.

and was sure I could use the experience I had gained to organize a good dance band of our own. All we would need was enough money to buy twenty band arrangements and a set of big band style music stands. I did some political lobbying groundwork before I brought up my proposal to the council and they approved the expenditure of about fifty dollars, as I recall.

That was in January. We were to play our first dance in April. I put together a group of four saxes, three trumpets, two trombones (including myself), piano and drums. Most had no dance band experience, but they were all good, or potentially good musicians in my mind. The only photo I have of the band was one where I had to replace three of the brass players who couldn't attend this particular dance with members of the Cathedral Latin H.S. dance band. I am proud to note that the band was fully integrated way back in 1946. In addition to the two black members, one of the regular members not pictured, were excellent girl trumpet players.

I felt I had arrived, at least as a well-known, if not socially popular student, when the Glenville Torch, our student newspaper, ran the headline on page one "Bill Nemoyten Leads Fourteen Piece Band." We rehearsed after school once or twice a week and it started to come together pretty well by March. The day of the dance was fast approaching and we had all twenty pieces in pretty good shape. I was getting very excited and so were all of the band members.

During that period I had begun to have a problem with a pilonidal cyst

High School Graduation Day

Marvin Shapiro, Bill, Larry Braun, Art Baum

Bill coming home with his diploma

Marvin, Bill, Natalie and Larry in 1997

on the base of my spine which had become infected, was very painful and needed to be lanced and drained once or twice. I thought the problem had gone away but it suddenly became very painful the week of the dance. I couldn't get an appointment to get it treated until 1:00 p.m. on the day of the dance. After the painful lancing the doctor put extra bandages on when I told him what I was going to be doing later that day. I got to school on time over the objections of my mother who was understandably very concerned. The band was a big hit and though in some discomfort, I lead the band, standing the whole time and playing my solos pretty well. I was simply too much involved in the whole experience to let anything distract me. When I got home I discovered that I had given up a lot of blood to those bandages and that some of it had soaked through to the back of my pants! Several months later I underwent the major surgery that would cure the problem, once and for all.

An Opportunity to Go on the Road

During the summer after graduation from high school I was invited to an audition for a dance band that was planning to "go on the road" along with Norm Strachan, a sax player who had graduated from Glenville a year earlier. The leader had been a member of some "name bands" but now wanted to strike out on his own. After the rehearsal he offered both Norm and I positions in his band and said we would be leaving in a couple of weeks. Norm accepted immediately, but although the idea of traveling around the country with a band, any band, was exciting to this eighteen-year-old, I said I'd like to think it over for a day or two. That was on a Tuesday. On Thursday a letter arrived from the admissions office of Western Reserve University stating that I had been accepted as a music education student at Adelbert College. At that moment I made a decision that would impact the rest of my life in many positive ways. But beyond the obvious reasons for choosing college over the "road," I suppose I had something to prove to myself as well as to the misguided guidance counselor, Miss Bushman, at Glenville High who told me my grades were not good enough to get into Western Reserve University, much less expect to graduate from such a fine institution.

I was to learn in a very dramatic way some years later that I had taken the right path. From time to time I heard about Norm Strachan as he toured the country and changed bands a few times. Once I even heard his name announced on the radio when, to my astonishment, he sang a novelty song with the band. At that moment I felt a twinge of regret that I wasn't in on the fun and glamour.

It was fairly common at the time to hear radio broadcasts, such as "And now ladies and gentlemen the Mutual Network brings you the Rippling Rhythms of Blue Baron and his orchestra from the Starlight Room high atop the Blackstone Hotel in Downtown Chicago" Then, for a long time I heard nothing about Norm until one day I met him at Local 4 of the musicians union in Cleveland. He related to me sadly that he had been on the road for ten years and had nothing to show for it but a few laughs and memories. The big band business had all but died. He had no education beyond high school. All of his friends were married, had good jobs, kids and their own homes. He was nearly thirty and had to start all over with his adult life.

College Days

College seemed like a continuation of high school at first. I was just taking a different bus. Later I found out how vastly different it was. It seemed that the university's mission was to convince me of how little I knew about the world, how much there was to learn and to instill in me a lifelong desire to learn. I like to think that they succeeded in that mission. Western Reserve (now Case Western Reserve University) is a private school and tuition was expensive. But I could afford it because I lived at home, earned money playing in dance bands, worked other jobs during the school year and during summer vacation and received some help from my parents when and if I really needed it. The music department was very small and was mainly located in an old house on Bellflower Road where most of the fraternity houses stood. It looked like it was built in the 1920s with a big front porch and several gables slanting this way and that. A few classes, the university band and other ensembles met in Harkness Chapel, an ancient ivy covered stone building that looked like it belonged in the old British film "Goodbye, Mr. Chips."

But I mostly remember Harkness because that's where the faculty and student recitals took place. Although we were not required to attend all of the programs the way many music schools do today, we soon learned that those recitals were an essential part of our education as musicians and were not to be missed. Harkness had a fine organ, a superb nine foot Steinway grand piano, excellent acoustics and incredibly uncomfortable church pews that prevented one from falling asleep during adagio and pianissimo passages. There were countless piano and organ recitals, string solos and ensembles, woodwind quintets, vocal solos, choirs, orchestra and concert band performances. The faculty had a "Collegium Musicum" ensemble that performed ancient music on ancient instruments; a harpsichord, viola da gamba and a viola da amore that I especially remember because it was owned and played by Dr. F. Karl Grossman, my favorite professor, and because it had a beautifully carved golden cherub as it's scroll.

The total music experience of the recitals at Harkness and other campus venues covered a five-hundred-year year span in the history of musical styles and forms. The quality ranged from good student work to top professional performances. I came to understand that attending those recitals was an integral part of learning what music was all about in order to become a more complete musician.

Often on Friday afternoons an announcement was posted on the music department bulletin board stating that there were free tickets to Cleveland Orchestra concerts available to us. They were nearly always for box seats where the wealthiest patrons sat, but chose not to attend because there was a guest conductor or a soloist that didn't have a big important name. We students would dress up in our finest clothes, bring our dates and imagine for two hours that we were also wealthy patrons of the orchestra. We were extremely fortunate to have that experience. Severance Hall, which is on the campus of the university and the exquisite home of the Cleveland Orchestra, is an aesthetic and acoustical wonder. Many of the world's great artists were the soloists and the orchestra was superb. Cleveland's orchestra was, and I believe still is, considered to be one of America's "Big Five" orchestras along with the Boston, New York, Philadelphia and Chicago symphonies. Actually, I believe there should today be at least a big six that would include the San Francisco Symphony!

The "Murder of Us All"

I believe it was in 1950 or 51 that the university music department, along with the drama department, produced the relatively new American opera "The Mother of Us All." It had been written five or six years earlier by the colorful author Gertrude Stein, with music by the well-known American composer Virgil Thompson. It was based loosely on the life of Susan B. Anthony, the famous woman who led the fight for the right of women to vote during the nineteenth century.

Most of the student performers hated the strange opera and so they dubbed it the "Murder of Us All." Virgil Thompson came to Cleveland to see the performance and was interviewed by the local music critics who made quite a fuss about him prior to the first performance. I was a member of the pit orchestra and the performance was at Severance Hall. In a scene near the end of the opera there was a solo for trombone accompanied by strings. It was written very high and was to be played softly. It was one of the greatest challenges I ever had as a trombonist. Not only was there a full house for the performance but the famous composer himself was in the audience! One cracked note would spoil the effect of the scene. Though I was a little shaky during the dress rehearsal, I played the solo perfectly at the performance. What a relief!

In the Cleveland Press and the Plain Dealer newspapers the next day the critics agreed. They hated the opera, but the performance was excellent. Virgil Thompson left town in a huff!

The Western University Band

At the beginning of my freshman year I signed up as a member of the university band, which rehearsed in what was called the "broadcast room" at Severance Hall. I presume that was because the room was used for some kind of radio broadcasts by the orchestra many years before in the "golden days" of radio. When I arrived for the first rehearsal I discovered that the band already had eight trombones, six of whom were seniors. I wasn't happy about the prospect of sitting at the end of the section playing the usually boring third trombone parts, especially because I thought of myself as a "hotshot" player who was one of the best to come out of a Cleveland school and had been seated in the first chair in my school bands from the ninth grade through high school.

I noticed, however, that there were only two rather weak baritone horn players in the band. I asked the director, Mr. Grant, who had been the conductor of the Cleveland Institute of Music student orchestra when I played there, if I could have the use of a baritone horn and join that section. He agreed and I began to teach myself the baritone. What I discovered very quickly was that there was an equivalent fingering for each slide position on the trombone. Notes in first position are played with no keys down, notes in second position with the second key down, notes in third position with the first key down, etc. I also gained an appreciation for the fine band parts that the baritone often played in the concert band. When we played music that had originally been written for an orchestra, the baritone played the cello part. Learning to play the baritone gave me a foundation in brass instrument fingering technique that helped later when I took up the trumpet, French horn and tuba, all of which I still play today. Later in that school year I had become the first chair baritone player and had many challenging solo passages to play. Neither Mr. Grant nor I were very happy with the dented old school-owned baritone I was issued. So one day he surprised and delighted me with a brand new university-purchased burnished silver King baritone. I showed my gratitude to him by volunteering to become the band librarian, not expecting the bonus that doing so would soon afford me.

The band library was in a back room off the broadcast room at Severance, where we rehearsed. It was reached by an elevator to the third floor. The security guard knew me after a while and I was admitted automatically. One day while working on the library by myself I saw a door at the back of the storage room that I had not taken notice of before. I tried the handle. The door opened and I found myself in the upper balcony of the hall. The Cleveland Orchestra was rehearsing under their famously austere conductor, George Szell. I immediately went down to my knees and crawled to the center of the balcony behind a barrier that hid me from the view of anyone who was on the stage. There I sat, entranced for the next two hours, observing the rehearsal technique of one of the greatest conductors in the world. I was to continue my visits to those rehearsals for the rest of that school year, undoubtedly hurting my grade point average! The maestro always wore a short-sleeved maroon sweater over his shirt as he relentlessly rehearsed the orchestra for greater and greater precision and balance. At that time the orchestra under Szell put out an enormous volume of great recordings, many of which are considered among the best ever by any orchestra.

Many years have passed and I have had the privilege of hearing, among others, the St. Louis Symphony under Walter Susskind, the Pittsburgh Symphony under William Steinberg, the Chicago Symphony guest conducted by Leopold Stokowski and the Orchestra de la Scala in Milan, Italy. This larger perspective has made me realize that the clean and absolutely precise playing by the Cleveland Orchestra was truly in a class by itself.

Kappa Kappa Psi

While a student at Western Reserve University in Cleveland, I was inducted into Kappa Kappa Psi, the honorary band fraternity. And I had the honor of being selected to represent our school band at the organization's national convention at Indiana University in Bloomington along with another band member, Mike Captain, a fine euphonium player. That was a really big deal to me for several reasons. Other than one trip to Columbus to visit a girlfriend at Ohio State one weekend, I had not been to any other big college campuses. Indiana's music faculty included many famous musicians and was rated one of the best in the country. There would be a convention band and I would be playing with college musicians from all over the country in a very large ensemble directed by Thor Johnson, conductor of the Cincinnati Symphony. I was also told the campus was very beautiful.

NATIONAL CONVENTION
KKΨ + ΤΒΣ
JULY 26-29
INTER-COLLEGIANTE BAND
INDIANA UNIVERSITY
BLOOMINGTON
'51

Kappa Kappa Psi Emblem

Mike and I drove to Bloomington, starting before sun-up on what became a cool and cloudy spring day. As we headed south from Indianapolis I was surprised by the verdant landscape of dark green rolling hills and valleys. It was as pleasant a countryside as I had ever seen. Soon we were at the University and I remembered that Hoagy Carmichael, the composer of "Stardust", "Old Buttermilk Sky" and dozens of other sweet, charming and sometimes quirky songs had walked the paths of that campus. Everywhere I looked there were handsome, warmly hued sandstone buildings among towering majestic trees. We registered and were assigned our dorm room. That was the first time I had ever stayed in a dorm room. I had always lived at home. I was thrilled to have that new experience too.

The next day we reported to the music building to audition for section seatings. There were ten trombone players, all male and from many different states. There were three judges. I was impressed to learn that the head judge was Newell Long, a member of the music faculty and the man who had written the *Rubank Beginner's Method for Trombone*, the first book I had studied from. We were told to line up in a straight line, shoulder to shoulder.

Somehow I ended up in the number one spot. That meant I would have to sight-read the music first—without having heard or seen it before. They had covered the title page of the book it had come from, but as soon as they put it in front of me I immediately recognized it. The music was from a book I had studied from perhaps four or five years earlier. Before I played, I did as my teachers had always instructed me to do. I scanned the piece, which was actually an etude or exercise, checking the key and time signatures and looking for any complicated rhythmic passages. I then asked what tempo or speed they wanted it played at since there can be a fairly wide range, even within one Italian language tempo marking, such as Andante or Allegro.

One of the greatest benefits of playing an instrument is the way it teaches you to focus your mind. There is no more focus motivating tool than an audition in front of judges and a group of your peers. I picked up my trusty King trombone, took a deep breath into my diaphragm and read through the etude nearly perfectly, nailing all the high notes, a particular strength I was fortunate to enjoy.

When I finished, I passed my music stand and music to the next person in line. I was surprised at how most of the others struggled through the etude. Some gave up altogether. When ten had played, the judge handed him a new piece which came back down the line ending with me. The second selection was easier than the first and I believe I played it perfectly. We were told the seating would be set when we got to the first rehearsal.

We were to report for that band rehearsal right after lunch in the huge cafeteria. There were about one hundred twenty-five players crowded onto the stage of the magnificent auditorium where Indiana U. presents complete grand opera performances. The trombones were seated and I was given the fourth chair. I was just happy to be there so it didn't bother me much, but I couldn't figure out how they had come up with that seating. I recall that the young man given the first chair was a tall Hispanic from Texas Tech who played pretty well. I think his name was Jose Mendez.

The rehearsal began. The conductor, Dr. Thor Johnson, was introduced. It's very unusual for the conductor of a major professional orchestra to agree to conduct a concert band. Many of them would consider it too low for their lofty status. But we learned that Dr. Johnson had been an army band conductor during World War II, enjoyed bands and was very familiar with concert band literature. He was one of the best conductors I have ever encountered. His baton technique was clear and precise, as were his directions. He had a good sense of humor and quickly developed a fine rapport with the players.

After about fifteen minutes of that rehearsal, Mr. Long, the head trombone judge, approached the trombone section. He came over to me and quietly said, "I'm sorry. We made a mistake in the seating of the section. We got some names mixed up. Please follow me and leave your music here."

I grabbed my trombone and followed him to the edge of the stage where the trombone section started. He bent over and whispered something into Jose Mendez's ear. Jose nodded, stood up, looked at me and pointed to his chair as he vacated it. I sat down and each of the other first four players moved down one chair. I was a little embarrassed about the way the episode played out, but very proud that I would be able to return to Western Reserve and tell them that I had been selected as the principal trombonist in the National Intercollegiate Band. Mike Captain, my room-mate had also made first chair euphonium, so we both had represented our university extremely well.

Following several hours of rehearsal, we presented a fine concert under Dr. Johnson. The piece I remember particularly was a splendid arrangement of the orchestral work "The Pines of the Appian Way," one movement from the suite entitled *The Pines of Rome* by Ottorino Respighi. The piece starts softly with a heroic martial theme and light percussion. It suggests the Roman legions approaching from afar. The volume builds gradually as various sections of the band enter. The music evokes visions of gleaming helmets, armor and banners. The air is dusty from the scuffling of boots. We can picture the battle-scarred faces of the soldiers as they move past us in column after column on foot, horseback and chariot. The French horns soar on high and the bottom feeding tubas and euphoniums thunder away. We count our rests until the moment when all ten trombones lift their slide bearing shiny lacquered instruments to join the fray, stating the theme in full fortissimo. Now the high flying trumpets barge in. There must have been sixteen of them! The woodwinds have come along for the ride, but the brass are carrying the day until the percussionists bear down on bass drum, snare drum and cymbals. They're giving all they've got and just when you begin to wonder if the building itself will survive the onslaught of sound, there is one more weapon added to the percussion arsenal. The great huge gong is struck over and over at the peak of the climax.

By that time, in the midst of the ocean of decibels, the hair on the back of my neck was standing up and the chills running up and down my spine. It's the ultimate high for a musician and hopefully, for the audience. I returned to Cleveland the next day with a feeling of exaltation about what I had experienced and a memory that would last a lifetime.

Going for a Scholarship

My grades during my first two years at Western Reserve University were pretty awful. In fact, I believe that if my counselor had been paying attention to them, I might have been booted out of the school at the end of my first semester. But gradually, over the period of those first two years, I began to figure out what this college thing was all about. Then, having gotten most of my liberal arts requirements out of the way, I was able to concentrate on my music education major and my grade point average took a big jump. In fact, I found my name on the Dean's List by the end of my junior year.

I had never paid any attention to those bulletin board notices about scholarships because I just didn't think Bill Nemoyten and scholarships belonged together. But now my attitude was beginning to change. When I saw that notice about "Ranney Scholarships" for musicians on the music department bulletin board I actually decided to go for it, even though the notice didn't say very much about what was expected of the applicants.

A week after I submitted my application I received a letter that shook me up. It stated that I was to report to the auditorium at the Cleveland Institute of Music in two weeks with fifteen minutes of music memorized and that I was to provide my own piano accompanist.

I hadn't prepared a memorized piece since my high school days and had nothing ready at that time. Then I thought about how treacherous memorizing music can be. The week before all this I went to a music faculty recital at an elegant recital hall. One of the soloists was Jeannette Cherubini, an excellent pianist well known in northern Ohio who was one of the three piano teachers on our faculty. Her second selection was a Bach prelude and fugue. She began the fugue and ran into trouble four times before she was able to complete the piece! She was obviously quite shaken by the experience and the audience felt very uncomfortable. I visualized that happening to me at the scholarship audition . . . ugh!

After contemplating the question of whether or not I should try to do it, I came to the conclusion that it would be a very great and interesting challenge. I really had nothing to lose except the time I would need to prepare the music. If I couldn't learn and memorize the music on time, I could just skip the audition. Of course, then there was the huge problem of finding the hours of practice time while carrying on my full college load, playing in the university band, doing dance band jobs on the weekends and my part time job mowing lawns at a big estate in Shaker Heights. There was also the matter of finding a good accompanist who was willing and able to put the time and effort in as well.

I looked through the college music library and settled on two pieces. The first would be a Cavatine by the eminent French composer Camille Saint Saens. It was four minutes long and not terribly difficult. My big show piece would be Paul Hindemith's very modern and very difficult bassoon sonata. It had three movements and ran about twelve minutes. Hindemith was a great contemporary composer who was German born and had come to the U.S. to escape the Nazis. He had written a sonata for every major instrument of the orchestra including the trombone. But I liked the bassoon sonata much more and found it to be very playable on the trombone.

The sonata had a fiendishly difficult piano part. I was having trouble finding an accompanist when my girlfriend Sally mentioned that there was a very talented exchange student from Naples, Italy who had recently moved into her dorm. Her name was Bianca Pellis. Bianca looked at the score and very graciously accepted the assignment. She was amazingly proficient with Hindemith's music. I set about practicing several hours a day by myself and then after about five days I set up a series of practices with Bianca in whatever practice rooms we could find. Bianca was a very attractive young woman with the most radiantly beautiful complexion I had ever seen. She was a brilliant musician, friendly, joyful and full of life. Spending all those hours alone in small practice rooms, it would have been very easy to fall in love with her. And in a way, I suppose I did to some degree in my mind for a while.

The day of the audition arrived and we were ready enough so that I knew I would no longer consider backing out. As I paced the halls of the music institute waiting for our turn, I listened to some of the other entrants practicing. In one room there was a marvelous violinist brilliantly sailing through the first movement of the Tchaikovsky violin concerto. In another, a clarinetist with a gorgeous tone, was rendering the slow movement of the Mozart concerto. Next I heard a pianist tackling Chopin's very challenging *Revolutionary Etude*. I began asking myself what I was doing in such company. How could I dream that I could compete with such talent and virtuosity?

The judges were running nearly an hour behind schedule, so there was lots of time to get as nervous as possible. Finally the call came to go into a warm-up room and then to the recital hall. I recognized the judges: Russell Gee was the music department chairman at Western Reserve University; Beryl Rubinstein was the famous director of the Cleveland Institute of Music and Louis Lane was the brilliant young Assistant Conductor of the Cleveland Orchestra.

I was intimidated. But then I had a conversation with myself. I said, "Bill you're a pretty darn good trombone player. You've been playing for nine years. You have a great teacher. You've been a professional musician and member of the musician's union for three years and have played alongside some great musicians. It's time to go out and show them what you can do. If they don't like it, too damn bad. Bill, you've got nothing to lose!"

We had taken the stage and I nodded to Bianca to play the introduction to the four-minute-long opening piece. I picked up my trombone to begin when suddenly Louis Lane stood up and said, "Please stop." "My God," I thought, "What did I do wrong?" Lane said, "You didn't tell us what you were going to play!" I nervously responded, "It's the Cavatine for trombone and piano by Saint Saens." A discussion by the judges followed. Mr. Gee said, "We didn't know Saint Saens wrote anything for the trombone." I informed the learned gentlemen that the composer had written it for the trombone examinations at the Paris Conservatory, of which he was the director. They all looked duly impressed.

Somehow that exchange put me at my ease and I sailed through the piece nearly flawlessly. When I finished and while I was getting ready for my big showpiece, the one that I expected to blow them away with, the judges were having a quiet discussion among themselves. Louis Lane rose and said, "Thank you Mr. Nemoyten. That will be fine. We're running behind schedule." I was frustrated, annoyed and also very relieved.

I returned to my regular school schedule which now felt like a breeze compared to the way I had been working the past two weeks. I had all but given up hope of winning a Ranney Scholarship but I was noting in which ways the experience had benefitted me. First, I learned that when I practiced enough I could accomplish something quite extraordinary. Second, I learned that I could perform well in a pressure situation. And third, as a result of all that practice I was in the best shape as a player that I had ever been in my life up to that time.

Ten days after the audition there was an envelope in my mail mailbox from the Ranney Scholarship committee. Frankly, I was expecting a form letter saying something like "Thank you for participating in this year's scholarship auditions, etc. . ." But the letter said, "Congratulations. We are pleased to enclose a check in the amount of three hundred dollars to assist you in your musical studies. That doesn't sound like much money, but this occurred in 1950. Today, in purchasing power, according to the Consumer Price Index, it would be worth about three thousand dollars. Another comparison is that my part-time job was earning me seventy-five cents an hour. It would have taken me four hundred hours to earn that three hundred dollars in 1950!

I played the Hindemith one other time. It was for my final exam, but Bianca had an exam of her own at the same time so she couldn't be there. When I explained that to the faculty, one member said he would play the accompaniment for me. After half a page, he gave up and said, "Play it unaccompanied." I received an "A" and never played the Hindemith again!

While winning the money was very gratifying, winning that scholarship did a great deal for my self-confidence. It taught me the important lesson that the building of self-confidence is an essential part of becoming a proficient professional musician.

The Buddy Murray Band

When I turned eighteen I joined the Cleveland Federation of Musicians, Local #4 and bought my first tuxedo at Richman Brothers factory store on East 55th Street in Cleveland. The jacket was all wool, double breasted and had wide lapels. I weighed around 205 pounds in high school, and weigh a little more than that today. I paid around twenty-five dollars for the tux, have worn out three pairs of pants, but still wear the jacket after sixty years!

I had joined Buddy Murray's band while in college. Buddy was a pre-med student at John Carroll University in Cleveland and a fine trumpet player who had just finished a tour of duty in a U.S. Navy band. When he left the navy he managed to bring with him a whole dance band library. This treasure trove of music had been created by some of the country's best arrangers who had been drafted and spent their navy time writing for the navy dance bands during WWII. Actually, it would be more accurate to say that Buddy had smuggled them out of the Navy. He had painstakingly blocked out all the "Property of U.S. Navy" stamps in each part!

The Buddy Murray Band
Bill is highlighted in the back row.

The group was a very professional ten-piece band with four saxes, three brass, bass, piano and drums plus a beautiful blond vocalist, Janet Grady who was the wife of our drummer, Bill Grady. We were a union band and played dances at several of the finest hotels and country clubs in the Cleveland area.

Accompanying a Jazz Great

There was one dance that will remain in my memory forever! We had been hired to play for the Homecoming dance held in the Western Reserve University Gymnasium. As part of the publicity, the organizing committee had announced that there was going to be an appearance at the dance by a very famous person at midnight. The big old gym, was usually used for physical education classes and the university held final exams there. But that evening, it was transformed into a romantic ballroom. An enormous sparkling mirrored ball threw swirling dots of blue, white and red light, like giant snowflakes over the room, generously festooned with balloons and crepe paper streamers in the red and white school colors.

The band played pop tunes of the day along with those great Navy arrangements of old standards. Even though I needed to concentrate on reading the music, I always sought opportunities to look out at the audience and see how we were connecting with them. I just plain liked watching the people dance—some graceful and really great show-offs and others stiff, clumsy and clueless. There was also the matter of appraising and appreciating the beautiful girls, how they looked and how they moved, an activity shared with enthusiasm by the whole band.

As midnight approached the excitement kept building. It was now ten past midnight. The chairman of the dance committee asked to take the mike for an announcement. He also requested a fanfare from the trumpet section and a drum roll. A spotlight was trained on the entrance to the gym. At first we couldn't make out who the person was because so many people were crowding around him. And then when he approached the stage I couldn't believe my eyes. It was the one and only Louis Armstrong, also known as "Satchmo," America's and the world's best known, most loved and admired jazz musician/ambassador. Armstrong moved quickly to the stage and greeted the surprised and delighted student audience.

He then turned to the band with his famous toothy smile and asked in his universally recognized gravelly voice, "Can you cats play Basin Street Blues?" Louie didn't have his legendary trumpet. He was going to sing. He had just played a long concert on his trumpet at the Cleveland Music Hall with an all-star jazz group organized by the famous impresario, Norman Granz, as part of his touring production called "Jazz at the Philharmonic." As it happened, we didn't have that song in our library. But we had one of those wonderful piano players who seemed to know every standard jazz tune that had ever been written. He nodded to Louie, and played a four bar intro. He was joined by the drummer and bass as Louie began the song and was soon joined by all of us improvising a background. I'm certain that no one in the band wanted to lose the "once in a lifetime" opportunity to be able to say that on one special and memorable frosty night in 1950 in Cleveland, Ohio, they played in a band that backed up the great Louis Armstrong!

Playing After College Days

When I started to teach, having moved to Holland, Ohio, I no longer had any local contacts to help me get playing jobs. The only playing I did was to use my trombone to demonstrate how I wanted my students to play a particular passage. When I returned to Cleveland the following year I checked in with my Musician's Union contacts and picked up a few jobs. When I learned that the Union had some money to put into concerts by a band that was to be known as the Cleveland Municipal Band, I was determined to do everything I could to land a position in the group. Sally was pregnant and we were expecting our first child in September. I needed to make as much money as possible that summer.

The Cleveland Municipal Band

The conductor was to be a man named Milton Foy. Foy was an older gentleman, who was unknown to most of the professional musicians in town, but who somehow had a lot of influence with the Union big wigs. He owned a large library of band arrangements, mostly very ancient transcriptions of orchestral standards; overtures, movements of symphonies, etc. They were very difficult pieces requiring the very best possible players, especially the woodwinds. I contacted Foy and convinced him that he needed a librarian for the band, an experienced librarian who would also play in the band and that the perfect candidate was me.

Foy wasn't a very good conductor and was a poorly organized person, so as the summer passed I became more and more valuable to him and to the band. Despite his incompetency as a conductor, the band played at a very high level because of the quality of the musicians. There were even members of the Cleveland Orchestra in the band because in those days, they were not employed the year round as they are today. The band only lasted through that summer and then was disbanded. When we moved the family to Peninsula, Ohio in 1955, I dropped out of the Union to concentrate on my teaching career. My next playing experience was with Chic Tesmer.

Chic Tesmer and His Band

The first rehearsal of Chic Tesmer's band was held in the basement recreation room of my home on Stine Road in Peninsula, Ohio sometime in 1955. I had been the band director at Boston High School in Boston Township, Ohio for three years and had recently moved into the house that I had contracted to build and had worked on myself. Having moved to this small town and now teaching full time, I could no longer be active as a

Ready for a gig

working musician in Cleveland which was twenty-five miles north and an hour's drive in those days before the interstate highway was built. I had always enjoyed playing in dance bands and had helped earn my way through college as a musician, so I missed the playing and the extra income.

I made friends with Chic Tesmer, a local musician who was the proprietor of the Hudson Watch Repair Shop in neighboring Hudson, Ohio. Chic was a good looking young man in his late twenties. A Korean War veteran, he was a local guy whose mother worked in the school cafeteria and whose father drove a school bus. Chic had a dry sense of humor with an occasionally slightly nasty edge to it He often made very funny comments, but

always with a straight face. We got together to organize the group and by mutual consent we decided that I would select the music and rehearse the band and he would be the "front" man; that is, since he was a well-known local person, it would go under his name, he would take care of the bookings and would act as master of ceremonies on the jobs. That was, if we had any jobs!

We gathered together enough band music to get started with a group consisting of three saxes, piano, drums, accordion and me switching back and forth between trumpet and trombone. Four of the players were local adult musicians and three were some of my very best student players. Chic played the drums and the lead sax player was John Chessar, a man I knew from high school days in Cleveland who had moved to Peninsula. The piano player was Bob Shuey, another local. Because you can never count on a place having a decent piano that is in tune, we bought a Wurlitzer electronic piano. It was one of the first kinds of electronic pianos to be developed, didn't sound too great and was incredibly heavy to haul around, weighing in at about eighty pounds! I wouldn't be surprised if many a hernia developed as a result of transporting that monster.

Gradually, over a period of a year or two, the band improved and the high school students graduated and were replaced by adults who lived in the area. Paul Duncan lived in nearby Northfield. He was a fine jazz tenor sax man. We also added a string bass player whose name I don't remember.

After a few months, we began to get dance and private party engagements and we were on our way. At first, by mutual consent, instead of getting paid, we all agreed to use the money we made to pay for music and equipment like a set of slick red and white dance band stands and eventually our own P.A. system. Next, we bought jackets. We found them in a catalog. They were cut like tuxedos, made of a hard shiny material and announced us in a most unsubtle way with a loud multi-colored plaid design.

Bob Shuey, our pianist, was the oldest member of the group and in many ways the least proficient musician. He had a very limited knowledge of the chords needed to play the music correctly and often played the wrong chords, which drove players who were trying to improvise on chord patterns crazy. Since I was the musical director, the job of letting him go fell on me. It was a particularly tough thing to do because Bob was a very nice person who was very dedicated to the group and was really doing the best that he was capable of doing. But I knew that it was impossible for the band to keep some of our better players and for us to keep improving as long as Bob was our pianist. I know that Bob was heartbroken the night that I gave him the word, and even though all the rest of the band agreed with action, Bob always blamed me for his ouster. But I had made the right move. We found a fine new pianist, held on to our best players and improved musically and financially.

Later we added another trumpet player by the name of "Buzzy" Buzzelli. He was called Buzzy because of his last name but also because he loved to play jazz solos so fast that he reminded us of a bee buzzing around. Over the next few years several other fine musicians came and went. A music teacher from a nearby school named Rex Mitchell played terrific sax and clarinet for us. He left the area to take a college job and later I saw some of his published compositions for concert band in music catalogues.

As is often the case, the musicians can be an eccentric, strange, slightly crazy group. Gordon Rowe, our excellent lead sax and clarinet player, who was the high school guidance counselor was fond of practical jokes. One beautiful afternoon when we were playing for an outdoor wedding reception, I picked up my trombone and began to play a solo right after an intermission and discovered that my sound was unaccountably thin and airy. Gordon, who sat in front of me was shaking with laughter and could hardly play as I discovered that there was a rubber band holding my water key open, which had caused the problem. It has the effect that you would have if someone made a hole somewhere in your horn. I quickly fixed the key and laughed about it, but planned my revenge.

Chic Tesmer and his band
Left to right: Bob Shuey, John Krusinski, John Chessar,
Chic Tesmer, Don Reinbolt, Frank Kaczmarski, and Bill

During the next break, I sprang into action when Gordon went to get a drink. I had remembered an evil trick I learned many years before. I removed the barrel to Gordon's clarinet, placed a penny into it and replaced the barrel. When Gordon returned and picked up his clarinet for a short solo his air stream stopped one inch into his clarinet. His cheeks puffed out, he turned beet red and I think I saw his ears wiggle! He never fooled with my horn again!

Paul Duncan, our jazz tenor man, had a serious drinking problem. What amazed me was that he could play so well while intoxicated. Yes, he played well, but he had another problem while under the influence. It was staying seated on his chair. The more booze he had, the more he kept sliding off of it.

Our bass player was a very respectable looking guy. He spoke and dressed nicely and didn't drink in excess, so we were shocked to learn that he had been arrested. I believe it was a "white collar crime" of some sort. When he got out of jail a year or two later, he rejoined the band.

The excellent piano player who had replaced Bob Shuey was a vocal music teacher in a nearby school system. He appeared to be a very clean cut guy. So we were even more shocked when we learned he had been arrested in connection with contributing to the delinquency of a minor, one of his girl students, the major "no-no" for a teacher. I believe he was given a long prison sentence.

It appears that the band was a very motley crew of low down characters, but that wasn't the way it felt at the time. Over the years, thirty or forty players circulated in and out of the group, almost all of whom were fine musicians and upstanding citizens. We made many friendships and were supportive of one another.

During the summer of 1964 I spent several weeks in the hospital while a squadron of doctors tried to figure out why I had a terrific pain in my hip and why my right leg had atrophied so badly. I was at a very low point one evening when the entire band came to Akron to visit me. They told me about their most recent engagement. It was on one of those very hot and humid northern Ohio summer nights. They were playing for a private party on a beautiful estate with a big swimming pool. The food and liquor were abundant and the heat overpowering. After they finished playing they stood around looking longingly at the pool. Then someone said, "Oh, what the hell!" and jumped in fully clothed. Not to be outdone, the rest of the band followed. Their description of how it happened was hilarious and gave me a real lift. I think it was the first time I had laughed in several days and I wondered for a long time if I would have been crazy enough to have jumped into that pool that night.

After the band had been going five or six years and had developed a good reputation and a small following, we landed a steady gig every Saturday night at the Peninsula Night Club, a restaurant and bar with a stage and a big dance floor right in the middle of the town of Peninsula. It was the kind of smoke-filled honky-tonk place that reminds one of one of those "roadhouses" you see in movies of the '40s, slightly disreputable, but not really dangerous.

In addition to our dance music we had worked up a kind of floor show that consisted of samples of some of the famous big bands of the '30s, '40s and '50s. Chic narrated as we did some Glenn Miller, Tommy Dorsey, Harry James, Guy Lombardo and, of course, Lawrence Welk champagne music, complete with a bubble machine. We also always included in our dance music a "Bunny Hop," a Mexican Hat Dance" and a "Hokey Pokey" which often turned out to be the hit of the night because of Chic's addition of three new verses. The standard words were:

You put your right hand in, you take your right hand out.
You put your right hand in and you shake it all about.
You do the hokey pokey and you turn yourself around.
That's what it's all about!

The next verses use your right hand, your left hand, your right leg, your left leg, your head, etc. Chic's version added your left knee, your right knee and, always greeted with a big scream from the women in the audience, your weenie, which stopped the action because no one knew quite what to do, or more correctly, what not to do!

The Peninsula Night Club job lasted about two years and the band continued to play quite often in the ensuing years. I dropped out of the group after about twelve years, largely because of the boredom of playing the same music year after year and also because I knew that they were at a point where they didn't need my help any more. The band went on for another fifteen or so years.

Chic stayed in Peninsula. After the band broke up, he joined with Frank ("Genie") Kaczmarski, a friend who played the accordion, and they played free of charge for nursing homes and retirement centers for ten years. I phoned Chic while I was writing this story at a time when he was in the early stages of Alzheimer's. We reminisced about the band and I was delighted to discover that his memory of those days, despite his affliction, was still sharp.

When I flew to Ohio to visit relatives and old friends. I phoned Patty Tesmer, Chic's wife, and arranged to see her at home on Stine Road. She told me that Chic, who was now eighty years old, was in the Alzheimer's wing of an area nursing home. After a number of incidents in which he fell and injured himself, including a tumble down the basement stairs, it had become impossible for her to give him proper care. She reluctantly placed him in the home. Knowing Chic as I did, I knew that must have been a terribly difficult thing to do.

The next day, I took a nostalgic ride through the lovely town of Peninsula. I drove up Stine Road past the house I had built in the fifties on my way to the Tesmer ranch house. Patty greeted me and we both walked out to the rear deck

Chic and Patty Tesmer in 1983

with our canes. We sat and talked a while about the old days, about some of the old gang and Patty shared some juicy new town gossip about one of my former students who now is probably in her seventies. I told her I would like to visit Chic later that day. She cautioned that he might not recognize me. I said I didn't care, I would still like to see him.

As we went back into the house and I prepared to leave, I sensed that something was amiss, even though everything looked the same as it did when I visited a few years before. Then I noticed the eerie silence and I knew. Chic, who had been a watch and clock repair man, had a large collection of clocks hung on the three walls of a room just off of the living room. Their tick tocks and hourly chimes filled the house as if they were its beating heart. Most of them required hand winding and resetting on a regular schedule. Now they were silent. When I noticed the silence, Patty told me she hadn't the strength or the patience to attend to those clocks that Chic had so lovingly maintained all those years.

Later that afternoon I met Patty at the nursing home. To get into the Alzheimer's wing we had to find our way through several doors that were locked to keep the patients from wandering away. When we reached Chic's room, he was lying on his bed asleep. He was thinner than I ever remember and very weak and pale. Patty woke him and said, "Chic, Bill Nemoyten's here to visit you."

He looked at me blankly and I wasn't sure he knew who I was. He said something I couldn't make out in a thin voice, barely audible. I moved my chair nearer to him and spoke the one thing I could think of that might get a response from him. "Chic, I'm Bill Nemoyten, the guy who fired Bob Shuey."

His face lit up with a grin of recognition and I knew the visit had not been in vain. For years after the famous firing incident, whenever I saw Chic he would take perverse pleasure in reminding me of the incident and tell me how well Bob was doing with his music. And then we would both laugh!

Three weeks later on September 3rd I received a phone call from Manny Goldman, an old friend from Akron whom I hadn't been in touch with for many years. Manny had been reading the Akron Beacon Journal obituary columns online from his home in Boca Raton, Florida for over a year. He had phoned because on that day he came across the name of Chic Tesmer, who he remembered had been my good friend from half a lifetime ago.

Chic had died on August 31, 2010, but because of the dreaded Alzheimers, in reality, he had all but left the living many weeks before.

The Cleveland Brass Quintet

Between 1967 and 1969 when I was running the Summit Music Project and then the Akron Symphony, I had a somewhat flexible schedule and I was invited to join the new Cleveland Brass Quintet.

The personnel were outstanding and I felt honored to be asked to join them. The first trumpet player and leader, Harry Herfurth, played in the Cleveland Orchestra and was a former member of the Boston Symphony. Frank Bradshaw, the other trumpet player was the principal trumpet of the Akron Symphony and taught at the Firestone Conservatory. The French horn player, Rick Solis, was the prize student of the principal horn player of the Cleveland Orchestra and a few years later assumed that chair himself. The tuba player, Donald Allcorn, was the tubaist in the Akron Symphony and a superb artist.

We rehearsed very diligently and frankly some of the literature was right at the edge of my technical ability. After a while we started to get some school engagements through "Young Audiences" and had some interesting experiences along the way.

On one occasion we were performing in a very upscale elementary school in Shaker Heights, a very wealthy suburb of Cleveland. We had designed our program in a way that engaged the students in carefully listening to specific elements of the music. We began a Bach fugue, a piece where the instruments come in one by one and weave a complex pattern. Then we asked the students to describe what they heard, expecting them to say "The instruments started to play one after the other until they were all playing at the same time," or some such thing. Instead, one little girl raised her hand and said, "One trumpet came in on an "F" and eight beats later the other trumpet came in on a "D," then six beats later the French horn came in on a "B flat." As we checked our parts we discovered that she had described everything we did accurately. Frankly, we were flabbergasted!

A week later we played in a tough neighborhood in the City of Cleveland that had a reputation for a lot of shootings. Our first trumpet player was demonstrating his horn and then pulled a mute out of his case and asked if anyone knew what you called it as he placed it into his horn. One particularly tough and grungy looking senior raised his hand and answered, "A silencer!"

On July 14, 1969, I sent my letter of resignation to the Akron Symphony. I had just been made an offer I couldn't refuse and the next chapter of my life was soon to begin.

Playing in "Pit" Orchestras

I had joined the Akron Musician's Union and picked up a few jobs. One of my favorites was playing for shows in the "Pit" orchestra. I was hired to play for the show "Most Happy Fella" at the Goodyear Theater. Goodyear at that time had a huge operation in Akron. In addition to the enormous tire factory buildings, there was the Goodyear Bank, the Goodyear Gym with their own basketball team, the beautiful Goodyear Theater and, of course, the Goodyear Blimp with its enormous hangar. The musical "Most Happy Fella" was written by the amazing Frank Loesser, who is most famous for "Guys and Dolls." The production was first rate in every respect and playing it was a fantastic experience.

My next pit orchestra gig was accompanying the New York road company performance of the hit musical "Mame," starring the well-known movie actress Janet Blair with her sidekick played by the now veteran Broadway star Elaine Stritch. The show was presented in a restored old movie palace in downtown Akron and drew capacity crowds every night.

A Short Trombone Sabbatical

When we moved to Quincy, Illinois, I put my trombone away for the next three years. I had become a professional Symphony Orchestra manager and an arts council administrator and while I was still very interested in performing, it somehow didn't feel right to do it there and then. By that time I was in my forties. Then, in 1972 we moved to Foster City, California, and I became the Executive Director of the San Mateo County Arts Council. I began to look around for some opportunities to play my horn again.

Back at it Again in California

Someone told me about the San Mateo based fifteen-piece band called the "Park Squires." It was also known as the "Doctor's Band" because it included four doctors and a dentist. I joined the group and was asked to play the lead trombone part. After a couple of years the leader moved away and I took that spot over as well. Playing in that band helped me to make connections with other musicians and at various times I played with other big bands on the Peninsula; the Serenaders and the Unicorns. We played at places like the Elk's Club and the Peninsula Country Club. Next I joined the Peninsula Symphonic Band and was quickly promoted to first chair in a section of seven trombones. One of my new contacts invited me to join a trombone choir made up of a dozen trombonists. Our biggest gig was playing the "Star Spangled Banner" at a Giants game at Candlestick Park.

I hung in with the Peninsula Symphonic Band for three or four years but became increasingly frustrated with the incompetence of the conductor. The band had about seventy members, many of whom were excellent players, so despite the poor conducting, the band played quite well.

The conductor would actually brag that he never looked at a score before the first rehearsal. He was the only conductor I have ever known of who appeared to learn the music by following the band. I'm told it's not supposed to work that way!

One time when we were playing the famous Rakoczy March by Hector Berlioz, the conductor kept losing the rhythm and messing up the big trombone section solo passage. Finally, in order to correct it, I passed the word down the line to other trombonists, "just play your part and don't watch him!" That saved it. At the end of my last season I told the band's manager that I could no longer go along with the conductor's incompetence. I resigned from the band and I asked him to contact me if and when they got a real conductor.

I missed the playing so I looked around for another group and joined the Foothill College Symphonic Band which had an outstanding conductor who chose very challenging music. That was a fine experience. It's funny what sticks in your mind. I remember posters hung on the wall at the Foothill College band room. One said, "Stamp out In the Mood," referring to that the old Glenn Miller favorite, played so much that it has become a cliché. The other said, "Play an Accordion, Go to Jail!" Enough said.

The Los Trancos Woods Community Marching Band

While I was running the San Mateo County Arts Council, a member of our staff named Kent Seavey, who was our art gallery director, mentioned that he belonged to the Los Trancos Woods Community Marching Band where he played the trombone. I was surprised to learn that Kent played the trombone and even more surprised when he told me he *didn't* actually play the trombone, but just carried it because he got such a kick out of being a member of the band. He also stated that it didn't matter that he couldn't actually play because many others couldn't play either. But he said enough members could play so they carried the rest of the band. It turned out that the Los Trancos Band is a genuine "anti-establishment" organization. The members are encouraged to wear whatever they want to—the more outrageous the better. After hearing his description I couldn't resist seeing it for myself and volunteered to play for the annual Redwood City Fourth of July Parade. When I asked Kent what music they played he said stuff like "It's a Long Way to Tipperary" and "Yes, We Have No Bananas!" They didn't pass out any music. You were just supposed to pick it up by ear as you went along. In order to get into the spirit I dressed in drag for the first and only time in my life. The band marched, or more accurately, strolled down the street. An alto sax player on roller skates weaved in and out of the band as he played. The back ranks were made up of adults and children playing kazoos. The drum majorette was the scruffiest excuse for a majorette I'd ever seen. Instead of clean white boots she wore worn out sandals and carried an ugly old twirling baton. Whenever there was slowdown in the parade, she would blow her whistle. That was the signal for the band to break ranks and head for the rear of the band where some family members pushed a colorful wheeled cart with a cooler full of beer and soft drinks which were generously distributed. Not only was it great fun to play with that group of delightfully nutty people, but it was also great to see how the audience cheered them on!

The Jeremiah O'Brien

While playing with the Unicorns big band on the Peninsula, I was involved in four appearances on the historic World War II "Liberty Ship," the Jeremiah O'Brien, during the 1980s. The last remaining ship of its kind, it is on the National Register of Historic Places and can be seen on Pier 45 in San Francisco. The volunteers who operated the ship, mostly sailors who served in the war, offered rides to the public complete with lunch and dancing on the deck to big band music from the 1930s and 40s. It was a fun gig except for the unpredictable weather. Often we were struggling to keep our music from blowing overboard. I learned, after the first trip, to prepare for the incredible temperature changes that occurred as you sailed through various sections of the bay. It was always very cold and windy near the Golden Gate Bridge and then twenty or more degrees warmer as we sailed into the Oakland Estuary. We weren't paid, but the band members were given a free lunch and we had a blast!

This was one more example of how being a musician took me to places I most likely would never have ever seen. Because musicians do a lot of networking, my connection with that band led to several gigs with another group called "The Serenaders," which consisted of five saxes, three trumpets, three trombones, bass, piano, drums and a male vocalist—fifteen in all.

San Francisco Union Jobs

Around the same time, I joined the San Francisco Musician's Union and picked up a few jobs. The most unusual was playing in marching bands at Chinese Funerals. The band would gather in front of the Green Street Mortuary in North Beach and march through Chinatown. We would follow the hearse, and as part of the parade there would be an open car with a big picture of the deceased on display. If the person was wealthy, there might be two or three bands in the procession. We would play pieces like "Onward Christian Soldiers" or "Nearer My God to Thee."

Another one of my favorite experiences was becoming a member of the "San Francisco Wind Orchestra." Wind orchestra is just a pretentious name for a concert band. It was an excellent ensemble with a fine young conductor, but the organizing group was clueless about finances and the appeal to the general public of such a group. They scheduled a concert series at the Herbst Theater, a beautiful, prestigious and very expensive hall to rent. The group went "belly-up" by the third concert.

The East Bay Symphonic Band

When we moved to Hayward in 1986, I looked around for a concert band to play in and heard about the East Bay Symphonic Band that was part of the Hayward Adult School. It rehearsed at the old Sunset High School band room. When I approached Beverly Johnson, the conductor, I told her I was interested in joining the band, but there was one condition. I wanted to know if it would be OK if I played different instruments from time to time. I was in the process of developing my Hornman Show and I wanted to strengthen my skills on all the brass instruments. Beverly welcomed me into the band and over the years I have played the trumpet, the French horn and the euphonium, which I am still playing today, some twenty-five years later. Even though I almost never played in the trombone section in that group, I have soloed on trombone and also played duets with a trumpet player on the trombone and the euphonium. I also performed my Hornman Show with them at the Union City Senior Center. I have enjoyed playing with that group because Beverly usually picks fine and often challenging music, and because she works hard at trying to craft good performances. The East Bay Band is now affiliated with Chabot College and presents three or four concerts each year.

The Duet

Sometimes I think, *I'm nearly 81 years old. Maybe I should just hang it up!*

As a performer I've been noticing certain age-related weaknesses creeping into my trombone playing. The most noticeable and frustrating to me is my inability to play long phrases without taking an extra breath or two.

My reflexes aren't as fast as they used to be and my hearing isn't as acute as it once was. I am further burdened by my partial dental plates. Yet, I still have the "fire in the belly" to get out there, put myself before an audience, and show them what I can do.

A few years ago, and over a period of twenty months, I had performed a duet entitled "Cousins," first with my trumpet playing son Mark and the North Bay Symphonic Band at Napa Valley College, then with the first trumpet players of the Pleasanton Community Concert Band and the East Bay Symphonic Band. The piece is a very pleasant selection with a flashy opening cadenza, some sparkling triple tongue passages and four high "C's" for the trombone. It was written by Herbert L. Clarke, a name well known to many brass players. He was a composer and a virtuoso cornet player during the "Golden Age" of the American Concert Band when he was cornet soloist in John Philip Sousa's internationally famous band.

Though I never get nervous when I am performing my Hornman Show with fourteen different horns, lately I have been getting a strong stage fright symptom when I am a featured soloist on the trombone. My mouth dries up. That can be a major problem for a brass player. Even though I talk to myself and say things like, "Bill, you've been playing the trombone for sixty-eight years and you're an expert performer. You've performed hundreds of times, once for an audience of six thousand!" But apparently I don't listen to me, because my dry mouth persists.

So what did I get myself into this time? On Sunday June 21, 2009, Father's Day, San Francisco's famed Golden Gate Park Band would be performing their usual Sunday afternoon concert. It would take place on the second day of the annual Golden Gate Park Band Festival. There would be an extra-large crowd, made up partly of musicians from all over Northern California who would be performing that day. My son Mark is the principal trumpet player in the Golden Gate Park Band. It occurred to me that playing a duet with him would be especially appropriate on that day. Mark agreed and so did Michael Wirgler, the band's conductor, who was familiar with the piece.

I got the music out several weeks in advance and began my practice routine. Of course, I knew that the best defense against nervousness is thorough preparation. At first I toyed with the idea of trying to memorize the piece, but abandoned the idea early on and just concentrated on consistency. At first I began having trouble with my triple tonguing technique. It just didn't come out well at all and I felt a little panic, thinking that I had lost that part of my technique entirely. But with a little patience and some slow practice it came back after a few days. Triple tonguing is a clever device designed to help a player more rapidly perform notes in groups of three. Instead of beginning each note by articulating single "T's," like "TTT, TTT, etc.," the musician articulates the groups with "TTK, TTK, etc."

As the time grew shorter and the day of the performance was close at hand, I thought about many things, but mostly that I didn't want to embarrass myself or my son. Then I thought proudly of what a fine professional musician Mark is and that in playing a duet with him, he is a rock of reliability. I was his first teacher, starting him at age ten. When he outgrew me I turned him over to a master teacher and he has had several fine teachers over the years. He surpassed me as a player long ago and is a fine teacher in his own right today.

The day of the Festival I drove to San Francisco to rehearse with the all-professional Golden Gate Park Band at their rehearsal room at the Randall Museum. We got through the rehearsal all right but my performance was a little shaky. The band applauded politely, but I wasn't satisfied with the way I played.

I greatly admire the members of the band. They do something quite amazing every Sunday from mid-April to mid-October. They rehearse music, most of which they have never seen before, for one hour and then go to the park and play a two-hour concert. Much of the music is very challenging technically.

Their concert began that day as usual, at 1:00 p.m. At about 2:00 p.m., I was introduced along with Mark as the special Father's Day feature. I don't know exactly how it happened, but at that moment I was filled with an overwhelming joy that seemed to whisper in my ear, "Bill—go for it and have fun doing it!"

The band played their short introduction. Maestro Wirgler looked over at me and I started my opening cadenza. As I had experienced a couple of times before when I performed with community bands in the historic

Mark and Bill playing "Cousins" by Herbert L Clarke
with the Golden Gate Park Band on Father's Day in 2009

Spreckels Temple of Music band shell, the acoustics were superb. The sound flowed out of my horn with great ease and I nailed the first of the high "C's" perfectly. Mark joined me in the cadenza and we harmonized beautifully. Next we were off on the flashy triple tongue section and I soon knew it would all go well. If my mouth was dry, I didn't notice it. We finished to thunderous applause .and several people came up to us to express their appreciation.

I guess I'll keep doing this a while longer.

Composing Aspirations

I suppose my love of classical music must have begun when, as a young boy, I listened to the 78 rpm records on the hand wound Victrola in our attic. That was in the house I grew up in on Olivet Avenue in Cleveland in the 1930s. My father Jacob was proud of his collection of records that included a Caruso, a John McCormack and various other great opera singers of the day. We also had a record of John Philip Sousa's Band playing the "Thunderer" and various orchestral classical standards. I remember a recording by Paul Whiteman's orchestra playing "Whispering." My aunt Bess, who lived downstairs, played classical pieces on the piano that fascinated me. Then there were the radio broadcasts by the NBC Symphony conducted by Arturo Toscanini and the Metropolitan Opera on Saturdays sponsored by Texaco. My father loved that music and early on I got the message that classical music was something to be appreciated.

But I believe my strongest influence came from the series of children's concerts that they took us to when I attended Parkwood Elementary School. We were given several lessons about the music we were to be hearing and listened to recordings in advance of the concerts. Miss Williams, our music teacher, was an attractive woman with a lovely singing voice and an abundance of enthusiasm.

The concerts were at Severance Hall, the home of the Cleveland Orchestra. I still can remember the feeling of awe when we entered the lobby. The pink marble columns, the gilded scroll work, the beautiful sculpture captivated me. Then, as we entered the hall itself and sat in the blue velvety oversized seats I was certain this was a place of magic even before the first note was sounded by the orchestra.

The Cleveland Orchestra, at that time, was conducted by Artur Rodzinski and was well on its way to becoming one of America's great orchestras. The music transported me to the tops of snow covered mountains and to sweet nostalgic scenes in gardens and forests. I saw the skeleton's dancing in Danse Macabre and the flowers waltzing in the Nutcracker. I was fascinated by the variety of instruments that were making the sounds and the incredible precision of the strings as thirty violins played as one.

One of my most vivid memories as a boy was going for walks on balmy summer evenings by myself and hearing beautiful melodies in my head, melodies I was making up. I was a good whistler and would whistle the tunes as I walked along, but being very self-conscious I would stop if someone was walking near me or sitting on their porch and might hear. I dreamt of one day becoming a great composer. When I was twelve or thirteen I enjoyed going to the library and reading books about Mozart, Beethoven, Brahms and many others. I remember thinking that they composed their music hundreds of years ago and that because the music was still performed today those composers had achieved a kind of immortality.

During the years that I was developing as a trombone player I pretty much put aside my dream of composing my own music and going for my own immortality. I knew very little music theory until I entered college. It was in basic theory and harmony that I discovered what a great handicap I had in not being a pianist. I took some extra piano training when I could, but never developed a good basic technique. I was a very average student in theory and harmony and soon came to the realization that I simply didn't have the talent and/or skills needed to be a serious composer.

But the seed of an idea that I could compose music never ever left me. In college I started to put down a few ideas and they developed into a short piece for string quartet that I called "Night Song." As a music education major, I knew lots of players. I gathered together a couple of good violinists, a violist and cellist, rehearsed them and made arrangements for them to perform my piece at the "Hillel House." It was well received, but although I didn't think it was a great composition, I had the satisfaction of having written a piece of music and actually having had it performed. It's difficult to express how powerful and intoxicating that experience can be. While it is somewhat akin to the feeling that must be experienced by a visual artist creating a painting or drawing or sculpture and displaying it, it is somehow different because it has to do with filling silence with sound, a sound that has never been heard before on this earth.

After college and during my early years as a teacher I put aside my composing urge for a while. Then one day I realized that our school, Boston High, didn't have a fight song. It took about a month for me to write a song I called "The Bostonian." I wrote the words as well as the tune and arranged it for marching band. We played it at football games for about three years. Then they built a new school and named it Woodridge High School, so I wrote "Woodridge is on the Go!" which was similar in style to the Ohio State University fight song. It was very peppy, well received and was performed many times over the years. Unfortunately, I didn't keep copies of either of those pieces and when I checked back, the Woodridge band directors were not able to locate them in their library.

Up until recently, the piece that I had the most satisfaction from was the Woodridge High Alma Mater. I wrote it sometime in the early 1960s. The school was new and a good school song would help to give it a

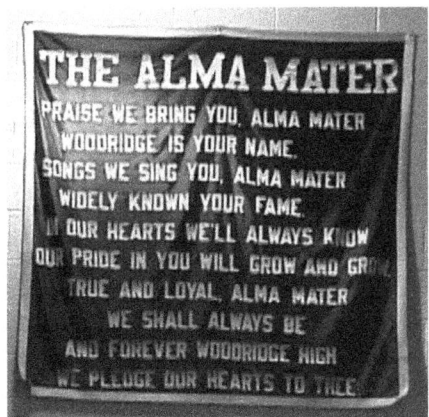

THE ALMA MATER

PRAISE WE BRING YOU, ALMA MATER
WOODRIDGE IS YOUR NAME.
SONGS WE SING YOU, ALMA MATER
WIDELY KNOWN YOUR FAME.
IN OUR HEARTS WE'LL ALWAYS KNOW
OUR PRIDE IN YOU WILL GROW AND GROW
TRUE AND LOYAL, ALMA MATER
WE SHALL ALWAYS BE
AND FOREVER WOODRIDGE HIGH
WE PLEDGE OUR HEARTS TO THEE

Banner on the gymnasium wall today

special new identity. Once I started in on it, the words and melody came rather quickly. We introduced it at a school assembly and it was accepted almost immediately. It has been played and sung at every football game and other events for about fifty years. The words appear on a giant banner in the school gymnasium:

> *Praise we bring you, Alma Mater, Woodridge is your name.*
> *Songs we sing you, Alma Mater, Widely known your fame.*
> *In our hearts we'll always know, our pride in you will grow and grow,*
> *True and loyal, Alma Mater,*
> *we shall always be,*
> *And forever, Woodridge High,*
> *we pledge our hearts to thee.*

Bill conducting the Alma Mater he wrote in the 1960s
with the 2006 Woodridge High School Band

I learned that a few years ago someone tried to change the Alma Mater, but there was a great swell of support for the song which will likely have a life as long as there are Woodridge High graduates who remember it.

Being a music teacher afforded me opportunities to write music that would have a chance of being performed. Another such opportunity came along when the Peninsula Players, our local barn theater group, decided *not* to produce a play about a notorious legendary local character named Jim Brown. The play was written by an elderly retired gentleman named Henry Boynton who had been a newspaper writer and local history buff his whole life. At one time he had been the Editor of the Akron Beacon Journal. I met with Mr. Boynton and proposed that we produce the show at Boston High School. He agreed and it was then that I learned there were lyrics for seven songs in the show that needed music to be written for them. I wrote the songs over a

Backstage at a performance of Money Mill
White-haired man standing on the left is Mr. Boynton. Bill is next to him.

period of several months and we performed the show which received excellent publicity from the Beacon Journal because of Mr. Boynton's connection with the paper. The songs included some solos, a duet and a dance number, all with piano accompaniment.

My next opportunity came a year or two later. We had lived in the small town of Peninsula, Ohio for nine years. We were the first to build a house on what had been the pasture of a local farmer. But soon there were houses on both sides of us. Our view of the Cuyahoga Valley was partially blocked. Stine Road was minimally paved and one of the last roads to be plowed in the winter snows. We wanted to be able to give our children a Jewish education. We began to feel that we had all of the inconveniences of living in the country and not many of the advantages.

After much deliberation we decided to move to Akron, Ohio, a distance of about twelve miles. I would commute to my teaching assignments. We sold the home I had designed and helped to build and bought a new house in Akron. We joined Temple Israel. The children were enrolled in the religious school. Sally became active in the Temple Sisterhood and me in the Temple Men's Club. I learned that the Temple had a very important occasion coming up. Plans were under way for a celebration of the 100th anniversary of the congregation.

There was to be a special service with a distinguished guest speaker, Rabbi Maurice Eisendrath, one of America's best known reform Rabbis and the president of the Hebrew Union College in Cincinnati, Ohio. I knew the Cantor of our temple quite well and had attended graduate school at Kent State with Wallace Nolin, the professional tenor with the choir. Some ideas for a choral piece started to roll around in my head. One day I sat down at the piano and started work on it. I recall being so into it that I spent the whole weekend at the piano and had it finished to my satisfaction in a week or so. I took it to the cantor and he presented it to the choir which gave the song an excellent reading and heartily accepted it.

Every seat in Temple Israel was filled for the 3:00 p.m. ceremony. My composition was performed following Rabbi Eisendrath's address. Unfortunately, in those days, it wasn't very common to record such occasions. But hearing my composition beautifully performed and appreciated by a large audience was all that I could have hoped for and all I expected. I had written both the words and the music for a four-part choir and organ. The words were as follows:

One hundred years Temple Israel
(repeated three times with slightly different music each time)
Out of the dreams of men of good will,
Out of the hopes of leaders with dreams,
Out of their vision, their love and their skill,
Beyond the heights of their loftiest schemes.
Before your Ark, and 'neath your dome,
Your people worship, your people pray
One hundred years religion's home,
To Akron's thousands you've led the way.
To Temple Israel we bring our hearts,
To Temple Israel we bring our hearts,
Bring our hands, bring our hope, bring our grief,
And lift our voices as we sing,
And lift our voices as we sing Shma Yisroel
To reaffirm our belief, affirm our belief, Amen, Amen.

The next composition I want to describe has had a long and continuing history. In 1964 I had an idea for a piece for concert band, part of which grew out of a piece I was writing for a trombone quartet. I abandoned the trombone quartet deciding to use it for the second part of a larger composition I called, rather pretentiously, "The Cuyahoga Valley Overture." Once again I took advantage of my position to get my music performed and played it with my own Woodridge High School Band at our winter concert. It went alright, but I didn't think it was very good.

I put it away and forgot about it for nearly forty years. One day I was going through my old papers and came across a large envelope full of music partly written in pencil and partly copied on an early copy machine. I had actually forgotten that I had written the piece and was surprised to find that I still had all the music. Just to satisfy my own curiosity I brought it along to a Pleasanton Community Concert Band rehearsal in 2003 and asked if the band could read it through one time.

The reading went well and when we finished, the conductor, Bob Williams said that he thought it sounded like it would fit in very nicely with the theme of our November 23rd concert. As it happened, that date was my seventy-fifth birthday. I agreed to have it ready to perform on that day, but decided that it needed a lot of work if it was going to be something I would be truly proud to have my name on. I didn't know it at the time, but it would eventually take hundreds of hours of work, and a trip to do further work on it with my music computer helper who had moved from Hayward to Mossy Rock, Washington. Eventually, there would be several other performances. The most significant decision I made was to change it from an overture into a three-movement suite which I call the *The Cuyahoga Valley Suite*.

The Cuyahoga Valley is an area between Cleveland and Akron and is the last remaining vast rural wooded area in that part of Ohio. The Cuyahoga River, which empties into Lake Erie at Cleveland, meanders through the area and passes through the village of Peninsula where we lived for several years. The remnants of the old Erie Canal Locks run next to Riverview Road on its way to Akron. The area was declared a national park about twenty years ago, so it has been preserved as a beautiful natural environment for future generations. The following is a description of the composition.

I. The Ancient Valley

It begins with a slow plaintive theme on the oboe followed by a French horn solo. The idea was to evoke an impression of the beautiful valley as it was in ancient times. The theme is then transformed into a faster, more rhythmic section with more instruments joining in. It ends with the same theme in a new key played by the flutes, bells and clarinets in the high register.

II. Song of the Vanished Tribes

The idea for this movement came from the Native American flute that I own and play. It was the Iroquois or Erie Indians who vanished from the Cuyahoga Valley over 200 years ago. The opening theme played by the flutes is based on the unique scale employed by Native American flutes. The sound of drums separate the various sections. Part of the movement is "Aleatoric" or chance music. It features a background over which various players improvise their solos based on the aforementioned scale. The result is that this movement never sounds the same way twice.

III. The River Bridges March

What I had in mind was the jumble of huge ponderous bridges that cross the Cuyahoga River in downtown Cleveland and further down the valley. It starts with a heavy low bass theme followed by percussion solos leading to an unusual march theme. Later the opening bass theme and the march theme are played together leading to the climax.

At this point, The Cuyahoga Valley Suite has been performed by the Pleasanton Community Band, the East Bay Symphonic Band, The La Honda

Music Camp Band, The Hercules High School Band, The Woodridge High School Band at the Blossom Music Center in Ohio, The Golden Gate Park Band and the California State University East Bay Wind Ensemble.

It has been a long time since I have written any new music, but there are some ideas still running through my head wanting to be put down on manuscript paper.

Bill conducting the Golden Gate Park Band
playing his composition, "The Cuyahoga Valley Suite" in 2008

Learning to Teach Music

Although I was very confident when I began my first teaching assignment and did a pretty good job in Holland, Ohio in the 1951-52 school year, I realized that I had a lot more to learn if I expected to do a really outstanding job as a music teacher. Now, as I look back on those twenty-two years of teaching, I have a pretty good idea of what it takes to be successful in that field. Admittedly, my learning curve was very steep for several years. Here is a lot of what I learned to do and what I believe.

Musical performing groups are not like other classes. While the individual is afforded an opportunity to learn and is graded based on how well he or she performs, unlike a math or history class, they must also learn that they are part of a group and that the success of the group depends on each of its members. One of the most important jobs the music teacher has is to build a sense of group pride or "esprit de corps." There are many ways to accomplish this. But the most important one is to persuade the members of the group that the only way to reach its goal of excellence is if each member takes personal responsibility for doing the very best they can on their individual part. In order to do that, it is necessary to build a way for students to value their status within the group. Some of the devices I used to achieve that are as follows:

1. I would hold regular tryouts within each section. I would turn around so I didn't know who was playing and have a student assign numbers to each player. That way everyone knew that the only way they were being judged was on how well they played the assigned passage and not on what grade they were in, how popular they were, etc. That system led to some very interesting situations where freshmen sometimes took principal seats away from seniors and everyone learned that complacency was not acceptable in our group.

2. I also encouraged students to challenge for higher seats in the section. Those challenges became an item for discussion among the other students and were watched by everyone with great interest.

3. Entering competitive festivals gave the students a chance to compare our group's level of achievement with those of other schools.

My philosophy of music performance is this: I believe that each performance is a search for truth. I define musical truth as a performance that is technically perfect, completely in tune, with perfect balance, at the correct tempi and most important, is consistent with the intentions of the composer. Achieving that kind of truth is virtually impossible except by the most talented and dedicated professional musicians.

But I believe that all serious musicians at all levels, including school bands, orchestras and choruses have the capability to perform at a very high level when challenged and trained properly. So, while admittedly achieving what I define as musical truth is virtually impossible for all except the very elite of musicians, seeking that truth is, I believe, what all musicians should always be aspiring to do.

I went to school in Cleveland, Ohio where the music programs were outstanding. That, plus my attendance at the Mid-west National Band and Orchestra Clinic in Chicago for several years, where the finest ensembles in the country performed, demonstrated to me that it was possible for student groups to perform at a very high level of artistry.

I don't believe that you can develop a fine music program in a vacuum. The students must be exposed to fine music in live performances. In Peninsula, Ohio we were in a small town where the only live music was in our schools. In order to expose our students to live music we did a number of different things:

1. We took them to children's concerts by the Cleveland Orchestra in both Cleveland and Akron.
2. I volunteered to take on the job of booking assemblies into the high school and saw to it that they included many fine music programs.
3. I invited performances by University bands that were on tour.
4. Every year I took the best high school performing groups on a tour of the elementary schools in our own district.

I discovered that you really need a number of different influences to have the chance of leading a student to a lifelong love of fine music. I returned to Ohio a few years ago and saw some of my former students, most of whom were in their sixties. A woman named Bertha Jones who had played cornet in the high school band in the 1950s proudly told me that she and her husband were Cleveland Orchestra season ticket holders. She then explained that what influenced her musically was not just the playing in the band or taking trips to children's concerts, but the fact that when she came over to our house to babysit for our daughter, she would listen to our collection of classical LP's on our stereo. She particularly remembered her love for Moussorgsky's "Pictures at an Exhibition." She also told me there were no classical records in her house when she was a child.

One of the basic jobs that a music teacher has that is very similar to that of a football, basketball or volleyball coach, is the recruitment and development of players in a way that will assure that as seniors graduate, their places will be adequately filled. I would contend that filling a bassoon chair in a band or orchestra is every bit as difficult as replacing a good ball handler in basketball or a running back in football.

This would be a good place to insert my bassoon story. It illustrates how the right investment of time and effort can pay huge dividends when it is invested in the right students.

In the late fifties at Boston High School our band was really beginning to grow and I was able to get the substantial sum of money needed to purchase a fine bassoon for the school. I convinced an alto sax player in the band named Paul Krusinski to switch instruments. Paul was an outstanding student, a fine saxophonist and a member of the varsity basketball team. The bassoon is really the oddest of all the wind instruments and requires very specialized training, especially in the matter of handling their double reeds. With Paul's parents' approval, I arranged to take him for lessons every two weeks to a professor of music at my university who was a double reed specialist. That was when I was taking my daughter in for her violin lessons nearby. Paul excelled on the bassoon and soon became a fine player.

Two years later, at the beginning of his senior year, I asked Paul if he would use the knowledge he had gained to start a new student named Dick Oliver. Dick had never played an instrument before but had convinced me that he really wanted to learn one and become a band member. I didn't bother to tell Dick, who had never heard of or seen a bassoon before, how difficult it was to learn to play. I only told him that that was the instrument we had available and that if he could learn it he would soon be in the band.

Dick Oliver, Paul's "student" practiced his bassoon very diligently and later, after Paul graduated, Dick took lessons from a local woodwind teacher, went to Kent State University, graduated as a music teacher and taught middle school band in Stow, Ohio until his retirement a few years ago.

When Paul graduated he went to Ohio State University where he played in the ROTC band and eventually graduated from medical school. He is now a professor at the University of Vermont Medical School. When he went to medical school he no longer had the time to play the bassoon or sax but he is now partially retired and I recently received a letter from him. This is the last paragraph of that letter.

"I've just bought a piano and am taking lessons now for the past nine months. After many years of just listening to music, it's great to play an instrument again. I think having played an instrument in treble and in bass clef have helped in my progress. It's really fun. I'm already playing a little Andrew Lloyd Weber and some easy classical numbers. I often think about you and the huge support that you gave us as a start up in music. It is appreciated. It has stayed with me as a lifetime enjoyment."

The next student to use that bassoon was Jim Cummings. Jim was already a fine alto sax player when I convinced him to try the bassoon. Dick would soon be graduating. Jim took to the bassoon very naturally and developed a gorgeous tone. I'm not sure where he went to college, but I know that he became a professional bassoonist performing in one or more of the great London Orchestras.

Reviewing what some of my former students did with their lives reminds me about the real privilege of being a teacher, and particularly an instrumental music teacher. At that very first lesson, when you are about to show those somewhat unruly and very excited fourth or fifth graders how to open their cases, how to put their instruments together and how to hold them, there is something of which I always reminded myself. Although they may not look it, there may be a child in that motley looking crew who will someday be a great musician. You, as the teacher, have the responsibility of bringing out the best in your students, and you never know when the best in one of them might turn out to be extraordinary.

I have been very fortunate, not only in having had many fine students, but in the fact that I have been able to track some of their accomplishments. Following are some more stories about my former students.

Jerrel Morgan was a third grader when I started teaching in Peninsula, Ohio. We had announced that you had to be in the fourth grade to start an instrument, but Jerrel's parents insisted that he be given a chance to start with the older beginners. He had a fine old silver plated Beuscher trumpet with gold trim that had been in the family for many years and Jerrel and his parents were anxious for him to start playing it. I bent the rules a bit and let Jerrel into

Boston High Marching Band
Early 1950s

the beginner's class. Not only did he do well, but by the time he was in high school, Jerrel was one of our very best players. Tall, slender and athletic, Jerrel was also on the school's basketball team. After graduation he attended Kent State University and majored in music education. He had a long and successful career as a high school band director in Ohio. After retiring from band directing he returned for several more years as a basketball coach. It was my pleasure to meet him last year and reminisce about those days in the early fifties when he was a child and I was a beginning teacher.

Fred Thiel must have been ten when he took up the baritone horn at Boston Elementary school during my second year at that school. Fred's mother was a talented pianist and piano teacher and was gifted with absolute pitch, that is, she could identify any note you were playing just by hearing it. Apparently Fred had inherited her considerable musical talent. In addition to school band classes, Fred studied privately with me. He progressed through the method book at a startling rate of speed and by the seventh grade had developed a technique equal to or better than any of our seniors. When he mastered triple tonguing technique I challenged him with a virtuoso solo, Herbert Clarke's arrangement of the "Carnival of Venice." Fred whizzed through the piece at breakneck speed and took top honors in the area solo contest.

In the ninth grade he left us for a fine private school, Western Reserve Academy in Hudson, Ohio where they had no band and no use for a baritone horn player. Many years later we met and this is what he told me. "I took up the French horn and went on to advanced study with Dale Clevenger, principal French Hornist with the Chicago Symphony. I was engaged to play with a symphony orchestra in Germany. A short time after I began with that orchestra I realized that playing in an orchestra was not what I wanted to do with my life. One day, in the middle of a rehearsal, I just got up, packed up my horn, left the orchestra and went home. I am now a very successful stock broker, have a beautiful home in Shaker Heights, and play chamber music with some fine musicians for my own enjoyment.

At spine-snapping attention Jim Klippert of the Boston Band undergoes inspection by C. G. Turner, commissioner of the All American Judges Association. Majorette Jeannine Darrahan watches.

Akron Beacon Journal, November 1, 1953

Jim Klippert in 1953
at the Fourth Annual Summit County Marching Band Contest
Boston High School Band won in their division!

Jim playing in 2012 at Café Borrone

One day I was listening to "A Prairie Home Companion" on the radio when Garrison Keillor announced the names of a national all-star traditional New Orleans jazz band that he was presenting that day. The trombonist was Jim Klippert, another former student of mine some fifty years ago in that small Ohio town. Jim was now living in nearby Moraga, California.

I had started Jim on the trombone in the fifth grade. He was a bright, but gangly, uncoordinated kid who was just beginning to make some good progress when he also left us for that private school upon reaching the ninth grade. Jim went on to earn an engineering degree at Cornell University.

Later, while doing graduate work at Harvard, he became involved with a group of musicians who played jazz in the traditional New Orleans style. Jim's interest in that kind of music came to him through his father, Mo Klippert, a fine amateur jazz clarinetist. Gradually Jim learned to improvise the standard jazz tunes and eventually he memorized hundreds of them. He moved to California and became affiliated with several fine bands over the years. His playing is represented on several Dixieland CDs and he can be heard playing with Clint Baker's Jazz band at Café Borrone next to Kepler's Book Store in Menlo Park most Friday nights. He not only plays, but also sings with the band. Jim told me "he makes his living as an engineer, but lives to play the trombone."

I have one sad story to tell about a former student. His name was Douglas Fazzino. Doug was a quiet kid. He had dark curly hair and a very ethnic Italian look. He played the trumpet, but wasn't one of our star players. He sat in about the seventh chair in a section of nine players. Many years after leaving the area I learned that Doug had served in the army during the Vietnam War and was killed in action. On a trip to Washington, D.C. I visited the Vietnam War Memorial Wall and found the name Douglas Fazzino among the 55,000 names engraved into the polished black marble wall. It is very difficult to explain how emotional the experience of seeing that name actually felt to me.

I believe very strongly that a music teacher should present him or herself to the students as a practicing musician. If they play a wind or string instrument they should have it available and play it often. If they are singers they should sing often. If pianists, they should use the piano as a musical tool of communication. Students need models of how musical passages should sound. While recordings are helpful, they are not as good as hearing live music. Another reason for the teacher to play their instrument is that it makes a statement about their own enjoyment of making music.

Putting together a symphonic band with full instrumentation is a daunting task involving money for the instruments, instruction for the students, and keeping a steady flow of replacements for graduates. Just what instruments are needed is dictated by what the composers have indicated in their scores.

A complete symphonic band should have the following in order to meet the criteria for most fine band pieces; four or five flutes and a piccolo, two oboes and one English horn, an E-flat clarinet, at least ten B-flat clarinets, a bass clarinet and a contrabass clarinet, two oboes, two bassoons, two alto saxes, a tenor and a baritone sax, eight trumpets some of which may also play cornet, four French horns, six trombones, two of which play bass trombones, two euphoniums, three tubas, a string bass, five percussionists and possibly a harpist and bass guitarist.

Even though producing professional musicians is not the main purpose of music education, it is always a possibility. And if not professional musicians, perhaps some of them will be fine amateurs who will enjoy playing their instruments for a lifetime. The least that will come of it is that they will

1952 Holland High School Concert Band
Bill is standing on the right.

1964 Woodridge High School Concert Band
Bill is in the back row in the white suit..

have a real first-hand knowledge and a deep appreciation of what it takes to be able to play an instrument and be an effective member of a musical group... and hopefully a lifetime love of fine music.

1962 Ohio State Fair
Woodridge High School Concert Band

First Teaching Job

It was the middle of June, 1951. I had just graduated with a B.S. degree from Western Reserve University. Married for five months, Sally and I packed our suit cases and headed west in our 1948 blue Dodge Meadowbrook sedan. It was a car Sally had inherited from her dad, Joe Fisher, who had died suddenly just a few weeks after out January wedding.

Young Sally and Bill
at Western Reserve University

I had been declared 1A by my local draft board, but the government had announced that deferments would be given to people who had jobs that were considered essential if the employer wrote a letter to your draft board stating so. I had no desire to be sent to Korea to fight in the so-called "police action." To me, this conflict was nothing like what had happened during World War II, when it appeared that the whole free world was threatened by the fascist regimes in Germany and Italy and the militaristic Japanese.

I would have been willing to fight in that war, but I was too young to join the army. Having just gotten married and loving married life, I would do everything I could to avoid having to leave my lovely young bride, Sally. I had gone to the university at the time when many World War II veterans were using the wonderful G.I. Bill to get the education they wanted, but in many cases would not have been able to afford without that help. My veteran classmates told me, "Serving in the military is a terrific experience, but avoid it, if at all possible." Even though I had passed my physical exam, I was certain that sooner or later the army would declare me unfit to serve anyway. My left leg is shorter by nearly an inch than my right, requiring specially made shoes without which my back is in excruciating pain.

I would have just thirty days to find a job that was considered essential, so Sally and I decided to head out on a tour of Ohio, stopping at all of the county boards of education until I landed a job. The day we left Cleveland on that journey was one of the most exciting days in my life up to that point. To me it was a whole new beginning as an adult, an adventure story with an undetermined outcome. We didn't know where this trip would take us or even if it would be successful.

Would anyone see my potential as a band director and be willing to actually pay me for the work that I was sure I would love doing? Would we find a nice place to live? Would Sally be happy there? Strange, but I don't remember being at all afraid of what was ahead. I felt that whatever it was, I could handle it.

I was only twenty-two years old, but I had a lot of life experience supporting me both in my aspirations as a music teacher and in life situations. By that time I had been a musician for ten years. I had performed as a professional in dance bands, concert bands, marching bands, and symphony orchestras. I had been the student conductor of both my high school and college bands and I had conducted the school band and orchestra nearly every day of my student teaching semester. All of those factors led me to believe that I could succeed as a music teacher.

As to life experiences, I had been working at one job or another since I was ten. One time I tried to recall all the jobs I'd had by the time I had graduated from college and it came up to about twenty. They included selling Liberty magazines door to door, selling ice cream cups off my bike, soda jerking in four different drug stores, packing chewing tobacco, delivering groceries for my uncle Dave's market, working at my uncle Harry's fur business and selling hardware at Sears Roebuck. I also worked in factories on kick presses and drill presses making car antennas in one place and jet engine carburetors in another. I worked in a rubber lab and handled steel in factories. I delivered electrical conduit, wire and fluorescent tubes for an electrical supply company and ran a jack-hammer and dug ditches for the Cleveland Electrical Illuminating Company. I delivered the mail for the U.S. Post Office at Christmas time. I had been a camp counselor, a playground supervisor and an activities director at an after school teen-canteen. I was a night watchman for the main administration building at my college and I cut the grass at the grounds of a large mansion in Shaker Heights. I taught dozens of brass players at two high schools All that was done over a period of twelve years.

Those jobs taught me a great deal. They taught me what real work was all about and helped me to understand what my strengths and weaknesses were. I learned to get along with people from all walks of life and how to handle all kinds of situations. The various jobs showed me very clearly what my life choice alternatives might be and helped me to realize just how much I really wanted to spend my life in music.

Looking for the Job

And so we drove west and away from our home with my mother Shirley in Cleveland. It was a bright and sunny day as we arrived in Clyde, Ohio, Sally's home hometown We stayed there with her mom, Norma and her aunt, Lil Kabb, on our first night. Did I mention that one of the things that intrigued and charmed me about Sally was that she had come from a small town? I had never known anyone at all from a small town and certainly not a person who was a member of the only Jewish family in a town. Sally's family operated a "dry goods and ready to wear" store in the center of Clyde's main street. It was called "Fisher's," after her father's name, Joe Fisher, a very nice and gentle man who I wish I could have gotten to know better. We only stayed the one night because there were no jobs available in the area so we continued west to Toledo and the Lucas County Board of Education. I had called ahead and managed to get a last minute appointment with the County Superintendent. The Lucas County Board of Education was in a shabby, old run-down government building and the superintendent's office looked shabby, and run down as well.

The superintendent's face was hard to read. Was he sympathetic to my situation or did he disdain me as a "draft dodger?" After he heard me out he consulted his files, smiled broadly and said, "I think you ought to call Mr. B.J. Bishop, Superintendent of the Springfield Local Schools in Holland. It's about ten miles west of Toledo on Route 2. He may have something for you."

Superintendent Bishop told me why they were looking for a new band director. He said, "Milo Barrett has been the band man here for twelve years and we like him just fine, but the state just passed a law saying that we're not allowed to pay teachers who aren't certified. "Heck," said Bishop, "Milo's not only *not* certified, I don't think he ever went to college and he's too old to start now."

Bishop told me he would check my credentials right away and if they wanted to hire me he would gladly write a letter to my draft board. We stayed in the area instead of continuing our tour and two days later got the news that I was to be hired at the less than princely sum of $2,400 for the year! As I recall, they also gave every teacher a $400 "bonus" at Christmas time.

We rented a furnished apartment in an old section of Toledo. The place was drab and the furniture old and rickety. The bed mattress was lumpy and uncomfortable, but it was all we could afford. We stayed there two weeks but the leaky plumbing, street noise and cockroaches quickly drove us out.

We were able to find a cheaper place in Maumee, a pretty town about two miles east of Holland. It was not far from the beautiful Maumee River on Key Street near the Lucas County Fairgrounds. We rented a basement room in the home of Dr. and Mrs. Garland Y. Green otherwise known as "Dixie and Donna" to us. He was a podiatrist and she a homemaker.

The Greens were very kind and that made living in their basement a little less unpleasant. They had two beautiful young children, a boy and a girl who we played with and babysat for. Babysitting was fine with us because we got to watch television and it was time we didn't have to spend in the dank basement. We watched things like the "The Jack Benny Show," "I've Got a Secret," "This is Your Life" and "What's My Line?" and I recall hearing the wonderfully nasty satirical songs of Tom Lehrer for the first time on their record player. That winter there was a lot of snow that piled up and blocked any sight of the outside from the basement windows. In the spring there were very heavy rains and one morning we stepped out of bed into three inches of frigid water.

Small Town Life

There were many things about the Holland High School community that were totally new to me, mostly having to do with small town rural life. I was really a "big city guy" and unprepared for the experiences that awaited me.

One day the band was on the field after school practicing for an important halftime show. I took attendance and discovered that Foster McCord, my best tuba player was missing and I was not pleased. I asked the band "Does anyone know where Foster is?" They raised their hands and then pointed out past the fence to the vast reaches of McCord's cornfield that surrounded the school on three sides. There, in the middle of the field, was Foster, wearing a raggedy farmer's straw hat and big smile on his round face as he sat atop a huge harvesting tractor. It seemed that at harvest time it was perfectly natural that he should be there, an idea that was totally acceptable to everyone but me.

On one football Friday night I learned how potent apple cider can be when it began to turn into hard apple cider. Some band members had brought along two jugs of the stuff for the long bus trip to Delta, Ohio. On the way home the cider, combined with the fumes from the bus and the rocky motion on the rough country roads was too much for the stomachs of five or six band members. The mess and stench were awful! Cider was henceforth banned!

There it was on the bulletin board, an announcement for the annual "Donkey Basketball Game" between the faculty and the varsity basketball team and coming up in two weeks.

"Are you kidding me?" I innocently asked, "What's a Donkey Basketball Game?"

It's simple, I was told. Each team gets five donkeys. You ride them and play basketball. I suppose I still thought it was some kind of a hoax so I didn't see any harm in signing up for the faculty team. Besides, I wanted to show them I was "one of the guys." The day arrived and when I saw the big van pull up to the school entrance with garish lettering proudly trumpeting the "World's Greatest Donkey Basketball and Baseball" (baseball, oh God, not baseball too!) I wondered what I had gotten myself into.

It wasn't pretty. I spent most of the game trying to mount the poor animal. When I finally succeeded, Horace (that was his name) wouldn't move. Along came one of the animal handlers with an electric shocking device that barely phased Horace. Such shockers would not be acceptable today. The whole scene was wild and crazy. Though I tried, I never touched a basketball at any time during the game. Naturally, the audience of students and parents loved every minute of it. I think the kids won, but did it really matter?

Another incident that didn't necessarily have anything to do with the rural nature of the school occurred at a football halftime show in Swanton, Ohio. I had just taught the band a maneuver called a collegiate counter march that I had incorporated into the evening's halftime show. The maneuver is a relatively easy way of turning the band completely around so that it is marching back in the direction where it came from. It looks complicated but is easy to do as long as the leader of each line in the first rank knows what to do and is followed by everyone else behind him or her. We went over it several times in practice until everyone knew what to do and it was running smoothly.

Holland, Ohio – 1951
Ready for half time show at Holland High School

Nothing could go wrong, right? The band had completed most of the show and the counter march was coming up. The drum major, a pretty blond girl named Mary Lou, was at the back of the band, which was facing in her direction. She was supposed to give the signal for an about face and then do a high kick step to the front of the band, signal for a roll off, and then do the counter march. But, instead, she gave the signal from her position at what was actually the rear of the band where no one knew how to start the counter march.

I wanted to let out a bloodcurdling scream. "NOOOH! DON'T DO THAT!" But there was nothing I could do except watch in horror and wonder what would happen. Keep in mind that the band was playing a march all through this maneuver. As the band started to march they seemed to morph into an amorphous mass that kept changing its shape. The first shape was a kind of raggedy oval thing. Then it looked like a worm with wings. Maybe the audience would think we were doing a picture of an amoeba! How clever! A couple of players bumped into each other and some strayed out of the central massed group. This went on for what seemed like an eternity to me as I was noting that in college they never taught us what to do in a situation like this.

To their credit, the kids kept playing. When the march ended, they started it at the beginning again. Then I saw it start to happen. The mass gradually reformed itself into a marching band shape and when it did, Mary Lou led them off the field with aplomb. To me it was some kind of a marching band miracle!

Later, Superintendent Bishop said to me, "That was some maneuver the band did."

I said, "Yes, it certainly was!"

Holland High School Marching Band 1952
Bill is on the top right. Foster McCord (the tractor driver) is the tuba player on the top left. And Mary Lou, the dangerous drum major, is behind the bass drum in front!

Creating a Balanced Music Program

Having just graduated from college, I was filled with all kinds of knowledge that I felt I simply had to use somehow. I determined that the school system didn't really have a well-balanced instrumental music education program and that it would be my mission to correct the situation. The band sounded like a glorified drum and bugle corps with all the emphasis on the trumpets and drums and no real balance to the sound.

The trombones and baritones were weak and needed beefing up so I did what I have done many times since with other bands. I challenged them to see who could play louder, me, or the whole trombone and baritone section. They accepted my challenge and the rest of the band was to judge. I won hands down but the challenge worked and the trombones and baritones began to realize how powerful they could be. I also started spending more time with the flutes, clarinets and saxes and let them know how important they were to building a full and balanced sound.

When football season ended, I began in earnest to try to build a concert band, but was frustrated because we were missing certain instruments that were needed to be able to play the music correctly. I went to Mr. Bishop and explained the problem to him. He asked me what we needed and I told him an oboe, some French horns and a bass clarinet.

He had no idea what I was talking about so I brought him some pictures of the instruments and some recordings of how they sounded. He said he would take the matter up with the Board of Education. They agreed to buying one oboe, one French horn and one bass clarinet. I was very excited and happy to get the news.

By February the band had worn off some of the rough edges and was starting to sound like a concert band. I wanted to take them to an Ohio Music Education Association band festival, but didn't feel we would be ready to compete with the other groups that have been taking their concert bands seriously for years. So instead, I entered some solos and small groups in the OMEA Solo and Ensemble Festival that was to take place at Bowling Green State University in April. I attended all the solo and ensemble performances that day that I could. We managed to get one or two "Superior" ratings and three "Excellents."

One more trumpet player was to perform. It was David Brown, a ninth grader. David was very nervous and it didn't help that he was to perform on the stage of the big auditorium instead of a classroom in the music building where most of the solos were played. David climbed up to the stage looking very frightened and faced the judge who told him he could start at any time. He nodded to his accompanist who then played the introduction. David struggled through a short cadenza and launched into the first section—so far, so good. Next, the piano by itself had a sixteen-bar interlude.

David began to fiddle with his first valve and started to unscrew the cap. I thought, "What in the world are you doing David? This is no time to take your valve out." David pulled the valve out and shaking with nerves, he promptly dropped it on the floor. I began to sink down in my chair. Next, as David bent over to pick up the valve, the spring fell out of the trumpet and rolled about fifteen feet, right to the edge of the stage. David ran over and retrieved it along with the valve and fumblingly put them back into the trumpet. In the meantime, the accompanist played the interlude again and again and again as I sank further into my seat. Miraculously, the valve still worked and David continued to play. But only about a third of the notes actually came out and many of the others were out of sync with the piano. Mercifully the piece ended and we all left the auditorium with as many words of encouragement for David as we could muster.

I taught music for a total of twenty-two years and every year entered as many solos and ensembles as I could. The festival performances are graded on a five-tier basis. I is superior, II is excellent, III is good, IV is fair and V is poor. David Brown had the dubious distinction of being the only student I ever had to receive the dreaded V.

Sally Gets Involved

At the end of January, 1952, Sally and I celebrated our first wedding anniversary by going out to a night club in Toledo. It was a very cold and snowy winter night. The headliner was a comedian named Jay Jayson who was actually very good, but it was hard to judge him fairly because the spacious room was nearly empty. We had a few drinks and a fine dinner. I'm not certain about this, but I believe that right around that time, Sally told me she suspected she was pregnant. Our first child, Jo Ann, arrived the following

September.

Earlier that evening I had given Sally her gift. It was an elegant and very warm sheared beaver fur coat. I could only afford such a luxury because several of my uncles were in the fur business in Cleveland where they both made and sold quality fur coats and jackets. Like many of my cousins, I had worked there while in high school. In those days there was nothing politically incorrect about wearing fur coats.

Sally got involved in Holland High School activities when I mentioned to one of the teachers that she had had a lot of theater experience. The teacher asked if Sally would be willing to direct a school play. There weren't any qualified teachers on the staff to fill that role so Sally agreed to do it and gave it her all. The play that the students had chosen, the name of which I have forgotten, was a comedy. It was one of those formulaic things that are ground out by the car load by hack writers that can be published and sold to schools much more cheaply than well-known plays by good authors.

Proud new parents and grandparents
Max, Shirley with baby Jo, Bill and Sally

Nevertheless, Sally did a fine job. She went about it very methodically, blocking every movement with great precision, supervising the construction of the set and advising the students on what to wear. She used her talent as an actress to demonstrate how she wanted the lines delivered. The kids were a little difficult at first, but she soon won them over. The play went off without a hitch and was enjoyed by all and Sally got a chance to do something she really enjoyed.

Going Back Home

The principal wanted me back the next year but I had no choice but to resign. We were barely making it financially and there would be another mouth to feed in the fall. The meager increase in pay wouldn't have been enough to get us into a better place to live than that basement. The draft was no longer an issue by then, so we returned to Cleveland that summer.

When we got back I looked around to see if I could renew some of my professional music connections and searched for a job. In no time I had landed a position as a brass teacher at the Higbee's Department store's music department. Higbee's was a fine old Cleveland store located in the Terminal Tower on the public square. The music department sold instruments along with ten lessons. It was my job to try to advance the students far enough so that their parents would buy their kids a fine new instrument by the tenth lesson. Although I only taught there from 4:00 to 8:00 on weekdays and all day Saturday I made more money than I had when I taught full time. But as September approached I began to yearn to get back into regular teaching. I reasoned that if I could find a part-time job teaching early in the day, I could do both jobs and make a better living for my soon to be expanding family.

I investigated and found out that a school in a place called Peninsula, Ohio was looking for a part-time band teacher. It turned out to be in the Cuyahoga Valley, about two thirds of the way from Cleveland to Akron. It was quite a drive at that time since there weren't any interstate freeways as yet. I still remember my first trip west on Route 303 off of Route 8 through the forested countryside and then reaching the top of the hill and looking down into the valley at that idyllic village with its modest church steeples. It looked like a picture postcard then and it still looks that way to me sixty years later.

And so the next chapter in my life began.

Boston and then Woodridge

Boston and then Woodridge Schools

In 1952, I began to teach part-time in Peninsula, Ohio at the Boston Township School. Peninsula is located in the Cuyahoga Valley about twenty-five miles south of Cleveland. The only actual towns were the villages of Boston and Peninsula and a smaller hamlet called Everett. It was the tiniest school system I had ever heard of. All the grades, K through twelve, were located in one building. And the total enrollment was about 125. The high school graduating class had seven seniors. The man who hired me, W.J. Gregg, was the superintendent, the principal and the seventh grade civics

BOSTON TOWNSHIP HIGH SCHOOL

teacher. We connected almost immediately and became life-long friends.

Bill Gregg's ambition to get the most out of that school was enormous. He wanted to provide as complete a program as he could for the children. Even as small as it was, the school had competitive football and basketball teams. They had also started a band program two years before I arrived. The teacher's name was Al Messmore and he had done a fine job of getting the program started. But Al had a bad case of Narcolepsy and would often fall asleep in the middle of classes. That's why I was hired. There were twenty-eight kids in the band which included Grades 5 through 12 and they even had new uniforms and a small library of band music. Our only equipment was music stands, drums and one beat up old baritone. We rehearsed on the stage with the curtains closed, often while there were gym classes going on. The loud sounds of basketballs bouncing around made it nearly impossible to hear what the kids were playing.

A Tough Schedule

I know the exact date when I was scheduled to begin my new job. It was September 8, 1952. I played hooky because, following a very long and difficult labor, Sally gave birth to our first child, Jo Ann. When I started my new part-time job, I drove each day from our rented home on 153rd off of

Kinsman Avenue in Cleveland, twenty-five miles south down Route 8 to Peninsula and began teaching at 10:00 a.m. In addition to band, I taught beginning band and started a girl's chorus. I finished classes around 2:00 p.m. but always did extra work until 3:00 p.m., when I left for Higbee's Department Store, taking Route 21 for twenty-five miles north to downtown Cleveland. I taught from 4:00 until 8:00 and then drove home, arriving about 9:00 p.m. It was usually twelve-hour days, leaving me very little time with

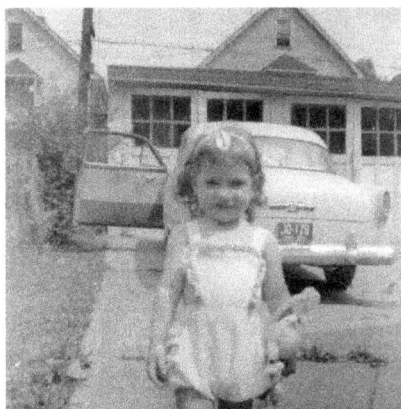
Jo behind house on Kinsman

Sally and our amazing new baby who, of course, many times kept us up all night. The traveling wasn't too bad in the fall, but it got very bad in the winter when the snow–covered roads became treacherous and the trips often took much longer. As we approached the second semester in mid-winter, I went to Bill Gregg and asked him if there was any way he might be able to arrange for me to be taken on fulltime. He seemed very receptive to the idea. A week later he called me into his office and made the following proposal: I was to teach band, elementary classroom music, beginning girl's chorus, art, and seventh grade civics. That last one was the clincher, because he wanted to be

relieved of that teaching responsibility. I found an art workbook to use that was fairly effective and managed to stay one chapter ahead of the civics class. I no longer had to deal with twelve-hour days!

The Coach Helps Out

I was asked to develop a marching band. But early on I recognized a disturbing problem. The football players and sometimes even the cheerleaders made fun of the band members. They were

Fluteophone lessons
were part of elementary classroom music

especially hard on the boys, calling them "sissies." That had to stop. So I went to see the football coach, Ray Brannon, and discussed the problem with him. I asked him to explain to the team that since we have such a small school, we needed to be united—all pulling together—and that the band would always be there to cheer for the team. Ray, a good guy, heartily agreed and after he spoke to the team the problem evaporated.

The Band Parents

I knew the Board of Education would not be able to provide all the funds needed for uniforms, percussion equipment and the larger or rarer and more expensive instruments like sousaphones, baritones, French horns, bass clarinets, oboes and bassoons. So I organized a Band Parents Association and they got to work helping the band. One of the first activities I remember was the annual Strawberry Festival. The strawberries were donated by the Krusinski family who lived in the village of Boston next to the town cemetery. I remember asking John Krusinski how it felt living there. His quick reply was. "No problem. We have quiet neighbors!"

The Krusinskis also had a small strawberry farm where they grew some of the most delicious strawberries imaginable. We played a concert on the grounds of the old wood framed former school building across

Jim Grinham receives the Arion Award

from the G.A.R. Hall while the town folks enjoyed strawberry shortcake and sundaes. The Krusinski's three sons, John, Paul and Ray, played in the band over several years. In addition to raising money for uniforms and instruments, the band parents held a potluck band banquet each spring where I made presentations to a number of band members in many categories like "Most Improved Player" and the "Arion" award for the most outstanding band member whose name would be inscribed on a bronze plaque.

Consolidation and the building of Woodridge

In the late 1950s there was a move on in Ohio to consolidate small school districts like ours with other small nearby districts to make them larger and better. Whereas we had a certified high school, our neighbors, the Northampton School District operated a K through 8 school, sending their ninth graders to Cuyahoga Falls High. The state of Ohio Department of Education ordered us to consolidate. We became the Boston Northampton Schools and tripled in size overnight! By that time the band room was no longer on the stage but in a brand new small building that had been built for music on one side and shop classes on the other. But after consolidation things really got moving. I was spending part of my days at Northampton and training far more future band members. We even added another music teacher to the staff. But most exciting were the plans to build a modern new high school on a lot on Quick Road where there would be plenty of room for future expansion. I received the news that I was to meet with one of the architects to give him my input into how the band room should be designed. The size in square feet that we were allowed was less than I would have preferred. Eventually I was proven correct in assuming that there would come a time when the band room would have to be large enough for 100 musicians, the present size of the Woodridge High Marching Band. But the room was large enough to accommodate us during the 1960s. The room I designed had a high ceiling and angled front walls. It had a director's office and three practice rooms with windows and soundproof doors. Walking into the finished room for the first time in 1962 was a great moment. Very few band directors ever get the opportunity to design their own room and I really savored the moment. Bill Gregg, the superintendent did a fabulous job in selecting faculty members. Arnold Lewis was an inspiring English teacher, Jim Wilsford, the math teacher eventually went into administration and once was named the outstanding superintendent in his state in the south. Gordon Rowe, formerly the junior high band teacher switched to guidance and earned a doctorate in that field. Robert Pletzer, a science teacher went on to teach at the University of Akron.

In future years I was to and still do visit Woodridge High. It has been my distinct honor and pleasure to have guest conducted the band several times at their annual spring concerts held at the Blossom Music Center, the spectacular summer home of the Cleveland Orchestra. A special bonus was the unique experience of conducting the *grandchildren* of some of my former students!

Marching Band

The band improved and the school spirit did as well. By my third year the band had grown to fifty members. We had acquired a sousaphone, some baritones, French horns, an oboe, and more drums. In addition to appearing at all football games both at home and away, we entered a marching band contest at nearby Copley High School and took first place in our division, which was of course, for the smallest schools. We needed a "Fight Song," so I wrote "The Bostonian" which we played frequently during the football games. When we moved to Woodridge High, I wrote "Woodridge is on the Go," a peppier march in the style of the Ohio State University pep song. As the years passed, the band got bigger but the marching band competition from most of the much larger schools with bigger bands was very tough. I had been putting much more emphasis on the concert band season and we had improved considerably in that area. But one day I came to the conclusion that if we were going to march competitively I would have to go all out to develop as good a marching unit as possible. Summit County, our area, was near to Stark County, where the Football Hall of Fame is located and big time high school football and marching bands such as the one in Massillon, Ohio operate. The schools in our area were heavily influenced by their neighbors, all of whom had big powerful and flashy bands. I knew I had to upgrade my marching band skills.

I signed up first for a workshop conducted by Bill Moffitt, a great marching band director and music arranger at Michigan State University. I incorporated some of his ideas and music, but I knew I needed more skill in designing marching formations, so I enrolled in a one week concentrated workshop by A.R. Casavant, the famous Tennessee band director who had invented the "Patterns in Motion" concept.

A Workshop in Chicago

Casavant had been trained in a military institution and had developed techniques for building "esprit de corps" in bands. The workshop was held at Vandercook College on the south side of Chicago. I drove there and remember parking on the street in front of the old Victorian building that housed Vandercook. I climbed the stairs and went to the registration desk. The first thing they asked me was where I had parked my car. When I told them they said, "You must move your car into the parking lot behind the building immediately before the contents are stolen. This is not a safe neighborhood. You must stay in the building or on the grounds at all times unless you are driving to another part of the city." What a great introduction to Chicago!

Halftime Show Special Effects

I learned a lot at that workshop and brought it back with me. Up until that time I would create shows that featured trick and novelty things like majorettes twirling flaming batons, using black lights for special effects and lights on our hats when we turned all the stadium lights off. I even had a lighted baton for those shows. One of the most successful shows I created I called "The Absent Drum Major." The band would march in a parade block down the middle of the field. Suddenly a crazy looking clown–like character wearing a long coat and a funny hat ran out on the field waving his arms and motioning to the drum major to stop. He then pantomimed that she had an urgent phone call, whereupon she handed the clown her baton and whistle and ran off the field leaving him in charge. Seeing the power he now had, he gave a wild signal with his baton and blew the whistle. The drums played a roll-off and the band did an about face, marching in the opposite direction of the new leader. He discovered that after marching several yards, and then turned around and ran wildly to catch up to the front of the band. That pattern was repeated several times until the clown leader is driven up against a fence with the bass drum pinning him there until he is rescued by the returning drum major. The audience loved the show and laughed a lot and the kids in the band had lots of fun too.

We Get Serious About Marching

After the Casavant workshop I came back with a new determination and first started to build the band spirit using new techniques. One example was when I spoke to the band during practice and I wanted their complete attention. I had them all crouch down so that everyone could see and hear me. It is also psychologically a way to clearly show who is in charge. I would get the kids pumped up just before they went out to begin their show by yelling, "What's the name of this school?" as loud as I could. They, of course, respond "Woodridge" as loud as possible. I would often repeat that two or three times. We learned from Casavant to march consistently eight steps to five yards. We memorized the music to our opening routine which started out with the band running out onto the field. Eventually we were not only competitive with the other bands in the area but were invited to play some pregame shows in the Rubber Bowl at the big annual Acme-Zip Game. We were no longer relying on special effects, but had a well-disciplined marching unit doing intricate formations. Meeting the band at the busses on Friday night trips to places like Hudson, Richfield, Twinsburg and Mogadore was always exciting and a little stressful because I was always concerned that someone essential might not show up in time for the bus. The kids would get very hyper on those trips and were very noisy. But one of my favorite memories was of my first trombone player, Bill Burr, who would stand up in the aisle and suddenly begin his very funny revival preacher sermon, evoking "Halleluiahs and Amens" from his appreciative band mates.

Band and Solo and Ensemble Festivals

I was a member of the OMEA (Ohio Music Education Association) and very much believed in the value of the competitive music festivals they sponsored. The band festivals were usually held at The University of Akron and the solo and ensemble contests at Kent State University. We entered the band and as many solos and ensembles as I could organize as possible every year. At that time schools were classified by the size of their enrollment into A1,A2,B1,B2,C1,C2. For the first three of four years we were in C2, so the standards were not very high. To enter the district band festival we had to prepare a required piece and two others of our own choice. After we performed for the three judges in the big gym, the band would be led into a separate room where we were given a sight reading test. As the conductor I was given two minutes to study the score and another two minutes to talk the band through the music and then we played it as well as we could. One time at the University of Akron I had sent the band to the sight-reading room and followed them a minute or two later to discover the whole band standing in a circle outside the room looking down at the ground. I asked what was going on and was told that Martha Kosar, our first clarinetist, had lost her contact and they were all looking for it. I joined the hunt, looked down, immediately saw the lens, picked it up and handed it to Martha and said, "Here it is Martha, now let's get going." Everyone looked at me as if I was some kind of wizard. I had just gotten lucky!

Building Toward Success

We entered the OMEA Band Festival all sixteen years that I taught in the system. The judges were pretty tough on us for the first two or three years. But those were all learning experiences. I learned what to do not merely by reading the judge's comments, but by attending the events and listening to the other bands. Gradually our ratings improved. We began getting more "superior" than "excellent" ratings, until we achieved our first all "superior" rating which qualified us for the state festival. By that time we had grown into the category "B2." It took another three years of dedicated hard work by everyone in the band to achieve the coveted "superior" at the state level. The method of learning what your rating was, was in itself exciting. Usually about once an hour someone would come into the hallway where the names of all the competing bands were posted on a large chart. They would then write the ratings of each of the three performance judges and the sight reading judge on the chart. You couldn't be certain of your rating until all of your numbers had been posted. The feeling of excitement when we had finally achieved our first state superior rating is hard to describe. There was a time when we looked to certain other bands as being the very best and now we realized others would be looking at us with that same special kind of respect. For me professionally, it helped me toward being elected chairman of District VI of the OMEA and qualified me to become a contest adjudicator, a job that paid well and was interesting and instructive.

Presenting Musicals

Since I was both the choir and band director, and since no one had ever put on a play or show with singing and music in the school before, I had an opportunity to pioneer something new. One day I was at Sheldon Music Company in Cleveland looking over band and choir music when I spotted a simplified version of the Gilbert and Sullivan operetta, "H.M.S. Pinafore." I looked it over and visualized which students might be able to handle the various roles. I had a special feeling about that operetta. When as a camper, and later as a counselor I attended Camps Baker and Wise, every year the counselors would put that operetta on for the entire camp. The songs were catchy, it had wonderful characters and a great twist at the

Eleanora Kubinyi

end. The only student I recall who was in it was Cynthia Wells, who sang the charming "I'm Called Little Butter Cup." The kids loved doing it and the people in the town did as well. I believe it was about then that I started to get help and advice from Eleanora Kubinyi, a wonderful choreographer and all-around great theatre person who mentored me in that field over the next several years.

Our next show was a "boiled-down" version of the hit Irving Berlin

Broadway musical, "Annie Get Your Gun." We bought the play books and just added the sheet music for the great songs, "Doin' What Comes Naturally", "The Girl That I Marry", "You Can't Get A Man With A Gun", "I Can Do Anything Better Than You Can" and, of course, "There's No Business Like Show Business." Sandy Wykoff was a terrific Annie and Dick Billings, a big strong football player, surprised everyone in town with his beautiful voice, singing and playing of the Frank Butler role. We did two other musicals. One was a school version of "Around the World in Eighty Days", and the other was an original play with original music called "Money Mill."

Money Mill

As mentioned in my story, "Composing Aspirations," Henry Boynton was an elderly gentleman who had been the editor of the Akron Beacon Journal newspaper and also a local history buff. In his research, he discovered Jim Brown, an extremely colorful citizen of Boston village in the late 1800s Brown had run a very successful counterfeit money operation out of his home, and his exploits in avoiding detection were legendary. They included the fantastic claim that he had ridden a horse across the frozen Lake Erie in mid-winter in order to establish an alibi by being seen in Canada. He also had taken a boat down the Mississippi River to New Orleans to pass his counterfeit in a place where no one had heard of him. Boynton wrote a play based on those exploits and tried to interest the

Henry Boynton
talking with 2 cast members backstage

Peninsula Players, who operated great theater in an old barn on Route 303, to produce his play. But those who ran the theater kept turning him down. I was curious about "Money Mill," and asked to see it. After talking it over with Eleanora Kubinyi, my friend and theatre mentor, I approached Henry and asked him if we could produce it at the high school. He agreed and then asked me who would write the music. He had written the lyrics to seven songs into the play. I told him I'd like to give it a try. He liked what I composed so we went ahead with the production. For many of the students, he was the oldest person they had ever met. It was a joy to see the respect they gave old Henry Boynton. We received excellent publicity from The Akron Beacon Journal because of Henry's connection with the paper, and the show got very positive reviews. I still dream of it being revived someday. I still have a copy!

The Three Sisters

Incredibly, over a period of about ten years, three sisters, Mary Ann, Susan and Molly Morgan, each performed the first movement of the famous, beautifully melodic and very difficult Grieg Piano Concerto with the school band. The sisters all studied with the same excellent private teacher and after Mary Ann had performed it, the other two sisters rose to the challenge. Remarkable! For each of them we secured a fine ten foot Baldwin grand piano. I have a vinyl record of Molly's performance and consider it one of my greatest personal musical treasures.

Starting an Orchestra

The Cleveland junior and senior high schools I attended had orchestras as well as very good bands. At Western Reserve I took string classes and was

Boston String Program
Bob Gref and Bill standing in back

taught that a well-balanced music department must include the teaching of strings. I had begun a string program in Holland, Ohio and felt that there was no reason not to try the same at Boston school. Superintendent Bill Gregg was supportive, if for no other reason than that he was at one time a violin player, (and I'll bet a good one!) I laid out my plan. I went to the band parents' organization and asked them to purchase two violins, one viola, a cello and a string bass. Compared to many of the larger band instruments, the violins and viola were inexpensive. The cello was costly and the most expensive was the string bass. There was a good reason to buy the bass; It could also be used with the dance band and the concert band. In addition to the instruments bought by the band parents, we put out a call for families who might have string instruments around their homes and/or families who wanted to rent them for their children. I taught the beginning string classes and we brought in a fine string teacher named Linda Bachlund who gave private lessons after school.

We were on our way. Our daughter Jo, by that time having studied violin with a great teacher at the Cleveland Institute of Music since she was six, was a great addition to our little orchestra. When the group reached Woodridge High we had twelve or thirteen strings, enough to put on performances at our annual concerts when we added some wind players. Although we were one of the smallest school systems in Summit County, which included the twelve school districts surrounding Akron, we were the only school with a string program, something

Jo practicing at age 9
Sister Sue wants in on the action!

of which we could we very proud. Sadly, my successor, Larry Cook, was not an orchestra oriented person and the program soon died.

The Dance Band

Today many large high schools have jazz programs and offer school time classes in jazz studies. No such thing existed in the '50s and '60s, so I organized a school dance band that met after school. It had the standard big band instrumentation of five saxes, four trumpets, three trombones, string bass, piano and drums and also a female vocalist. With the help of the Band Parents Organization we purchased dance band jackets, music stands and arrangements. The band played for school dances and appeared with the other school groups in concerts. It was another way to challenge and further develop some of our best players. Each year I made arrangements to have the

Woodridge Dance Band 1965
That's Ray Krusinski in front, leaning on the piano.

dance band play for the patients at Hawthornden State Hospital, an institution for the mentally ill! As we were setting the band up on the stage, the patients came into the auditorium. There seemed to be three different groups. One group sat on chairs and wheel chairs around the perimeter of the room. They were very docile and almost zombie-like. They looked pale and weak and hardly moved the whole time we were there. They probably were heavily medicated. A second group was a little more active and walked about either talking to others or themselves. The third group came over to the stage and asked me and members of the band questions about who we were and what we were going to do. They were animated, well dressed and cheerful and in some cases very attractive looking individuals. They appeared, in every way, normal. I'm certain the visits to Hawthornden was an intense experience our students never forgot.

Building Our Peninsula Home

Over the years there were several local families who were represented by two or more siblings in the band; Frank and Bob Kaczmarski, John, Paul and Ray Krusinski, Don and Jim Reinbolt, Susan, Linda and John Philips, Bertha and Janice Truxell, Judy and Jim Montaquila and Cynthia, Cleon and Yvonne Wells. The families of some of those mentioned were involved in the building of our home on Stine Road in Peninsula in 1955. I came to see that I had found a wonderful place to teach and also to raise a young family. I wanted to move closer and not to have the long commute from Cleveland anymore because my job involved many after school activities. When the word got out in the community that I was thinking about locating close by, Cleon Wells, a local carpenter came to me after a school event one night. He told me that Mike Manz, a farmer on Stine Road had decided to subdivide and sell his land for the development of new housing. Wells told me if I purchased one of the lots at $1,000 at that time I would be able to pick the best one. He also showed me the blueprints of a house he had recently built in Solon, one with a design he thought we would like. The next day we went out to look at the lot which was nine –tenths of an acre and had a view of the Cuyahoga Valley off in the distance. We visualized a big picture window facing east and a cozy living room with a brick fireplace to warm us on cold winter nights. The idea of actually designing our own home, contracting the workers and working on

Stine Road house under construction
Bill taking a photo in the foreground

it myself during the summer and on weekends was a great challenge, one I was ready to take on, and so was Sally.

I scraped enough money together to buy the lot and have a down payment for a loan from the bank in Hudson. My mother went to the I. Singer Unity Club our "family club", and got some money from them. I also got a $1,000 loan from my uncle Dave Saltzman who never told his wife, my Aunt Minnie about it, for fear she would disapprove. Altogether, the total cost for the land, materials and labor was a little over $17,000. It was very exciting to walk out on that acre of pasture land and know that we owned it. As we inspected it and the surrounding countryside Sally and I dreamt about the beautiful home we would build for our family. It would have a large open space that included the living and dining areas with cabinets built next to the fireplace that housed a TV a record player, radio and stereo system. The kitchen would be behind the fireplace and have a very large stainless steel sink that Sally insisted on. She wanted to use it to bathe her babies. It would

Baby Mark by picture windows

have three bedrooms. An unusual feature we came up with was a closet that connected the two children's bedrooms like a "secret passage." There would be one full bathroom upstairs and a toilet in the basement. The basement ran the whole length of the house and included a two-car garage, a laundry room and a recreation room. The exterior would have vertical redwood siding and a hip roof that would extend out far enough to protect us from the sun.

Looking for Water

I recall the day that Cleon Wells said the first thing we would have to do is find water, because there was no city water in Peninsula, Ohio. He knew the land and was very confident we would find water. We met at the property and he did something I had heard of, but frankly didn't believe would work. Cleon looked around for some twigs. When he found what he was looking for he tore all the leaves off and ended up with a "Y" shaped branch. He had created a "divining rod" used for detecting where water lay underground. He moved about the property in an area in front of where the house was to be built holding the two branches loosely. After about fifteen minutes of searching, the twig suddenly pointed down toward the ground and Cleon declared, "Here it is!" The next day we called the well digging crew. They dug down thirty-five feet and struck a flow of water that would easily be adequate for our needs. However, a lab test revealed that the water was very hard, meaning it was full of minerals. Cleon said that was not a problem, we just had to get a water softener. We learned many new things about living in the country. The water softener had to be serviced regularly to keep the water tasting good. Because we were a long distance from any super markets we bought a large freezer and stocked it with meat. Since there was no sewer system, we had to install a septic tank and a leach bed to treat the waste water. With nearly an acre of land I had to buy a riding lawn mower to keep ahead of the grass and weeds. As the kids grew up I would often hook their wagon to the mower. It was a special treat having daddy tow them around with his tractor.

Getting Started on the House

After laying out exactly where the house would be situated I hired a man with a backhoe to dig where the foundation and basement would be. We ordered the bricks and cement blocks and framing lumber from Terry Lumber and Supply in Peninsula. Next I hired John Bistro, a crusty, ill-tempered and sometimes very funny plumber. There was cement block work, and I distinctly remember coating the outside of the basement walls with tar to water-proof them. Once the foundation was up, Cleon Wells and Luther Park, another local "old-timer" carpenter, were ready to get to work on the floor and framing. However, the local electric company hadn't installed electricity as yet. Undaunted, Cleon and Luther set up a saw horse, sharpened their handsaws and got to work without the benefit of electric saws and moved forward at an amazing rate of speed. When school was out I was able to help out in any way I could, carrying lumber to them, hammering nails in and mostly seeing to it that they received the supplies they needed. Cleon was great on mentoring me in who and how to contract good workers and what supplies were needed. On his advice I hired Mr. Eggleston, a local electrician and then hired two high school students, Bob Kovach and John Puchalsky. They were two strong young men, both football players. One day when we got to the part where we were putting up the sheet rock, I bent over to pick some of the heavy slabs of sheet rock and felt something in my back snap. Actually, it felt as if I had been shot in the spine! I was bent over and could literally not move. I called Bob and John for help. They had to pick me up and put me into Bob's car. They drove me to the office of Doctor Doron, an osteopath, who had an office in town. After his treatment I was able to walk out of his office without pain. Building the house was a great education that would benefit me all the rest of my life. I learned how buildings are built, what is inside the walls, about electricity, plumbing and heating, sewage systems, mortgages, utilities, appliances and a myriad of things that are mysteries to many people. Those lessons served me well in the future, especially when dealing with workmen where I was managing agencies that had buildings to maintain. I remember thinking that the total experience was worth at least a year or two of college.

The Peninsula Players

Today if you drive down Route 303 toward Peninsula, you'll see an old barn with an extension built on to it, painted in a faded shade of grey. There is a sign on the building that reads: "Player's Barn." But the building appears to be abandoned, having at some time in recent years served as an antique shop. The Peninsula Players, former residents of the

Honoré Guilbeau in 2006

barn, was quite an extraordinary community theater in its heyday when we lived in Peninsula. At that time a small group of highly talented and accomplished artists lived in the area. The foremost ones were Eleanora Buchla Kubinyi and Honoré Guilbeau Cook. Eleanora's credentials were described elsewhere in this book. Honoré was a multi-talented artist who

worked equally as well in just about every artistic medium you could think of. For the Players, she designed, constructed and painted sets. She also designed and made costumes. Her art work adorned the programs, and all of the above were done with originality and style. Honoré lived a long and very active life, creating art well into her nineties.

On a trip to Ohio in 2006, accompanied by my son, David and grand-daughter, Sarah, we visited her as she worked in her garden. Three days later we learned that she fell while hiking near the "Deep Lock Quarry" and had died the next day from her

PENINSULA PLAYHOUSE

Program cover 1960 Season
Art by Honoré Guilbeau

injuries. She was ninety-nine years old! Eleanora directed many plays and designed the choreography and staging. Soon after we moved into the community Sally and I became deeply involved with that wonderful group of people. We both appeared in plays.

Sally as ingénue
in *Tobias and the Angel*

Sally made quite an impression as a maid in the Moliere's farce, *Le Bourgeois Gentilhomme* (*The Would Be Gentleman*). She had a laughing scene that nearly stole the show. She also appeared as the Narrator and several other roles in *The Thurber Carnival* and starred as the ingénue in *Tobias and the Angel.* She had roles in *Of Thee I Sing, Summer and Smoke, The Shoemaker's Prodigious Wife* and the old time melodramas, *Because Their Hearts Were Pure* and *The Secret of the Mine.*

I appeared in *The Girl of the Golden West* in a minor part. I came on stage in the first scene and told everyone I was going home. I would then take off my costume, remove my make-up and drive down the hill to the

Peninsula Night Club and join Chic Tesmer's Band. In Garcia-Lorca's *The Shoemaker's Prodigious Wife,* I played the Sashmaker's apprentice and pursued the beautiful wife of the Sashmaker around the stage on my knees in my vain attempt to seduce her. In Jean Anouihl's *Thieves' Carnival,* I was positioned in a tiny Gazebo mid-stage and played a variety of instruments, using them to musically comment on the strange goings on in the play. One of my better roles was as the grocer in William Saroyan's *My Heart's in the Highlands.* I played the scene with young Eric Conger, who was about nine at the time. Eric grew up to be a professional actor. He has appeared on many TV dramas and co-narrated a tape of the life of the famous film star Anthony Quinn.

Sally stole the show with her laughing scene in Moliere's *Le Bourgeois Gentilhomme.*

A Thurber Carnival

But it wasn't just the plays we were interested in. It was the fascinating group of people who interested us. They had great parties. A favorite was their annual celebration of "Ground Hog Day." One memorable evening near the end of a party just up the hill from our home on Stine Road at Milt and Betty Garrett's spectacular contemporary style ranch house, Sally had a little too much to drink. Our friend, Elaine Boose and I had to practically carry her home and put her into bed. That was the one and only time I ever witnessed Sally overindulging. But I remember that she was a pretty funny drunk that night!

Alpha Rex Emmanuel Humbard, 1919-2007, the Evangelist

So what did I have to do with a Pentecostal evangelist preacher? The once internationally famous television preacher, who officiated at Elvis Presley's funeral, Rex Humbard, lived in our school district. His two sons, Rex Junior and Donald were in my Woodridge High School Choir. Both played football as well. I believe this occurred in 1962, the year the building of Woodridge was nearly completed except for the gymnasium/ auditorium. Humbard offered the school his "Cathedral of Tomorrow" for our commencement ceremonies. Built in 1958 at a cost of four million dollars, the church seated 5,400 and was designed to accommodate television equipment, crew, and chorus. Paul Padrutt, the school principle, accepted the offer and told me to contact Humbard about the logistics for the band's part of the ceremony which was traditionally to play a selection or two at the beginning, "Pomp and Circumstance" and a recessional at the end. Humbard greeted me warmly, showed me around the cathedral, and then took me to the incredible stage area. He demonstrated how their platform on which a pit orchestra was designed to move up to the level of the floor in front of the stage and asked me if I would like to use that feature. I, of course, said yes, thinking correctly that I would never ever get another chance to have the band perform in such a facility. The day of commencement we had a large audience of parents and I suspect lots of people who were just curious about what the inside of the building looked like. My band members were very excited about playing in such a venue. We took an elevator down to the level below and in front of the huge stage and every one took their place. Upon my signal, the Cathedral crew member threw the switch and we began our opening piece as we were slowly lifted into the vast hall.

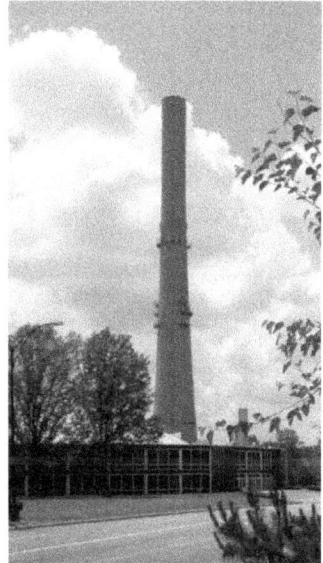

"Rex's Erection"

One other memory of Humbard stayed with me. He attended most football games when his sons were playing. One Friday night we were playing our arch rival, Mogadore. Donnie Humbard, a good "hard-nosed" ball carrier had been tackled and was lying on the ground when a Mogadore player deliberately kicked him in the head. Rex was so outraged that he came charging out on the field swearing at the officials and had to be grabbed by our coach Ray Brannon before the situation got out of control. So when put to the test, the evangelistic preacher was somewhat wanting in his demeanor.

Rex had plans to build a rotating restaurant, high atop the tower he built near the cathedral but never completed it under questionable circumstances. The photo was taken in 2012 of what all the locals call "Rex's Erection!"

Random Memories

I remember going into the faculty room on November 22, 1963 at Woodridge and hearing that President John F. Kennedy had been assassinated and going in to teach my next class and with a heavy heart announcing it to them. But what I remember most clearly about the experience is that one of the students, Linda Parry, a trumpet player, got very angry with me. It was a classic example of someone not being able to handle the bad news and wanting to, at least symbolically, "kill the messenger."

I remember the day when Barbara Lindley, an alto sax player, was bursting with enthusiasm about a new singer I had never heard of. His name was Elvis.

I remember someone calling me up to tell me that they wanted to donate a xylophone to the band. I drove to their home and they gave me a big cardboard box full of metal pipes and wooden bars that looked like a pile of junk. When we got it back to the band room and put it all together we had a perfectly serviceable xylophone we used for many years.

I remember climbing the stairs to a high platform and being given the honor of conducting the "Star Spangled Banner with massed bands of several schools in the "Rubber Bowl" for a University of Akron football game.

I remember getting together with the band directors from Revere, Copley, Stow, Northfield, Manchester, Mogadore and Hudson at Roland Gamble's house to talk music and drink beer. And then being invited down to his basement where the most clean-cut looking of the group, "Rolly" Gamble, would show us the latest in his collection of porno films!

I remember being called into our new Principle, Clair Muscaro's office and being severely "dressed down" by him because I dared to wear a new style of shirt that was made to be worn without a tie! Muscaro was not my favorite administrator.

I remember working very hard on half time shows until we had them perfected and getting to the field after a heavy rain and being unable to present the show because the field had become a quagmire.

But mostly I remember the hundreds of students who played in our bands and orchestras, the kids who sang in the choirs and the ones who acted and sang and danced in our musicals. And I remember a great deal of the music; the blasting of the brass and the pounding of the drums at football games and parades, trying to get the flutes and oboes to play in tune in concert band, seeking a balanced sound in the choir, looking for the right music for each group and each occasion.

And I remember hoping that the experience I gave each of my students would in some way enrich their lives.

Frankenstein Comes to the Party!

This occurred nearly sixty years ago, but it still remains vivid in my memory.

The band always needed money for one thing or the other—uniforms, instruments, or band music. Someone came up with the fundraising idea of having the band put on a Halloween party and dance.

A committee was organized. Some great ideas came forth from the students. We would use our band risers to make a spooky tunnel that everyone had to crawl through in order to get into the gym where the dance was to be held. There would be lots of icky things hanging down inside the tunnel and one of the kids offered to make a tape of scary sounds that would be piped into it. The menu would be simple; apple cider and donuts. There would be recorded music and a best costume contest. The decorations would be orange and black streamers and balloons, spider webs and a couple of skeletons, eerily lit. Of course, everyone was expected to come in costume.

The publicity worked. All manner of creatures appeared promptly at 7:30, ready for the fun. The tunnel was a big hit and the party was going well. At 7:45 a person arrived alone, dressed in a spectacular Frankenstein costume. He wore a scary full head mask that covered him down to his neck with, of course, the obligatory metallic knobs protruding out on either side. The mask had the classic Frankenstein look: a heavy sinister overhanging forehead and brow, the flat top of the head with matted down hair, skin with a sickly greenish color and tiny eye holes that only revealed the pupils of the mysterious wearer. His black jacket with huge shoulders looked exactly like Boris Karloff's in his famous frightening films. The picture was complete with heavy black shoes with a two inch build-up making the person appear monstrously huge. He walked with the accomplished stiffness of the legendary Mary Shelley character.

We wondered which student this could be. We welcomed him and asked who he was. No answer. He just handed over his admission money and proceeded down the tunnel. His appearance was menacing enough to evoke screams when he emerged from the other end. He lurched about the room talking to no one for about an hour and then left, again without a word spoken. That seemed odd. He paid his admission but didn't eat, drink or socialize. We couldn't find any student who knew who was under that costume.

The following October we held our second Halloween party using the same basic format. The crowd was larger and noisier. At 7:45 we spied the approach of Frankenstein once again. He paid his admission again in silence and repeated his lurching about of the previous year. We still weren't able to figure out who he was and why he had come at all since he didn't participate in the party in any way, but merely walked or stood around and once again left early. Somehow he looked more frightening than ever even though his costume hadn't changed.

When we started advertising for the third annual Halloween party we realized we had a very special feature to promote the event. The school paper headline read, "Who is the mysterious Frankenstein and will he appear again?"

The third party was the best attended. The moonless night was frighteningly dark and stormy. There was an unusually heavy downpour. Thunder and lightning shook the old brick school building. 7:45 came and went, but no Frankenstein. We were both relieved and disappointed. Then, at 8:20, we heard that sound we remembered from before—those heavy shoes trudging up the stairs. Once again he was silent. Once again he entered the tunnel and lurched about silently. But his time some of the more aggressive students, filled with curiosity, started to harass him and even tried to rip his mask off. He skillfully evaded them even with the clunky shoes he wore.

At 9:30 he came out of the gym and left the building. A few minutes later two students came to me to tell me that Logan Zintsmaster, a senior student and the band's drum major, who had his own car, had followed Frankenstein as he drove away amid the thunderbolts and lightning flashes.

Our imaginations ran wild. Who was that person? Was he a student, or an adult and what would Logan do if he caught up to him? Perhaps he was not from the school at all, but a predator looking for prey! Speaking of prey, we prayed that Logan would return unharmed. Thirty minutes passed. The dance was winding down and most of the kids were leaving. A group of concerned students and parents who had heard about Logan's chase stayed in the building. The storm raged on. The tension grew. We were contemplating calling the town's one police officer.

Meanwhile, Logan had followed the car down to Riverview Road where it turned south in the direction of Akron. At the little town of Everett the mystery car took a sudden hard turn to the right and headed

Bill with Logan Zintsmaster

toward the ancient narrow covered bridge that only had room for one vehicle at a time. It slowed as it entered the bridge and Logan got his best look at the car. As he did, he thought he recognized it as a car he had seen many times before. He couldn't identify it but had a strong gut feeling that the person to whom it belonged was not to be messed with. That's when he made his decision about what he would say when he came back to the school.

At about 10:15, Logan drove into the school parking lot. Relieved, we rushed out to ask him what happened. A breathless Logan said, "I followed him up Riverview Road. He must have noticed me behind him because he suddenly veered off at Everett and headed for the old covered bridge. Just as I entered the bridge there was a blinding flash of lightning and then he just disappeared. It was dark and pouring very hard. I kept looking up and down the road but there was no trace of him. I can't figure out where he could have gone."

If the mysterious person was one of our students we were certain he would eventually come forward to brag about how he had fooled everyone. But time passed and that didn't happen. The following year we moved to a brand new high school building and many things changed, including the demise of the annual band Halloween party.

Many years passed and scarcely anyone remembered those Halloween parties and the visits by the mysterious Frankenstein. After teaching there for sixteen years I had just resigned to take a new job. It was my very last day and I stopped in to say goodbye and reminisce about the old days with Paul Padrutt, the principal who had been a colleague all those years. As the subject of the Halloween parties and the appearance of Frankenstein came up, a small grin on his face grew into a broad smile and I knew I had, at last solved the mystery.

Paul said he had been concerned about certain students who were not band members making trouble at the parties and wanted to be on hand if there were any serious problems from outsiders. I suspect he secretly was hoping there would be a problem, so like a superhero, he could dramatically rip off his mask, reveal his true identity, and deal with the culprits!

Sometimes, when I think about the long ago magical mood of childhood "Trick or Treat" Halloweens, with black cats, witches, skeletons and monsters, I wish our Frankenstein was still one of life's unsolved mysteries.

Mezzo McClure

Becky was one of nineteen girls in the fourth-period chorus at Woodridge High School. She was a tall skinny girl with a ready smile and reddish hair. As the school year progressed I began to notice first her enthusiasm for chorus, and later her light and sweet voice which, unlike many of my other ninth grade singers, was always right on pitch.

Near the end of her second year in chorus Becky came to me after class one day and said, "Mr. Nemoyten, I really, really want to learn how to be a good singer!" Whereas I conducted private lessons on several instruments every Saturday with many of my band students, I didn't feel qualified to teach vocal students privately.

I was essentially a "band and orchestra guy." Woodridge was a small school and I had to do chorus work as well as instrumental. I was well aware of my shortcomings as a choral teacher. I had been a member of my high school choir and sang in the Kent State University summer choir while working on my master's degree, and that was about it for my training. But I did know something about the area voice teachers. So I said to Becky, "See if you can get your parents to sign you up for vocal lessons with John Stein this summer. He teaches at the Firestone Conservatory of Music at Akron University." She promised me she would follow my advice.

After school on the first day of chorus in the new school year Becky, who seemed to have grown both prettier and more confident over the summer, came to me and said, "I really loved working with Mr. Stein. He helped me a lot. Would you like to hear me sing?"

I said, "Of course, Becky." She asked me to play the accompaniment. I'm a very poor piano player, but the piece was fairly easy and I plunked away at it as well as I could on the Hamilton studio piano in one of our practice rooms. Becky was directly behind me as I struggled through the introduction. Then she began to sing. Was that really Becky, or had a mature woman singer snuck into the room? I was astounded. The voice was full, dark and rich. The diction was clear, the pitch right on!

I stopped and turned around to face this new phenomenon and said, "Becky! That was terrific! You have a wonderful voice. I hope you keep studying."

And keep studying she did. She became a very strong leader in the choir and also started to enter solo contests, always winning top honors. During Becky's junior year, the Piccolo Opera Company of Wayne State University in Detroit came to our school to do a chamber opera school assembly program. They had performed for the school once every other year for several years. I had gotten to know the singers pretty well and told them about Becky. I asked them if they would be willing to listen to her sing and they agreed to do so. I had asked Becky in advance and reminded her to bring her music to school on assembly day.

After the opera performance I invited the singers into the music room. Becky came in, but had forgotten her music. Actually, she was a typical teenager and a bit flaky at times. The pianist with the group asked what she was planning on singing. She named an aria from *Orfeo* by Gluck and the pianist said, "No problem, I know that by heart." He sat down at the piano and began the introduction and Becky sang. I watched the faces of the singers but wasn't sure what they were thinking. Had I gotten carried away in my estimation of just how good I thought Becky's voice really was?

Woodridge Girls Ensemble
Becky is in the back row on the left.
Next to her in the back row is Margaret Pettingill.

Without hesitation, all of the singers plus the one stage crew member, rose to their feet and gave Becky a rousing standing ovation when she finished. They then went up to her to ask her if she would like to come to Wayne State University and talked to her about the scholarships they could offer, actually vying with one another to see who could win her over as a student for themselves. It was then I knew that my judgment was correct. We had a very special talent in our school.

Becky did not go to Wayne State. She won a full scholarship to the Oberlin College Conservatory, one of the finest small school music departments in the country. She was to study voice with Richard Miller, a famed tenor and voice teacher. She went off to Oberlin, a school located about 80 miles to the west and dropped me a line from time to time. Everything went well for the first few months, but then Becky became ill and missed some school. It affected her throat and she was unable to sing for several months. She called me up at the beginning of summer vacation and said there was something she wanted to tell me. We met at the school. She recounted her health and voice problems and told me she had become very discouraged. She had a job in a bank and planned to drop out of school. She wanted me to know, said she was sorry and told me she had appreciated all the encouragement I had given her.

I heard what she said and then asked the most important question I could think of. "Becky, did they take away your scholarship?"

She shook her head. "No, they didn't."

"Then why are you quitting? They didn't take away your scholarship because, despite the problems you have had, they still believe in you and your great talent, just as I do. An important part of the learning process is overcoming adversity. You have another new opportunity awaiting you next fall at Oberlin. If you don't take advantage of that opportunity, all your life you'll wonder if things could have been different for you. No, Becky, you should definitely not quit school. You go back in the fall when you'll be fully recovered and give it your very best effort."

Becky took my advice. She went back and worked very hard. In her senior year she sang the lead in the opera *Ormindo* by Cavalli. The college had no tenor who could match her power, so they brought in a tenor from the Julliard School in New York. I attended that opera and was thrilled by Becky's performance. At the end of her senior year she applied for and won a Fulbright Scholarship to study opera in Europe.

But there is something else quite remarkable that I must mention here. That same spring another young woman, Margaret Pettingill, who had been a member of our Woodridge High School Choir graduated from Ashland College in Ohio where she was also a voice major. Margaret also won a Fulbright Scholarship to study in Europe. Becky was absolutely thrilled about that and has always brought that up as a highlight when speaking about her Fulbright honor. It was extremely unusual for two singers from the same school to win those awards, especially from a school as small as Woodridge which had about four hundred students at that time.

But my story about Becky doesn't end there. I moved to Illinois and then to California and lost track of Becky. I heard she was in Munich and doing some recording for Deutchagrammaphon Records. That was all I knew until several months ago when my son Mark forwarded a message to me from a Rebecca Norberg who was trying to locate a Mr. Nemoyten who had been her music teacher in Ohio in the 1960s. Since then, Rebecca and I have become reacquainted through email and phone.

I recently asked her to recount what happened in her life from the point when she left for Europe. The following email was her reply.

Hello Mr. Nemoyten (my Mr. Holland),

Thank you for writing last week! It is so good to hear from you! I'm glad your heart is doing better. Do you have a photo of you which you could send to Kevin and me?

I'll answer the questions as best I can. I entered Oberlin at age 17 in 1966. After graduating in 1970, I went to Europe on a D.A.A.D. (Deutscher Akademischer Austaushdienst) scholarship (Fulbright) and studied at the Brannenburg Goethe Language Insititute and then at the

Hochschule für Musik in Munich. While there, I sang with the Bavarian Broadcasting Company, recording for Deutsche Grammaphon and with the Munich Bach Choir. While in Munich, I studied with a student of Kirsten Flagstad (the Wagnerian soprano with the "largest voice in history"). I worked for a film company, screening movies all over Europe to be brought back into Germany (they couldn't make any decent movies themselves). I was to have lived in the Olympic Village where the Munich Olympic massacre took place. But, having been promised the world by an American talent agent, I decided to move back to America instead (in 1972).

For many years, my husband and I traveled across America, acting and singing for churches, camps, conferences and conventions. We sang on the CBN, TBN, PTL and Family Networks. Most of our lives, we have directed and produced mega musical/drama productions.

After freshman year at Oberlin, I decided to quit. I got a minimum-wage job at an Akron bank—until you talked me into going back (for which I shall forever be grateful)! How in the world can you remember *Ormindo* by Cavalli????? I'm so impressed! I played Sicle in that opera.

Oh, yes, you remember the pie-in-the-face escapades in my Christian club at Woodridge. It was called Youth for Christ.

I've been teaching at North Central University for five years now. I teach the teachers (Vocal Pedagogy), Music History, Music Appreciation (for about ¼ of the student body), Music Theater, Diction for Singers (multi-lingual) and Voice and Diction (for public speakers). I LOVE IT!

I also have about twenty-five private voice students this semester. This Easter, here in Minneapolis I will be portraying Jesus' mother Mary in a huge Passion Play for the eighteenth year. There are roughly 450 in the cast, flying angels, camels, donkeys—you name it. I am the main woman soloist, and my husband Kevin has the major male role. The music is really demanding. It runs for a month starting on Good Friday.

I don't know if I told you, but I went back to Oberlin a couple of years ago for a refresher course (School of Pedagogy) with Richard Miller. Did you know he is THE main authority on how the voice works? He has written some of the most respected resource books which are used in the major colleges and

Rebecca today

universities around the world. At age eighty-three, he is still amazing and sounds like a thirty-five year old. Speaking of singing, I'm still (at age fifty-seven) in really good voice. Mr. Miller was really surprised (he cried) when I sang a Wagnerian aria for him during a master class. When you are taught right, you keep your voice. I teach both classical and jazz/Broadway voice types. It's nice to be needed.

I'm sorry we can't get out to California. Kevin's and my businesses both keep us really close to home. If I ever do travel, I go see my Mom and Dad in Ohio. They are both in good health, but they are about eighty now, and I spend as much time with them as I can.

Well, I didn't mean to write a novel, but since you are personally responsible for most of the wonderful opportunities which have come my way in my lifetime, you should know what has been happening. Again, I am so appreciative for what you have done for me!!!!

Becky (McClure) Norberg

The New York World's Fair

After we decided to take the Woodridge Band to the New York World's Fair in 1965, I think it's possible that the average weight of the citizens in our school district increased considerably. Our main source of income for the trip was the sale of "World's Finest Chocolate" bars. We sold the calorie packed milk chocolate bars by the thousands and raised enough for the historic trip. One of the factors that encouraged us to mount such an ambitious undertaking was that during the previous three or four years the band had begun to perform at a very high level, having consistently been awarded superior ratings at district and state festivals. We applied to perform and were accepted two years prior to the Fair. We received approval and backing from the school administration, the Band Parents Association and the whole community.

Big Trouble

A week before we were to leave on the trip there was an incident that nearly scuttled the whole project. After a special evening rehearsal of the dance band, three students went into the store at Quick Road and Route 8 and stole some merchandise. They were caught by the owner and arrested. The result was that those students would not be permitted to go on the trip to New York. One of the students was our first chair clarinetist, Ken Gallegly. Fortunately we had two other fine first clarinetists who could handle his part. Another of the perpetrators was Howard Grether, a trombonist. I lost track of Gallegly, but I know that Grether became a Lutheran pastor. I don't remember who the other person was.

The Trip Begins

We left at 6:30 p.m. on June 10 from the Erie-Lackawanna railroad station in Akron, Ohio. The idea was for the kids to sleep in their seats on the train. Pillows were provided. The excitement level was through the roof and not many managed to sleep until well past midnight. We arrived in Hoboken, New Jersey at 8:30 a.m. Hoboken, incidentally, was one of the most depressing looking cities I have ever seen. Next we took a short bus ride and then a ferry across the Hudson River to New York City. Then sightseeing busses took the group for a trip to Chinatown, the Bowery, the Battery and to another ferry to the Statue of Liberty. At noon we arrived at the Piccadilly Hotel on 46th Street just off Times Square. Everyone unpacked and many got a little rest. There was more sightseeing after dinner. The chaperones accompanied the kids. Sally and I, along with our twelve-year-old daughter Jo, had other plans. We had purchased tickets to Broadway's most popular show, "Funny Girl," starring a sensational new young star named Barbra Streisand! We were able to get a babysitter to watch sons Mark, ten and David, seven Four-year-old Susan remained back in Peninsula with a neighbor. We only could afford side balcony seats, but it didn't matter. We could see and hear very well in what turned out to be the greatest stage performance by an actor I have ever seen in my life.

My Painful Condition

A few months before the trip I had begun to have a great deal of pain in my left hip. I was on pain killers all day and night without any relief. The doctor wanted to hospitalize me, but I told him that would have to wait until the trip was over. I asked him if there was something he could give me to help get through the five days. He prescribed Prednisone and it did the trick. That first night, I recall patrolling the halls of the hotel until 2:00 a.m. without feeling pain or fatigue and feeling that the students were all exhausted and safely asleep, I went to bed.

Thirty years later, on a visit to Peninsula, Gary Boodey, a trumpet player in the band at the Fair, told me the following, "Mr. Nemoyten, do you remember that first night in the hotel when you were patrolling the hall so late?" I said, "I certainly do." "Well after you and the other chaperones went to bed, a bunch of us went down to Greenwich Village!" Upon hearing that, I pointed my finger at him and putting on my sternest "I'm still your school teacher" expression, admonished fifty-year-old Gary, saying, "Mister, you are in big trouble!"

The medication did a wonderful job of keeping me going, but when we returned and I stopped taking it, I had a near collapse. A week later I was in Akron General Hospital and remained hospitalized for several weeks until a correct diagnosis was made and treatment started.

The next day in New York we took a bus to the Fair and performed twice; first at the nearly empty Tiparillo Pavilion and later for a good sized audience in front of the very impressive United States Pavilion. We opened that concert with the Star Spangled Banner, followed by the Navy Hymn "Respectfully dedicated to the memory of President John F. Kennedy," whose assassination in 1963 was still a powerful memory. The other selections included the "New York Suite", "Bugler's Holiday," "Mancini," and "Stars and Stripes Forever." The band played very well and the whole experience of playing in such a place was one of the greatest memories I have ever had as a teacher.

On Sunday the students were given the whole day to enjoy the Fair. At various times that weekend we toured the United Nations, the Museum of Natural History, the Hayden Planetarium, Rockefeller Center and Radio City Music Hall.

I'm convinced that, for some of our students, the trip was a life changing experience. It opened up a world of greater possibilities to those whose world was limited to what they had experienced in their own small town and occasional visits to Akron, Canton and Cleveland.

WORLD'S FAIR CONCERT
PRESENTED BY THE
WOODRIDGE
HIGH SCHOOL CONCERT BAND

William Nemoyten   Director ■ Robert Gref   Assistant Director

United States Pavilion
The Honorable Norman K. Winston, Commissioner
June 12, 1965 5:00 P.M.

STAR SPANGLED BANNER · · · · · · · · · National Anthem

NAVY HYMN · · · · · · · · · · · · · · · · · · Dykes
Respectfully dedicated to the memory of
President John F. Kennedy

CASTLE GAP CONCERT MARCH · · · · · Clifton Williams

FANFARE AND RONDO · · · · · · · · · · · · Fritz Velke

NEW YORK SUITE · · · · · · · · · Campbell Ponerty Azzolina
I.   Empire State
II. Broadway (featuring Stage Band)
III. United Nations

THUNDERBIRD · · · · · · · · · · · · · · · Frank Erickson

BUGLER'S HOLIDAY · · · · · · · · · · · · · Leroy Anderson
Trumpet Trio
Jeff Brown, James Bendett, Stan Robinson

THE BLUE AND THE GRAY · · · · · · · · · Clare Grundman

WORLD'S FAIR MARCH · · · · · · · · · · · Alfred Antonini

"MANCINI" · · · · · · · · · · · · · · · · Henry Mancini Arr. Reed

STARS AND STRIPES FOREVER · · · · · · John Philip Sousa

Woodridge High School
Paul B. Padurf, Principal

Boston-Northampton Local School District
W. J. Gregg, Executive Head
3313 Northampton Road
Cuyahoga Falls, Ohio 44221

Woodridge High School with an enrollment of 430 students in grades
9 through 12, is located 10 miles north of Akron in Peninsula
Ohio. The band, one of many fine organizations representing the
school, numbers 63 and has won many honors for Woodridge including the coveted Superior Rating in the State Contest in 1965. The
support displayed in sending the band to the World's Fair is a sin-
cere expression of pride in this group by the entire community.

Program from World's Fair Concert

Big Changes

Bill outside Twin Pines Manor
when he was Executive Director of the San Mateo County Arts Council

Pivotal Moment

I can trace my life back to the exact event that changed everything, that made me think of myself in a different way, changed what my wife and kids would do with their lives, led to incredible new experiences and eventually brought us to the "golden city" of the "golden state."

It all began on a Sunday morning in Akron, Ohio, "The Rubber Capital of the World" where we had lived for about five years. I had decided to attend a meeting of the board of the local Musicians Union. Nothing that happened that morning hinted at what this would all lead to. Toward the end of the meeting some of the "officials" were grousing about how the Cleveland Musician's Union was getting lots of federal grant money to employ musicians for school concerts, while none was coming to them. They said they had contacted the county school superintendent, but he was not helpful. That's when I told them I was a fellow member of the Union who was also a music teacher and that I knew the superintendent personally. I volunteered to contact him and see what could be done.

The year was 1966. John F. Kennedy had been assassinated and "Camelot" was no more. President Lyndon Johnson was riding high with the "Great Society" slogan. There were federal grant programs blossoming all over. Jim Wilsford, an English teacher at Woodridge High, a rural on the way to becoming suburban school where I had taught for fourteen years, had just won a $100,000 grant to develop a new English curriculum for small Ohio high schools.

I phoned Ralph Gilman, the county superintendent and made an appointment to see him. Ralph was one of the few music teachers I ever met who became a successful school administrator. I never heard any performing group he developed and don't know whether he was any good at music. I always wondered why, except for the money, any self-respecting musician would want to spend his or her days as a "paper pushing" administrator. But Ralph looked like a superintendent. Superintendent, hell, Ralph looked like he could have been an English lord! He was in his early fifties, six feet two inches, trim of figure, handsome, had a full head of reddish blond hair and always dressed as if he were doing a "man of distinction" ad for a major magazine. He was the most damn distinguished looking man outside the movies I had ever seen.

After some brief but necessary small talk, I told Ralph about the Union meeting. He explained that in order to get funding, the county would have to come up with a proposed project that involved hiring musicians to do something in the schools. There would be applications to complete, statistics to be cited …tons of paperwork. It wasn't simply a matter of just asking for the money.

I set up a meeting with the aforementioned Jim Wilsford to find out more of the details of what was given the catchy name by the Feds of "Title III of the Elementary and Secondary Education Act." Jim was generous and helpful and incidentally an outstanding teacher.

A few days later, while home with a bad case of the flu, it came to me. Ensembles like woodwind and brass quartets and/or soloists would do assemblies that included narrations that somehow tied in history, science, math and other curriculum subjects with the music to be performed. It would be called "Curriculum Oriented Music Assembly Programs," an awkward title, but it told the story. I phoned Ralph Gilman with my idea. He liked it and asked me to come in to his office as soon as I felt better.

A week later Ralph introduced me to John Mayhew, the Assistant Superintendent and told me that John would help me through the voluminous federal forms. There were statistics to gather and plug in and pages of descriptions to write. We spent most of the two weeks of Christmas vacation on the project and finally sent the application off to the regional office in Columbus. Mayhew was amazing when it came to steering his way through red tape. He was also a great guy and a pleasure to work with.

Though we sent the application in on time in January, it took until May to get an answer. John Mayhew called and gave me the news. The letter said we were turned down. The reason given was that the program "wasn't innovative." John said I had a choice to make; forget the whole thing, go back to the drawing board or go to Columbus and fight for the program. I chose to fight.

I made an appointment with the Ohio director of the federal grants program and drove to Columbus. After a two-hour drive during which I went over my "plan of attack," I confronted the director with this question.

"Our program was denied funding because it was declared to be 'not innovative' which means that someone else is doing such a program. Can you therefore please tell us about who is doing it so we can learn more about it from them?"

The question seemed to make him uncomfortable. He picked up his copy of our application, wrote a note on the cover and then looked up at me with a relieved expression on his face. "As it happens," he declared, "our district supervisor from Washington is visiting today. I'm going to invite him into our meeting."

Wanting to add some weight to my cause, I reminded the Washington man that I represented the Summit County Schools that consisted of the eleven school districts surrounding Akron and with an enrollment of over 25,000 children. I then posed my question about wanting to know who else was doing our "not innovative program."

The Washington man looked over our application for about a minute. He then declared. "I don't like the title, it's too long." I agreed and said we could change the title. Then came the real surprise. He said, "I don't think you can do it for the stated budget. It should be about $5,000 more." Again I agreed that he had a good idea. I thanked him and said I would make the revisions and resubmit. A month later the approval of the *Summit Music Project* came and my life changed forever.

After the approval came, Superintendent Gilman called me into his office and let me know that he wanted me to administer the program that would be a full time job for 6 months. I arranged to get a leave of absence from my teaching assignment and went to work in my new job. After the story appeared in the Akron Beacon Journal the word got back to me that certain other Summit County music teachers resented that I had been appointed to that prestigious job and wanted to know why they picked me. I knew why and was determined to prove myself worthy.

I went about the job very systematically. I rented office space, bought used office equipment, installed phones and hired a secretary all with my eyes focused on staying within my budget. I lined up performers; Nick Constantinidis, a superb blind concert pianist, The Kent State University Trio, string, brass and woodwind ensembles from the Akron Symphony and the symphony's concertmaster, Andrew Galos, a great violinist who had performed in the NBC Symphony under Toscanini. We also had a fine harpsichordist who was willing to transport her very beautiful and very expensive instrument around the county.

In that brief six month period I had organized the program, worked with the musicians to be sure they were carrying out our mission and contacted the

Nick Constantinidis at piano with Andrew Galos conducting
Akron Youth Symphony concert ~ Jo Nemoyten second chair violin

schools to schedule the assemblies. I had also made an attempt at getting an evaluation of the effectiveness of the program with a survey that was designed by a Dr. Blackwell, a University of Akron professor who said he could computerize the results for us. Keep in mind that this was 1966. Computers were still in their infancy and punch cards were the state of the art. He made several attempts at the project, but finally had to give up, most likely because the computers of that time simply did not have the required memory for such a task. But the bottom line was that we had presented ninety-nine programs in seventy-five schools in grades K through twelve, while providing part-time employment for twenty professional musicians.

When I began, it all felt peculiar and uncomfortable to not be answering the call of the school bell. I wondered what I was doing there instead of teaching as I had for the past fourteen years. After all, the only thing I had ever wanted to do was to be a good school band teacher. On some days I would say to myself "Bill, what do you think you're doing? You don't belong in an office. You should be out there training the marching band or conducting the concert band!"

This was a strange new world to me, but one that I discovered I was well suited for. Each day I seemed to know what I needed to do next. My new title as "Director of the Summit Music Project" was opening new doors to me every day. I was the same person I had been a few months earlier, but suddenly I was being treated with greater respect. As time passed and I felt more at ease in the job, I began to think about the fact that I wasn't getting any younger and that in a few years it would be very difficult physically to be chasing a marching band up and down the field. Also, there was the painful realization that while I was at the top of the school pay schedule and was earning extra money giving private lessons and playing professionally, I was still struggling to make a decent living for Sally, Jo, Mark, David and Susan. Now, for the first time in my life, I saw the possibility that I could earn a living, and possibly a much better living, by entering a new profession that I somehow seemed to be well suited for.

As the program was winding down in December, I decided to investigate other jobs in the field. I had recently read an article about the manager of the Chicago Symphony. His name was John Edwards. His was the only name of a person in the field that I had heard of, so one day I phoned him "person to person" at his office. I told him about the Summit Music Project and about my interest in arts administration. He listened very patiently and then advised me that the American Symphony Orchestra League would be holding their annual orchestra management seminar at Steinway Hall in New York during the first week in January and that I should enroll in it.

I took his advice and enrolled after arranging a one week delay in returning to my school position. I took a Greyhound Bus to New York City and stayed at the YMCA to save money. It has always been hard for me to sleep the first night that I arrived in New York. The electric energy in the air and the feeling that there was an incredibly dynamic night life going on all around me was overwhelming. Steinway Hall is on West 57th just down and across the street from Carnegie Hall. We entered through the vast piano showroom of magnificent Steinway grand pianos. The classes were held in a meeting room on the second floor near the intimate recital hall. The classes were fascinating, with a roster of the top symphony orchestra managers in the country as our lecturers. The students were just as fascinating. They were a group of highly intelligent, sophisticated men and women, many of whom were already in the field but wanted to upgrade their skills. Much to my surprise I discovered that one of my classmates was David Rockefeller, Jr. who was, incidentally and perhaps surprisingly, just a regular guy and very friendly. On one occasion the whole class went on a field trip to view a rehearsal of the American Symphony Orchestra conducted by Leopold Stokowski. Though a frail old

Ron Caya, Bill and David Rockefeller Jr. in 1966 at the Orchestra Management Seminar in New York

man by then, he rehearsed the orchestra with great energy and full command.

Some evenings I entertained myself by seeing the last half of Broadway shows. It started one evening when I went for a walk in the colorful and exciting theatre district. There was no way I could afford those pricey theater tickets. But I noticed that during the intermission, the audience members flowed out onto the sidewalk to smoke and talk about the show. Without really being concerned with what might happen, I joined the crowd as they re-entered, then stood in the back of the orchestra seating section grabbing the closest unoccupied seat when the house lights were dimmed. Of course, there was no room in the big Broadway hit shows, but I do remember seeing Melina Mercouri (the great Greek star of *Never on Sunday* and many other movies) perform in a show about the Sabine women who withheld sex from their husbands to prevent them from going to war.

A week after I returned to our home in Akron I received a surprise phone call one evening from Mrs. Mabel Graham, the Grande Dame of Akron's musical life and president of the Greater Akron Musical Association which operates the Akron Symphony, Akron Symphony Chorus and Akron Youth Symphony. I was astonished when Mrs. Graham told me that the Board of Directors had voted to offer me the position of the first part-time paid manager of the association. I had no idea that anything like that was being considered and though I was flattered by the offer, I phoned Mrs. Graham the next day and told her that I had two problems. First, that I didn't believe it would be practical to try to do the job on a part-time basis. Second, I already had a full time job with a lot of responsibility. However, I told her that since I was interested in entering the field of symphony management, I would consider the job if it were on a full time basis and if the association would match what I would be making as a teacher in the coming year.

She called a special meeting of the executive board of the association and a week later I was offered the job as their first full-time manager. A new chapter in my life was about to begin.

Running G.A.M.A.

The Greater Akron Musical Association operated The Akron Symphony, the Akron Symphony Chorus, and the Akron Youth Symphony. It had a board of directors populated by some of the most influential citizens of the City of Akron and surrounding suburbs. Metropolitan Akron has a population of nearly 700,000.

My appointment as manager of the organization perhaps wasn't as much of a surprise as it appeared in the previous chapter. I had been serving as the chairman of the Akron Youth Symphony for the past two years which entitled me to a seat on the board of directors of G.A.M.A. I had learned how the organization worked, who the "movers and shakers" were and what roles they were playing. And, most importantly, the board members knew me and so did several members of the symphony.

I started my duties in August of 1968. My office was in a fine old house on West Market Street in a semi-round, well-windowed section of the house that jutted out even with the large first floor porch that greeted visitors. I had a wonderful secretary, Mrs. Sykes, who had been "holding down the fort" mostly by herself for several years, but was now genuinely happy to have my help and counsel.

The eighty-member Akron Symphony was and is a part-time, but very professional orchestra with a season of seven concerts at that time. The musical director was Louis Lane who was also Associate Conductor of the Cleveland Orchestra. Early in his career he made his mark as a pianist performing with such conductors as George Szell, Igor Stravinsky and Ernst Ansermet. Working with Lane was thrilling and challenging, as it would be with any perfectionist!

The first concert of the season featured the rising young opera star, Marilyn Horne. I have written a separate story (right after this one) about my interaction with Ms. Horne entitled "The Yellow Cadillac Convertible."

On November 25th after having spent about three months as a symphony manager I wrote a letter to my former colleagues at Woodridge High School where I had taught for sixteen years. The following is an excerpt from that letter:

> *"Since leaving the profession, I have learned a sad truth. It's one I suspected, but while a teacher, refused to believe. I have encountered a kind of respect afforded to me in this new position that was not forthcoming when I was 'only a school teacher.' Although I enjoy the new found respect, I perhaps naively find it hard to explain. I am essentially the same person I was a year ago. I probably contribute no more to society than I did as a teacher. Perhaps I contribute less. I have made no dramatic financial gain, and I am not, as yet, (but have ambitions to be) at the top of the orchestra management profession.*
>
> *What I am saying is that being a school teacher does not afford one the kind of*

respect that it truly merits in our society. Although this experience may be mine alone, I suspect that it is not. As teachers, I feel you must find ways not only to upgrade your financial position, but seek out ways to make being a teacher mean more than it presently does in today's values-disoriented society.

I wish you much success, not only in your teaching duties this year, but also in your search for the recognition and status that is rightfully yours."

Louis Lane had done an excellent job with the orchestra during his tenure and had brought in superb guest artists. We had a good subscription base and attendance was respectable. But at that time the concerts were being held in the Akron Armory, a huge barn of a place that I had thought of as "America's ugliest concert hall." While the acoustics were surprisingly fine, the hall was aesthetically more suitable for circuses and live-stock shows.

Over a period from my early twenties to my thirties I had become interested in the possibilities innate in the interrelationship of the arts. I theorized that if I couldn't do anything about the ugliness of our auditorium, maybe there was a way to distract attention from it. I received approval from the board to install art exhibits into the vast area on the first floor where the audience enters. Our first exhibit was provided by Akron's premier gallery. They brought in a fine print show with signed works by Chagall, Miro, Picasso, Vasarely, Warhol, Dubuffet, Dali and others. Several works were sold, we received some commission funds and the project was a great success. The gallery had set up their exhibit on their own panels and had handled all the logistics.

The next month's show was to feature a prominent local artist named Marc Moon. We were to provide the free-standing panels and he was to install his paintings. I was able to borrow the panels from a local artist's group, but we had to transport them to the armory. We, of course, meant me, since I had no other staff to help out and a very limited budget.

It snowed heavily on November 19th, the day of the concert. Early in the afternoon I drove over to the truck rental agency. The only truck available was twice as large as we needed it to be and had seven gear positions. In those days rental trucks with automatic transmissions weren't easily available. Somehow, with a few words of advice on how to drive it, I managed to get it home and into my driveway. In the meantime, the snow was piling up in huge drifts. When it came time to pick up the panels I climbed back into the truck cab. After several tries, the cold engine finally turned over. My next problem was to figure out which of the seven gears was reverse. Over the next few minutes there was the cacophonous din of gears grinding as I pushed and pulled until I finally found the reverse and backed out of the driveway, ending up in a huge snowdrift across the street. Then the process began again as I searched for first gear and managed to stall the engine four times. Just when I was beginning to sense panic, the gear responded and I was out of the snow bank and on my way. After loading up ten free standing panels and then unloading them at the armory, I wasn't noticing the biting cold anymore and was thankful that there would, after all, be another art show to go with the music that this time would be the Poulenc "Gloria" and the Brahms Violin Concerto among other selections.

In December I was asked to go to Severance Hall in Cleveland, the home of the Cleveland Orchestra, to meet with Louis Lane and Michael Charry, an associate conductor who was the conductor of the Canton, Ohio Symphony. We were planning our joint concert in January. The Canton group had no manager so I was handling all of the logistics. After about 30 minutes of discussions, Charry accused me of somehow being devious in my dealings with him. I remember being surprised by the accusation and also somehow pleased. No one had ever so accused me of such a thing. I never thought of myself as being clever enough to be devious.

At that same meeting, Lane was trying to figure out what conductor he could ask to fill in for him at a future concert. I suggested the other new young associate conductor of the Cleveland Orchestra who both Lane and Charry referred to as Jimmy. Lane replied, "No, Jimmy would never agree to conduct any orchestra that wasn't a full time professional group at the highest level." The Jimmy he was referring to was a virtuoso pianist in his twenties named James Levine, the famous long time musical director of the Metropolitan Opera, now conductor of the Boston Symphony and recognized internationally as one of the world's great conductors.

Late on the afternoon of January 28, 1969, a blizzard hit northeastern Ohio, with the worst of it concentrated on the west side of Cleveland. That was the night of our joint concert with the Canton Symphony. As concert time approached we had two main concerns. Would we have an audience, and would all of our musicians be able to get to the hall?

We were pleasantly surprised with the audience and the players were arriving with a few telling of harrowing experiences on the snow covered highways. About twenty minutes to eight we received a frantic call from two of our players. Akron's first oboist and second French horn player were stuck in Bay Village, about forty miles away. The roads were still unplowed and there was no way they would be able to reach Akron in time for the concert. Each of them had the only copies of their music.

The conductors, Louis Lane and Michael Charry and I got together to figure out what could be done. We had plenty of fine professional players, but not the music. The first piece on the program was for double string orchestra, so that wasn't a problem. But next up was Richard Strauss's very tricky, oboe solo laden *Till Eulenspiegel's Merry Pranks*. After the intermission it was to be Tchaikovsky's very dramatic Symphony No.4 with lots of oboe and horn passages.

Suddenly, Charry asked me "Can you read a conductor's score?"

I said, "Yes, of course, why?"

He replied, "We have two scores to each piece. I'll conduct the Strauss from memory. I'll give my score to the second horn player and you turn the pages for him"

Not to be outdone by his younger colleague, Lane declared that he would conduct the Tchaikovsky from memory and that since we still had three oboes available, the third oboist could turn the score pages for Canton's first oboist who would be sight-reading her part from one of the scores.

The two conductors meeting the challenge of conducting, from memory, two lengthy and complex works was quite extraordinary. But keep in mind that Lane was the associate conductor to George Szell and Charry was an assistant conductor. Szell was considered one of the world's greatest conductors and often conducted major works from memory. Naturally, the people he would choose to be his colleagues would be extraordinarily gifted musicians.

In addition to the "high wire" act of the conductors, there was the challenge of the players reading their parts off of a huge score of music picking out their part from the 30 some staffs and finding their place again after the page was turned as rapidly as possible. What they had on their side was that while they hadn't played those particular parts before, they were familiar with the overall sound of the music. Following the score and turning the pages in time took great concentration. By the time the concert was over I felt mentally exhausted. Sally was in the audience and after the concert, she asked me what in the world I was doing sitting in the middle of the French horn section. She was amazed when I told her what we had to do because she said the orchestra sounded terrific and there were no detectable mistakes on the part of the conductors or players.

For that concert I had prepared a short essay about the music world's many Strausses that appeared in the printed program as follows:

Tonight's concert features *Till Eulenspiegel's Merry Pranks* by Strauss. Now the question is—which Strauss? Let me see... There was Johann Strauss (1804-49) of Vienna. He wrote waltzes, polkas, galops, marches, and quadrilles, led his own orchestra and fathered Johann Strauss II (1825-99) who wrote *The Blue Danube, The Emperor, Tales from the Vienna Woods, Die Fledermaus*, and many more. He is the Strauss we refer to as The Waltz King.

His brother, Joseph Strauss (1827-90) did his share by conducting the family orchestra and composing nearly 300 pieces including (with Johann II) the familiar *Pizzicato Polka*.

Then there was brother Eduard (1835-1916) also a noted composer and conductor. He led the family orchestra until 1902. Remember *The*

Chocolate Soldier? Oscar Straus (1870-1954), also of Vienna wrote the famous Nelson Eddy—Jeanette McDonald style operetta. He was a one S Straus, unrelated to Johann and his progeny.

Now we come to Richard Strauss (1864-1949) from a musical standpoint the most profound bearer of that famous surname. Born in Munich, Germany, and also unrelated to Johann's clan, he nevertheless managed to compound the confusion by composing *Der Rosenkavilier*, an opera with a wonderfully nostalgic set of waltzes that evoke the spirit of old Vienna. However, he is the Strauss who composed *Till Eulenspiegel*. Freshest and most spontaneous of the Strauss tone poems, it relates musically a well-known German folktale. The orchestration is imaginative and challenging to any orchestra, but perhaps not as challenging as keeping your Strausses straight!"

Later in the season I addressed the fact that we had a lot of paid for, but empty seats at the concerts by writing the following poem which appeared in one of our programs.

THE SAGA OF AN E.S.* (Empty Seat)

A short and sad tale in very free verse.

There it sits!
Proud that someone has financed it
for an entire glorious season and yet,
tonight sadly filled not with its owner
but with empty loneliness.

How awkward to have its venerable
wooden slats, nakedly staring at the musicians
enjoying making their music, but
enjoying it less when gazing at this emptiness.

If only he had seen to it
that another filled this void tonight.
Seats all about are ensconced with
their cheering patrons who would dare
not miss the moving music and the
works of art, leaving this ancient
rustic seat alone,
unoccupied and unloved.

For the February 25, 1969 program we had booked the Jose Limon Dance Company. Jose Limon was one of the true giants of modern dance in America. He had been a teacher of dance at the Julliard School in New York who had influenced thousands of dancers. He was not only a great dancer but a "force to be reckoned with." He was not a tall man, but appeared so nevertheless because of his magnificent bearing. When he entered a room all eyes were upon him. We met and went over the logistics of the program. It was then that I learned he wished to change the order of the music that was, of course, already printed in the program.

I carried his message to Charry who was our guest conductor that evening. Charry was not pleased and told me to ask Limon to reconsider. In addition to the printed program problem there were some staging adjustments and instrumentation changes that would have to be made. Limon was not interested in reconsidering. He insisted on starting the program with his most famous piece, *The Moor's Pavanne* which was his dance interpretation of Shakespeare's *Othello* set to the music of Henry Purcell. It was scheduled to follow the intermission.

It had been announced that this would be his farewell tour and the last time he would perform the intricate and moving part of the "Moor." In the end Limon won out. In situations like that, the guest artist is in the position of power and will usually win their point. I spent several stressful minutes caught between two powerful personalities. That was not enjoyable. But by the end of the program, the stirring music and exquisite dance programs won the day and all conflict was forgotten.

We didn't know it at the time, but Limon was suffering from prostate cancer. He died three years later.

There were two other particularly memorable things that happened that season. G.A.M.A.'s women's committee sponsored a symphony ball with the theme "Fiesta de Mexico." It was held at the Statler Hilton Hotel North. Dance music was by Lester Lanin's society orchestra flown in from New York for the occasion. The special guests were the ambassador from Mexico and his wife, who were flown in from Washington by the Goodyear Tire Company whose home office was in Akron. This was an example of an organization using its connections to create a win/win situation. The orchestra benefitted financially and so did some of the large local industries who used the occasion to have their top executives make personal connections with the ambassador and investigate trade and manufacturing opportunities.

Keep in mind that this was Akron, Ohio—not California. Mexico was pretty exotic to our people at the time. It turned out to be a glorious evening. There was fine dining, the women in their beautiful ball gowns, the men in formal wear, and terrifically danceable music filling the ballroom, colorfully decorated in the Mexican theme. During the course of the evening my wife Sally danced with Mexican Ambassador Margain and I danced with Senora Margain. The occasion was probably the biggest social event of the season in Akron and a smashing success for the organization. I take no credit for any of it since it was organized totally by the women's committee.

Near the end of what turned out to be my first and last year as manager of the symphony I learned that the University of Akron had received a large grant to build a performing arts hall on their campus. The Akron Symphony was to be one of its principal tenants, with the opening of the E.J. Thomas Hall targeted for 1971. Initiating a new hall is a perfect occasion for the commission of a new work for orchestra. I investigated possible sponsors and wrote a request to a local women's service organization called "Witan." Within a month we had our answer. We were to receive a grant of $5,000.

We met with Louis Lane for his input and he suggested that we contact Leonard Bernstein, saying we had nothing to lose by at least asking. Bernstein turned us down as did some other big name composers. It wasn't until I had left Akron that I learned the commission had been accepted by Mexico's leading composer, Carlos Chavez. I was told later that the piece he wrote for the opening of the hall was very well received. It saddens me to know that though I secured the grant for the commission, I never heard it performed.

The Yellow Cadillac Convertible

The year was 1968 and it was going to be a big deal. Mabel Graham, president of the Greater Akron Musical Association, announced it at the Trustees meeting. Allied Chemical had given the Akron Symphony a $3,000 grant to pay for a "name" soloist for the 1968-1969 concert season. On the advice of the music director, Louis Lane, the orchestra had hired a singer who he said was a rapidly rising star. Her name was Marilyn Horne, a name only vaguely familiar to me. But I wasn't going to admit that I really knew nothing about this "famous" singer of choice.

I had just been hired by the orchestra. It was my first position as an orchestra manager. For some reason, I felt the necessity to give the impression that my knowledge of the field was practically encyclopedic. In the ensuing weeks when the subject came up, the admittedly less knowledgeable (and less hypocritical!) would say things like, "Never heard of her, are you sure you don't mean Lena? She's great!" or, "$?!? That's a lot of money for someone nobody ever heard of!"

Ordinarily, I'm not one of those kinds of people who goes at a job in the "established procedure" way, that is, by the book. I never seem to remember what it said in the book at the precise moment when the problem arises. But this time it would be different. I had taken an intensive one week seminar on symphony orchestra management in New York a few months earlier. The right stuff was still in my head. All I needed was an opportunity to try it all out. I was armed with copious unintelligible notes, pamphlets, brochures, newsletters and article reprints from dozens of orchestras.

One of our seminar leaders had spent hours advising us on how to handle our guest artists. This was the glamour part of the job. He said we should research biographical information so we could carry on a conversation with the artists on their favorite subject—themselves. All the advice was very good, but it lacked one essential element. What kind of music did they make?

I asked Louis Lane, our conductor, about Marilyn Horne's recordings. He recommended an album called "Souvenir of a Golden Era." I listened to it, and frankly, she blew me away! That's the best way to describe it. The voice was rich and smooth, but I took it for granted that it would be. It was the range and technique that astounded me and made me realize immediately that we really were dealing with a heavy weight artist. Marilyn Horne sang the very difficult Rossini arias, some of the greatest show pieces ever written, as if old Giacomo had written them just for her.

After listening to the album a couple more times I made a point of raving about Marilyn Horne to everyone I met, with little regard as to whether they were really interested or not.

I was so impressed that I went back to those unintelligible symphony manager's seminar scribblings and took special note of the part about how you were supposed to line up community resources to give your guest artist the VIP treatment.

Following the example I liked best, I made an appointment to see the general manager of Dave Towell Cadillac. Putting on my most important looking three piece suit, and assuming my most confident air, I laid out a convincing set of reasons why providing a new Cad for our star would be of enormous benefit to his agency. I raved ad nauseum about the merits of our operatic artist to this man whose main interests lie in the Akron University Zippers football team and squeezing sales of luxury cars out of a blue collar town. He said he'd think it over and let me know.

The next day my secretary relayed the message. You can pick up the car any time. It turned out to be a gorgeous lemon yellow convertible! I congratulated myself continuously until I learned that an influential member of our board of trustees had called Dave Towell the day before.

Miss Horne was scheduled to arrive at the Akron-Canton Airport at 8:16pm on Sunday. I had the Cad washed and polished, put on my "gonna meet a VIP suit" and shoved a small newspaper clipping with a photo of Marilyn Horne into my wallet. I had had experience booking all of the Lyceum Bureau attractions for school assemblies at Woodridge High School. I learned early on that the actors, musicians, magicians and jugglers never updated their 8 x 10 glossies. In person, they generally appeared to look like what you might imagine their parents looked like.

I arrived at the Airport at 7:45 p.m. Her plane was to arrive at 8:15. After about five minutes there was an announcement. Flight 221 from Chicago had been delayed. It was now scheduled to arrive at 9:00 p.m. I read the Akron Beacon-Journal for the better part of an hour. Another announcement. The plane was delayed again and would arrive at 9:40 p.m. I began to worry about what I would talk about with this lady with the awesome talent. I had lots of time to worry about such things.

It was now 9:45 p.m. and at last, flight 221's passengers were disembarking. I stood close to the exit and looked carefully at the arriving passengers. Maybe she was wearing dark glasses. I heard she was pretty short and "full-figured." They kept coming, but I saw no one who resembled Marilyn Horne either as she looked in her photos or as I imagined she looked. I went to the ticket agent. Did he know if a Marilyn Horne was on the flight that just arrived? No, he had no record that she was on the flight.

Then it struck me. My God! I had lost my first artist! It was obvious. I was in deep shit! My new career as a symphony manager was over before it really got started. How the hell would I explain this to the trustees? Wait a minute... I'm thinking only of myself. What about Marilyn Horne? Wherever she is, what is she doing? Is she lost? Upset? Don't panic! Stay calm. There's a logical explanation. But no books or courses tell you what to do in this situation. Then the darker side of my mind really started taking over and ran wild. She's been kidnapped, of course. The symphony is probably receiving the call about the ransom right now. No. That's not it. I know, she... wait a minute. What am I doing? I've got to think logically. That's it. Call the Mayflower Hotel.

"Hello, can you tell me, has Marilyn Horne checked in? (very long pause) She has? When? Thanks."

I'm doing eighty-five down the freeway. In this baby it feels like twenty-five in my Ford. Wish I could enjoy it... What the hell is she doing at the hotel? Did she walk past me? Am I going nuts? Now I'm in the hotel lobby. The Mayflower is old and has that comfortable but no longer elegant feel to it. The desk clerk told me Miss Horne is in Room 611. I called her on the house phone.

"Hello, Miss Horne? I'm Bill Nemoyten, manager of the Akron Symphony. I was at the Akron-Canton Airport to meet you."

She interrupted, "Damn that Colbert Management! They didn't tell me anyone was going to pick me up. When the plane was delayed for an hour I caught one that was going to Cleveland. I'm terribly sorry you had to wait."

"Miss Horne, there are several things we have to get arranged. Can I see you now?"

She replied, "I'm very tired and I just got undressed, but you can come up for a few minutes."

Her speaking voice was like a "regular" person. So were her words. She didn't sound at all theatrical or in any way different—certainly not the kind of different that set her singing apart from every other human being.

I remember my first impression very clearly. She was wearing a silky, filmy, light blue negligee sort of thing that preserved her modesty while nicely displaying her femininity. She was a short buxom woman in her middle thirties with a pleasant round face and a warm and lovely smile. If you saw her shopping on the streets of Akron, you wouldn't notice her. She could be your wife, your mother, your sister, anyone but a great singer of great operas.

After a few awkward getting acquainted minutes rehashing how we missed connections I began to feel very much at ease with her. She was very real and easy to talk to, a person not overly impressed with her own importance. After succeeding in sounding reasonably competent and professional while going over her schedule for the next few days, I confessed that I was new at this business and shared with her how I had secured a beautiful yellow Cadillac convertible just so that Marilyn Horne, my first artist, could ride in style. She laughed good-naturedly, encouraging me to confess how new I was at this sort of thing.

"You're my first artist and Tuesday's concert is my first with the symphony. You might say I'm a virgin manager."

She threw back her head and laughed with a richness of sound that hinted of powerful breath support as she responded, "Well I want you to know that I'm not a virgin singer!"

My too loud laughter was fired up by a mighty burst of released tension. We relaxed into easy, more personal conversation. She went on endlessly about how her husband, the conductor Henry Lewis, when I asked her how long she'd been touring. Not a person to hide her feelings, her love and admiration for Henry (at that time perhaps the only black conductor of an American orchestra at the level of the New Jersey Symphony) gleamed in her face and the words she sang/spoke. I told her I had been a music teacher and she shared stories about her school days in California. I left her room on a high note worthy of stratospheric trumpeters and coloratura sopranos.

I phoned at 6:30 on Monday to confirm picking "Jackie" (her nickname) up in the yellow Cadillac convertible for the rehearsal.

"Louis is here and we're going over the music. He's taking me."

The rehearsal began at 7:30 on the stage of Akron's National Guard Armory, the home of the Akron Symphony.

After warming up the orchestra on the program's opener, Verdi's overture to "La Forza del Destino," Marilyn Horne was introduced to the orchestra by Maestro Louis Lane. I'd learned that only a few members of the orchestra had ever heard of Marilyn Horne and even fewer were familiar with her artistry. The orchestra played at a very competent level. Many players were local musicians and teachers. Some of the principals were Cleveland professionals and others were the prize students of Cleveland Orchestra players. Several of those young students have gone on to positions in America's and Europe's great orchestras.

Marilyn Horne sang Rossini's *Una Voce Poco Fa* facing the orchestra. Her full throated natural sound, even though it was directed backstage, reached the back wall where you enter the Armory. A few minutes into the rehearsal, it was apparent that something was wrong. At times it sounded like part of the orchestra was playing a different piece. The entrances after long solo passages were incredibly ragged and Lane was having problems keeping the ensemble together. The music wasn't technically demanding, so it was difficult to understand the cause of what was becoming a major musical embarrassment to Lane and the orchestra. Lane could, on occasion, unload merciless torrents of sarcasm. But with Horne standing beside him he chose more prudent methods of gaining control and finally, after some very tense moments, achieved a result that appeared to assure a competent performance on Tuesday.

It wasn't until later that I figured out what had happened. Marilyn's singing had intimidated and distracted the orchestra! Once they had a chance to hear and fully understood her talent, they were able to settle down and rehearse. Though they accompanied many first rank artists that season, none had so affected them.

That evening, I told Marilyn that I had read that everywhere she sang she evoked a tremendous response, and invariably, a standing ovation. I didn't have a handle, as yet, on our audience's responses, but I had the impression of never having witnessed a wildly enthusiastic standing ovation for anyone within those cold armory walls. So I put the question to her.

"How would you feel if you did not receive a standing ovation?"

When I look at it written here it seems like a stupid and boorish question to have asked, but I admired her answer which helped me to understand more about Marilyn Horne and other great performers I was to know in future years.

Without hesitation or a hint of arrogance she said, "Assuming that I had performed well, I would believe there was something wrong with the audience."

We had nearly a full house for the concert on Tuesday evening. Apparently, there were a great many opera lovers in the Cleveland/Akron area who did know who Marilyn Horne was. Dr. Bruce Rothmann and his wife were scheduled to host a private reception at their Silver Lake home for the artist and a few of the trustees after the performance, so I was told that they would drive her to and from the concert. I drove to the concert in the yellow Cadillac convertible with my wife Sally and two of our kids, Jo and Mark. They loved it!

The concert was a triumph in every way! The orchestra's concentration on their task was a complete turnaround from the evening before. Each of Marilyn Horne's offerings was greeted with thundering waves of applause seldom heard before at any concert in the Akron Symphony's history. Her final piece was followed by what seemed like a standing ovation long enough to qualify for the "Guinness Book of Records."

One of the special guests invited to the very private reception at Dr. and Mrs. Rothmann's home was Beverly Barksdale (a male Beverly), manager of the Cleveland Orchestra and an old friend of Marilyn's. After most of the guests left, Sally and I joined Barksdale, Marilyn, Louis Lane and our hosts around the kitchen table. Over tea, coffee, and wine, Horne, Barksdale and Lane relaxed and began trading symphony and opera stories. The conversation was full of juicy tidbits about the famous and soon to be famous, about ego and temperament and idiosyncrasy. It had become a "Can you top this?" thing brimming with fun and laughter. It was, in some ways, like hearing a group of stand-up comedians unload a rapid-fire stream of jokes, clever quips and wonderfully funny stories. You want so badly to remember everything, but your brain becomes too involved with the sheer enjoyment of the moment and you remember only the sweetness of the cake and none of its ingredients.

Marilyn's plane was to leave from Cleveland Hopkins International Airport at 9:30 on Wednesday morning. We had been up until 3:00 a.m. on that previous night. This time, no one would pre-empt me with offers to transport our celebrity. I arrived at the hotel after scarcely sleeping more than a couple of hours. I was still very hyped-up with energy left over from the previous evening. The gleam of the yellow Cadillac convertible on that sunny fall morning was like some kind of "eye opener" drink, or splash of cold water on my face that helped get me going. Marilyn very kindly made a fuss over the Cadillac, without overdoing it.

The traffic that morning was, for some unexplained reason, heavier than

Autographed photo of Marilyn Horne
For Bill
Warmest best wishes for a great success in this old business & thank you so much for "thinking big"
Marilyn
1968

usual. We approached the airport about 8:55, but were stopped at a railroad crossing behind a line of forty or more cars less than two miles from our destination. The train track was elevated enough so that I could see that it was one of those freight carriers that looked like its caboose was just leaving Elyria, some fifteen miles west. Determined that the return of our artist would be better than her arrival, I looked for an opening on the crowded highway, executed a rapid, wheel screeching, illegal U-turn, and headed for an alternate route I remembered. We arrived at 9:15, just in time for Marilyn's flight. She thanked me for the exciting way in which I arranged to get her to her plane, for the yellow Cadillac convertible and for everyone's warm hospitality, and then planted her bright lipstick print on my cheek.

Three years later, Marilyn Horne made her debut in Carmen at the Metropolitan Opera, with Leonard Bernstein conducting. I saw her at various places over the years; at the Chicago Lyric Opera with Joan Sutherland in "Norma" and also in "Italian in Algiers" in Chicago; in recital with the San Francisco Symphony at the Concord Pavilion in California, and countless times on television. I'm certain she wouldn't remember me. But whenever I see her, or hear her voice, all of these memories, feelings and thoughts come to me again and I wonder, like a jealous lover, how many managers over the years shared a few days in her life, and did any of them ever offer her such a snazzy yellow Cadillac convertible?

Heading for the Mississippi

There were three reasons why what happened next took place. The first had to do with the symphony management course I had taken in New York the year before. I mentioned that we had many fine speakers, most of whom were managers of major orchestras. But the most interesting and stimulating to me was not a symphony manager.

His name was Ralph Burgard. He was the Executive Director of the American Council for the Arts. This was in the late 1960s at the time when the community and state arts council movement was just beginning to take hold in the country. Ralph was the "Pied Piper" of the arts council movement. To me he was the most inspiring, articulate and persuasive speaker on the docket. I had for several years been interested and involved in the inter-relationship of the arts. Ralph showed us how an arts council could strengthen all of the arts institutions in a community. He turned me on to such an extent that I asked him several questions and when the class ended I followed him as he was leaving, still peppering him with more questions as we walked down West 57th Street.

Just before he headed down the stairs to the subway station, Burgard turned to me and said, "Bill, if you are really that interested you should go to the Palace Theater building in Times Square where our offices are located and join the ACA." Following his advice, as I did that very afternoon, once again changed the course of my life. I began receiving the ACA Newsletter which included announcements of openings in arts councils all over the U.S.

The second reason had to do with my surprising discovery that my services as a symphony manager had a market value, even though I had been at it for less than a year. I had attended that year's national convention of the American Symphony Orchestra League in Denver and met and talked to a lot of people. One of the sessions was about the fact that ASCAP (American Society of Composers, Authors and Publishers), was awarding cash prizes to the major, large budget orchestras to reward them for performing American music by live composers. I rose to speak on behalf of the smaller budget orchestras, stating that there were a tremendous number of such orchestras, and that since they also perform a great deal of American music, ASCAP should broaden their range and reward those orchestras as well. A year or two later I learned that ASCAP did start to make cash awards to smaller budget orchestras.

Apparently, someone from the Portland (Maine) Symphony heard my argument and was impressed, and perhaps they did some investigation of my background. About a month after I returned from the convention there was a letter from them inviting me to consider becoming their new manager.

I was pondering the Portland position when an intriguing notice appeared in the ACA newsletter. It stated that the Quincy Foundation had just made a grant of one million dollars in support of the arts in Quincy, Illinois over the next five years. It also said that they were seeking applications for the position of Executive Director of the Quincy Society of Arts which included managing the Quincy Symphony, among other duties.

The third reason this all happened had to do with my desire to improve our financial situation. The announced salary was $3,000 higher than my present salary. I phoned the man whose name was given as the contact person. His name was George Irwin. When I look back on it, I can't believe how much chutzpah I had in those days. The conversation went something like this:

"Hello. Is this Mr. Irwin? My name is Bill Nemoyten. I'm phoning about your opening for an Executive Director. I read the job description and I believe I'm your man."

Mr. Irwin asked me a few questions about my present position and background and then said, "Send me your resume." About a week later he phoned and invited me to come to Quincy at their expense. He said I was one of four candidates they had selected to interview. Instead of flying, I chose to drive the 600 miles with Sally. I recall most vividly that when we drove into Quincy on State Street and down to and around the town square which was four blocks east of the Mississippi, I turned to Sally and said, "If they do offer me the job, I really don't think I'd like to move to a place like this." Sally was a little more open minded about it, perhaps because she had grown up in the much smaller town of Clyde, Ohio.

The next day we were taken for a tour around the town. We saw the offices of the Quincy Society of Fine Arts located in the rear of the historic State Savings Bank, a beautifully restored pink granite building from the 1900s on the square. The front of the former bank was now a splendid art gallery. We visited the Historical Society of Quincy and Adams County; a Greek revival style mansion built in 1835 by John Wood, one time governor of Illinois and friend of Abraham Lincoln. We drove by the Quincy Community Little Theater and were told about their season of plays and musicals. We visited the Quincy Art Club located in an old carriage house. But perhaps most impressive were the several blocks of magnificently maintained large old homes, some dating back to the late 1800s, all adorned with spacious lawns and tasteful landscaping.

One of the most splendid of those homes was the mansion of George Irwin, where the interview took place. George, a bachelor, lived in a home that had been built in the 1890s. He was a multi-millionaire whose family had founded the Quincy Compressor Company and the Irwin Paper Company. George had recently exchanged his holdings in Quincy Compressor for Colt Industries stock, increasing his fortune greatly.

Not only had he spared no expense in renovating his home, but had filled it with a world class art collection that ranged from signed drawings by

Pablo Picasso to a huge oil landscape by Alfred Bierstadt and a modern sculpture by Louise Nevelson. The occasion was more like a gallery opening reception than an interview. There were delicious hors d'oeuvres and fine wines. Those invited to attend were officers of the various arts organizations and their spouses. They were knowledgeable and artistically sophisticated people. The group from the Quincy Symphony seemed to take the greatest interest in what I had to say, while the Little Theater people focused on Sally when she told them about her interest and experience in the theatre. I confess that I was very impressed with the people we met and the amazing amount of arts activities in Quincy, a city with a population of about 45,000.

By the time we left Quincy I was seriously considering taking the position if it was offered to me. A couple of days after we returned home I received a call from George Irwin offering me the job. I later learned that the two most important factors in my favor were my symphony orchestra experience which none of the other candidates had, and that I was the only one who had brought his wife along. Apparently, Sally made quite an impression on everyone. I told George Irwin that I wanted a day or two to think it over because it would be quite a stressful thing for our four children to make such a move. They would be leaving their schools and many close friends.

When we talked it over with the family, I'd like to think the children understood what a great opportunity this was for me and that they also understood how I had been struggling to make a living for the family. But I know the move was very difficult for them, especially for Jo Ann, who was sixteen, and for Mark, who was thirteen.

When I did call back I told Mr. Irwin that since I would be losing my professional performing connections the differential in the salary being offered was not enough to make the move worthwhile. He asked me how much it would take to get me to come to Quincy. I said, "$18,000, a good fringe benefit package and moving expenses." I had thrown out that figure thinking it highly unlikely the organization would agree, since it was three thousand dollars more than the job announcement stated. And, after all, that amount was one and a half times what I had been making as a teacher just two short years ago.

George Irwin said he would get right back to me and the answer was affirmative the next day. What I hadn't understood was that George was the organization. If George said yes, then yes it was. That amount made me one of the highest paid community arts council directors in the country at that time even though I had absolutely no experience in that field.

The Quincy Society of Fine Arts, established in 1948, was the oldest community arts council in the United States. It was certainly one of the best funded, mainly because of George Irwin. George was not only the chairman of the Quincy Society of Fine Arts, but also of the Quincy Foundation. He was on the board of the Illinois Arts Council and American Council for the Arts and was a member of the U.S. Bicentennial Commission, having been appointed by Richard Nixon.

As it turned out, I had four different jobs to do: executive director of the Quincy Society of Fine Arts, manager of the Quincy Symphony, booking agent for the concerts put on by the Quincy Civic Music Association, and administrator of the Historical Society. The job sounds impossible, but it wasn't because I had a lot of help and didn't have to spend time raising money as is true with most non-profit arts organizations.

Although I soon came to realize that I was in a very special situation, I had no idea that in the next three years I would be meeting and/or working with many famous people, attending a reception at the White House, flying around in chartered planes and spending a month at Harvard University. I also had no idea how much family turmoil would impact our lives during the coming years!

When we arrived in Quincy we bought a large brick house in a newer neighborhood. It had four bedrooms and two baths on the main floor and a spacious basement with another bedroom, bathroom, a recreation room and laundry room. It cost $40,000. I also bought a beautiful new blue Buick Le Sabre four-door sedan. It was the finest car I had owned up to that time, definitely not a schoolteacher's car.

The office support staff of the Quincy Society of Fine Arts consisted of two middle-aged women. Carolyn Eldin had been in charge of the office for about five years and now suddenly I was to be her boss. Margaret Weltin was a very efficient secretary and was able to skillfully operate our small offset press and all of the other equipment we owned. Since Carolyn had been in charge for some time I presumed she could provide me with the basic information I needed about the community, the arts organizations and the people I would be dealing with every day. She didn't seem to resent the fact that I was now in charge and, in fact, appeared relieved that she would no longer have as much responsibility.

After a week or two on the job I became very puzzled by her behavior. Nearly every time I asked her for routine information about matters she would have been dealing with on a daily basis for several years she was unable to give me the information. Or was she unwilling to give it to me? At first, since I didn't really know her, I was very surprised and confused. One afternoon when Carolyn was out of the office I approached Margaret with the question, "How is it possible that Carolyn doesn't seem to know anything about what we are doing when she has been running the office up until now?"

Margaret seemed relieved that I had asked her the question. She said, "I'm very worried about Carolyn. There is something wrong with her. She just isn't the same as she was a few months ago. Up until recently she has been very sharp and now she seems confused all the time."

I called Carolyn into my office later that day and asked her how she felt and if she had any concerns about her inability to remember routine matters. She confessed that she was indeed very concerned but simply didn't know what to do. I suggested that she make an appointment to see her physician and told her I would give her the week off with pay. Carolyn never returned to the office. The doctors eventually concluded that she had a blockage in the artery leading to her brain and recommended surgery. The surgery didn't solve the problem and eventually Carolyn was placed in an institution. I strongly suspect that she had an early onset of Alzheimer's, many years before that dreaded disease had been identified.

My letting go of Carolyn so early on was a bit of a problem. She was a native Quincian, had many friends and connections in the community. To some, I was the outsider who was the villain that had fired their old friend. Gradually, as the word about her health problems spread, people began to understand what had happened and I was vindicated.

My Four Jobs

The first and most important of my four jobs in Quincy was as executive director of the Quincy Society of Fine Arts. At our offices at 428 Maine Street on the public square we produced and distributed a monthly calendar of arts events in and around the city. We provided printing services for the arts organizations and worked at promoting all the arts in the community. But the fun part was working with the many artists who were brought into town. Here are some examples;

Thiebaud

We hosted a week residency by Wayne Thiebaud, flying him in from his home in California. At that time he was one of the best known "Pop Artists" in America. Famous for his paintings of ordinary items like pies, cakes and gum ball machines, Thiebaud had taken his place in the forefront of America's top modern artists such as Andy Warhol, Jim Dine and Roy Lichtenstein. I recall his doing a painting demonstration in which he painted a picture of a neck tie on a piece of Masonite. He took a lot of time to create a beautiful rendering of the tie, fascinating everyone with his skill and his insightful comments about art. Then, when he finished it, to everyone's astonishment, he picked up his palette knife and scraped all the paint off of the surface as everyone gasped. He explained that he wasn't satisfied with the work and that was that! Thiebaud was a joy to work with. In 1994 he was presented with the National Medal of Arts by President Clinton.

Slam

Slam Stewart was the most recorded jazz bassist of the 1940s. He visited Quincy around 1970 when, after having played with many of jazz's greatest artists, he added classical music to his repertoire. I arranged a tour of the area for him with a string quartet from Western Illinois University. Stewart, a terrific man to work with, had developed a unique jazz technique that was all his own. He had perfect pitch and hummed along an octave higher as he bowed improvised solos. Over the years he had worked with a "Who's Who' of the jazz world including Benny Goodman, Gene Krupa, Art Tatum, Charlie Parker and Dizzy Gillespie, Zoot Sims and scores of other greats.

Snodgrass

W.D. Snodgrass, American poet born in Pennsylvania, was invited to Quincy not just because he was a great poet but because he had won the Pulitzer Prize for Poetry. That fact made it helpful to get audiences out to hear him read. What I remember most about Snodgrass is driving him around the city and listening to his comments. He was the most sensitive person I had ever encountered. It was as if all of him was constantly being over-stimulated by everything he saw and felt. His biography reveals that he had been married four times. I can imagine from my brief experience with him that he must have been very difficult to live with. He was best known for his books of poetry "Heart's Needle" and "After Experience."

The Quincy Symphony

I was the manager of The Quincy Symphony, which was made up of local amateurs, school music teachers, Quincy College and Western Illinois University faculty members and a few outstanding high school musicians. The orchestra performed four concerts a year at the very large Quincy Junior High Auditorium. My first year in Quincy we had a "fly-in" conductor. In other words, he flew into town for rehearsals and performances.

Gates

His name was Crawford Gates. He taught at Rockford College in Rockford, Illinois and also conducted the Beloit Symphony in Wisconsin. Dr. Gates was a devout Mormon who was well known in that religion as a composer. He had written the music for a large Mormon pageant that takes place in Palmyra, New York every summer. His compositions have been performed by many major orchestras and there are recordings of his works by the Mormon Tabernacle Choir. Dr. Gates' very mild manner was apparently very different from that of the orchestra's previous conductor. It took some getting used to. Instead of yelling and cursing at them when they failed to get something right as the previous conductor had done, Crawford would gently say things like, "I invite you to try it this way."

He was a joy to work with, a true gentleman and a very fine musician. What could go wrong? As it turns out, only one thing, but that was a biggie. Dr. Gates had worked out his own unique system for memorizing conductor's scores using various colored pencils and symbols. He had managed to memorize several major works which he had conducted with the Beloit Symphony, an orchestra that was no doubt more accomplished than the Quincy Symphony. But since he had those pieces memorized they were the ones he insisted on programming. So, instead of selecting music to fit the capability of the orchestra, he expected the orchestra to play what he had memorized whether or not they were up to it. He opened the season with Richard Strauss's fiendishly difficult tone poem, "Don Juan." Don Juan lost. When the season ended we looked for another conductor.

Ritter

George Irwin came up with the idea of hiring a conductor/composer in residence. It would be someone who was capable of conducting the orchestra

Ritter composing at his home in Quincy with his cat, Napoleon. The piano originally belonged to A.O. Dengler, who sent it to Ritter when he was living in D.C. It remained a favorite, and he composed most of his scores using it. Above the piano is Ritter's Picasso.

who would spend the balance of his or her time composing music and perhaps doing some teaching. The Quincy Foundation put up the money to back that very exciting idea. I placed an ad in the newsletter of the American Symphony Orchestra League. The results were astounding. We received inquiries literally from around the globe. Musicians who wish to become orchestra conductors have so few opportunities to do so, that even a partly amateur orchestra in a small mid-western city that only did four concerts a year had enormous appeal.

After sifting through the pile of resumes, we offered the position to Dr. Thom Ritter George, then just twenty-seven years old and already a successful composer. He had been a composer/arranger for the U.S. Navy Band in Washington and performed as a violinist at the White House many times during the Lyndon B. Johnson administration. Ritter, as he liked to be called, was a perfect fit for the orchestra and Quincy was a perfect fit for him as a composer. Today he has over 350 compositions to his credit, many of them published and several recorded. After leaving Quincy, Ritter became a professor of music at Idaho State University and conductor of the city of Pocatello's orchestra. Barbara and I became good friends with Ritter and his wife, Pat and visited them in Idaho on two occasions in

Ritter conducting a rehearsal of the Quincy Symphony in 1970.

our motor home.

Ritter now lives in Appleton, Wisconsin and still composes and guest conducts. His wife is editor of "Flute Talk" magazine and has written many books about flute playing and technique and his three children are all music professionals involved in performance, composition and education.

Ritter graciously agreed to write the Foreword to this book.

How I won a prize that cost me money at the Symphony Ball

Each year the Women's Guild of the Quincy Symphony would organize a symphony ball at the Casino Star-Lite Terrace, a surprisingly large party room that looked somewhat like the show rooms in Reno or Las Vegas. It was one of their main fund raising projects. The tickets were twenty-five dollars per person which included dinner, dancing and chances on several door prizes, the main one of which was a trip for two to Bermuda. In the past they had always given complimentary tickets to Carolyn Eldin who had functioned as the orchestra manager. For whatever reason, they didn't give any to me, so I bought tickets for Sally and me. Keep in mind that a twenty-five dollar ticket at that time would be comparable to around a hundred-and-fifty dollar ticket in 2012 money.

Sally and I had an extraordinary evening at that ball. I was shocked when my ticket number came up for the first prize. If we hadn't had to buy our own tickets I probably would, as an employee of the orchestra, had declined to accept the prize. But under the circumstances, I felt I was justified in accepting the first door prize, which was the trip to Bermuda. The next prize was a beautifully hand woven afghan. Imagine our shock when Sally's ticket number came up for that. She graciously declined, feeling we had won enough already.

After the ball, Sally and I talked about when we would like to go to Bermuda and contacted the travel agency that had donated it. Since truthfully a weekend in Bermuda had pretty limited appeal to us, we were delighted to learn that we could use the $450 value of the trip as partial payment for a seventeen-day seven country trip through Europe. That summer we visited London and Amsterdam, cruised, the Rhine River, stopped in Frankfurt and Heidelberg, Germany, spent a night in Innsbruck, Austria, took a train through the Gotthard Pass in Switzerland, saw the Coliseum in Rome and the Grand Canal in Venice and attended a naughty show at the Moulin Rouge, visited the Louvre and viewed Paris from the Eifel Tower. The $450 prize ended up costing us another $2,000!

The Historical Society of Quincy and Adams County

Another of my jobs was to serve as administrator of the Historical Society. The Society owns the most historically significant building in the city. It is the John Wood Mansion at 12th and State Street. Built in 1835 by John Wood, Governor of Illinois and a friend of Abraham Lincoln, the wooden structure is in the Greek revival architectural style with a set of impressive columns adorning the front of the building. The main parlor inside the front porch entrance is a room restored in great detail with furniture and paintings of the mid-nineteenth century as are the upstairs bedrooms. But most of the rest of the building was organized as a museum with a collection of articles of historical significance from all over Quincy and Adams County. There were three items I was told were of special value. They were connected with the trial of the accomplices of John Wilkes Booth's assassination of Abraham Lincoln, with the balance of that collection located in the Smithsonian in Washington, D.C.

As a very old building, it was always needing repair of one thing or another, but one evening I received very disturbing news. The caretaker called to tell me the entire plaster ceiling of the dining room, which housed many of the artifacts, had collapsed. Thankfully no one was in the room at the time. To help pay for the upkeep on the ancient building, the Historical Society owned a commercial building on the edge of the property facing State Street. It had three storefronts on the street and five small apartments above on the second floor. No renovation had been done on any of the units and no rental rates had been raised in at least fifteen years. I set about to remedy the situation, arranging remodeling and increases in rent, which made the best business sense but didn't endear me to the tenants. When I visited Quincy a few years ago I discovered that the commercial building had been demolished. Apparently the society had found enough money to operate without it. And now the lawn is much larger and the building looks more stately than ever.

Sitting outside on the grass next to the mansion I remembered a striking piece of stonework that I was told was a capitol from the old Mormon Temple that had stood in Nauvoo, Illinois about thirty miles north on the Mississippi. Nauvoo was the place where Joseph Smith, the Mormon religion founder was murdered. A few years ago I was startled to come across that same capitol sitting on the floor at the Smithsonian Museum of American History with the acknowledgement that it had been contributed by the Historical Society of Quincy and Adams County, Illinois

Filming the Lincoln Douglas Debates

I believe it was in 1972 that we were contacted by Time-Life films. They wanted to use locations in Quincy to create a film about the Lincoln-Douglas Debates. Washington Park in Quincy was one of the sites of the six famous debates that elevated Abraham Lincoln from an unknown young Illinois lawyer to a national figure. I was to assist the film crew in finding suitable places to film the debates. Since Quincy had many fine old buildings, as I recall it, they filmed scenes representing all six Illinois cities in Quincy.

Lincoln was played wonderfully by the well–known movie and TV actor John Anderson. Anderson was one of those actors who everyone had seen many times in many roles, but few people could tell you his name. At the time I didn't know that John had actually grown up in Quincy. Anderson had appeared in over 500 TV shows, including *MacGyver, The Rifleman, Gunsmoke, The Big Valley, Star Trek* and *The Twilight Zone*, plus many films. His portrayal of Lincoln was excellent. He was a thoroughly professional actor and a fine person to work with. Douglas was played by Eugene Roche, a lesser known, but fine professional actor as well. Roche appeared in many TV shows including *All in the Family, Magnum, P.I., Soap and Star Trek*. He was also in many movies including *Slaughter House Five*. We became pretty friendly. He told me he had nine children back at his home in Boston. I remember being pleased to hear a year later that he landed a regular spot on a TV sitcom

The film crew asked me to play a member of the audience in one debate scene. They gave me a period costume and placed me on a bench. Just before the filming began I asked the director if he wanted me to react to the debate. He said no. So there I sat with a blank expression on my face. I never saw the film, but am hopeful that my scene was cut.

The Quincy Civic Music Association

Another of my jobs was to assist the board of the Civic Music Association in booking artists for the coming season. Established in 1927, the CMA has continuously presented concerts by many of the world's great concert artists and ensembles. Some of the attractions I was involved in booking for them were the Saint Louis Symphony, The Chicago Symphony, the Minnesota Orchestra, the Goldovsky Grand Opera Theater (in a performance of *Rigoletto* in English.) and the Norman Luboff Choir. I recently came across a letter to me by the CMA from their president, Dr. Richard Cooper dated September 13, 1972. He wrote:

"If you recall, the CMA was very low when you came to Quincy. Your help in writing up the proposal for a grant from the Quincy Foundation was the beginning of an upsurge by the CMA. We appreciate your advice, interest and very hard work on our behalf."

Quincy Community Little Theater

Although managing the Quincy Community Little Theater was not a part of my job, Sally and I became very involved in the organization. Sally, a very talented actress, landed principal roles in three plays. They were the female leads in "The Solid Gold Cadillac", "A Majority of One" and the role of Golda in "Fiddler on the Roof."

I had done a little acting in Community Theater in Ohio, but nothing of any consequence, so when I was beat out for the role of Tevye in "Fiddler" by, of all people, the Unitarian minister. I was neither surprised nor crushed. The minister, with whom Sally and I became friends, was a very experienced character actor and did a fine job, but his Yiddish accent could have used some improvement.

Sally (left) as Golda in "Fiddler on the Roof"

A year later I did get a good part in a show. It was the off-Broadway hit musical, "The Fantasticks." The truly exciting part was that the theater had managed to hire a man named Donald Babcock who had played one of the principle parts in the New York production for the past eight years. He knew every subtle nuance needed to put the show over.

We were able to get a fine cast together and an excellent group to do the musical accompaniment. I played the part of the father of the girl, who was performed by a beautiful young teacher named Sandy Million. The boy was played by a handsome young Franciscan priest who taught at Quincy College.

My role required some singing ("Plant a Radish") and dancing as well as acting. As the rehearsals went along we began to feel that we really had something special going on. As I had mentioned, I had acted in a few plays before, but I had never experienced the sheer joy and excitement that I was getting from "The Fantasticks," a truly magical show. For the first time in the theater I was feeling a special excitement on the day of a show, the kind where you can hardly wait for the day to be over so you can fly down to the theater, put on your costume and make-up, and become, for two hours, a character in a romantic place and time that never existed.

The show was a smash hit! We had standing room only audiences every night and had to put on two extra shows. On the last night of the run we had a rollicking cast party. I was pouring the champagne, using large plastic tumblers. I recall that I didn't get to my office until three the next afternoon and that Sally didn't speak to me for a couple of days. I still don't remember what it was that I did at that party, but it must have been a doozie!

The Quincy Art Club

John Arthur was hired as director of the Quincy Art Club around the time of my hiring. We worked together on many shows. John was a colorful character. He hailed from Oklahoma and was part Native American. He was very attuned to the latest movements in art and connected wonderfully with the artists who came to town and with young people.

John's taste in art was more sophisticated and certainly more avant-garde than what many Quincians had experienced. The Art Club was located in a quaint old carriage house that had been very tastefully converted into a fine gallery space. One of the first shows I recall John organizing was of wildly imaginative colorful paintings and sculptures of erotic "Funk" art which was popular in the '60s and '70s. According to Wikipedia, "Funk artists treated their work with humor, confrontation, bawdiness and autobiographical references." That show was certainly filled with bawdiness. It was infused with lots of sexual content like tongues and phallic symbols.

Quincy Art Club opening receptions were major social events among the wealthier old line Quincy families. Mrs. Elizabeth Sinnock, the very proper old president of the club, who lived in a large, very old home a block or two away, always took her esteemed place as the pourer of tea at the openings. And as was her custom, no doubt for many years, she smiled at everyone saying things like, "Aren't the paintings lovely?" Lovely would not have been the appropriate description, but you see, Mrs. Sinnock was going blind and had no clue as to the nature of the art in the show.

John Arthur, in order to interest young people in art, would invite many of them to his home after the formal openings where things other than tea were served. He moved on to Boston a couple of years later where he established a solid reputation in that city's art community.

The New Quincy Trio

One evening I received an unexpected call from George Irwin. He told me he wanted to have the Quincy Foundation sponsor a trio of musicians who would be in residence for a year. He gave me an outline of what he wanted and told me he wanted a proposal to the foundation on his desk as soon as possible the next day. That was the beginning for "The New Quincy Trio", which became Steve Wiseman, Oberlin trained pianist and native Quincian, Brooklyn born violinist Paul Statsky from Julliard and Indiana University, and Ohioan Mark Simcox, cellist trained at Oberlin College Conservatory. The group performed standard classical piano trio works and a few contemporary pieces with Statsky and Simcox also joining the Quincy Symphony as part of their duties. The first few months went smoothly, but after a while the members of the trio began to resent the way George was treating them—as if he were the king and they were his personal court musicians. They were pleased when the year ended and they could get on with their professional lives.

A Month at Harvard

As I entered the gateway to Harvard Yard and gazed at the ancient ivy-covered walls, I wondered what lay ahead for me in the next 30 days. I pondered the unlikely set of circumstances that found me in this most famous of educational institutions. And I wondered, *'Will I be lifted to a higher intellectual plain? Will I be up to the challenge?'*

It was 1970. I was working in Quincy, Illinois at my multiple jobs in the arts when we learned that Harvard University was going to present its first ever Institute in Arts Administration and that it was to be taught by the prestigious faculty of the Harvard Business School.

And now, here I stood in Cambridge, gawking at the sights like a country yokel. They had assigned me to Wigglesworth Hall Dormitory, one of the oldest on the campus. It borders on Massachusetts Avenue, Cambridge's most famous street. My second story window, just over the brick wall, afforded a perfect view of the hubbub on Harvard Square, Cambridge's busy commercial district just off the campus. As I strolled through the ancient halls on the way to my room I felt the unseen presence of the generations who walked those corridors in pursuit of an education that often lead to lives of fame, wealth and privilege.

My dorm room was Spartan, but certainly not lacking in character. The dark oak furniture was from a different era and bore the carved scars inflicted by the hundreds of students who came before. On the first day, two other institute class members joined me, but apparently they were not pleased with the accommodations and had other choices, so I found myself all alone with the imaginary spirits of the former students night after night.

Walking across Harvard Yard to my class each day was always invigorating. In addition to just enjoying the ivy-covered wall ambience of the place, there was an abundance of earthy bra-less coeds who were always championing some new cause as they pushed flyers at me about one demonstration after another. This was the tail end of the wild '60s and there had been nearly as much ferment on the Harvard campus as there was at Berkeley. Late one afternoon I returned to my room to find myself inhaling the last fading fumes of tear gas that had floated through my window following a demonstration in Harvard Square that had turned violent.

The forty or so students in my class came from a variety of arts institutions: museums, dance companies, theater groups and arts councils. They were from a wide range of locations, with the largest number from the northeast. The faculty employed the famous "Harvard Case Study Method' as their principal teaching strategy. Instead of lecturing on the facts of a particular subject they employed a printed scenario which we were to read. Each scenario was a story of an actual problem that had occurred in an arts institution. That problem always had to do with one of the major areas that concern all organizations whether for-profit or non-profit such as: marketing, financial, personnel, legal issues, leadership, boards of directors, etc.

The professor would lay out the case and then ask the class members to discuss and analyze it in a way that broke down the various components of the problem. We were then asked to offer possible solutions that were dissected by both the teacher and the class members. At various times the faculty would pull surprises on us. They would lead us into a case where the principal party was faced with a particularly thorny problem. The students were often very critical of the actions taken by that character in the story. And then, when the discussion had heated up to its highest pitch, the teacher would stop the discussion and introduce that protagonist who had been sitting in the back of the class and who had been flown in by the university so they could tell their side of the story. More often than not, after hearing the other side of the story, we changed our minds about the actions that were taken by the protagonist.

I remember very well a particular case because I became very involved in the discussion. The focus of the case was arts criticism and relationships with the press. It was about a review of a concert presented by the Boston Symphony, one of the world's great orchestras. The famous and suavely handsome Italian conductor, Carlo Maria Giulini, had been the guest conductor and apparently had done a very inferior job of interpreting the music because the music critics of Boston's two leading newspapers both wrote very negative reviews.

The older critic, Michael Steinberg of the *Globe* was very critical, but in a subdued and scholarly way while the young critic of the *Herald*, George Gelles wrote a "take no prisoners" scathing review that had the Boston Symphony's Board of Directors extremely upset and agitated. After discussing the review at a meeting they instructed the orchestra's manager to write a letter to the *Herald* demanding that they fire their young critic because of his incompetence. While the manager felt the importance of the bad review had been overblown, he was obligated to carry out the wishes of his board. Because the Boston Symphony is such a revered organization, the newspaper caved in and fired Mr. Gelles.

A very heated discussion erupted about the freedom of the press and the need to protect critics from the pressure of powerful organizations. Almost everyone in the room was highly critical of the symphony manager, who by the way was perhaps the best known and respected manager in his field. At one point I felt that I must enter the discussion because I was the only symphony manager in the class. I became the "devil's advocate" as I defended the manager. My position was that one of the manager's main duties was to protect and preserve his institution. Also, since he works for his board of directors he is obligated to carry out their instructions. Both critics wrote negative reviews, but the orchestra only attacked Gelles, the newer, younger of the two because he had stepped over a line in his review. The line was in a different place for the older, more experienced Steinberg. After I finished my statement the professor turned to me and said, "Mr. Nemoyten, I want you to meet Mr. George Gelles" as he pointed to the young man sitting next to me on my left. Mr. Gelles was actually a member of the class. Gelles smiled broadly, and we shook hands.

I lost track of George Gelles, but learned years later that he had moved to San Francisco and had become the manager of the wonderful Philharmonia Baroque Orchestra. He had also become a widely respected musicologist and a contributing editor to music encyclopedias.

The classes consisted of morning and afternoon sessions five days a week so I had lots of time in the evenings and weekends on my hands. I visited the museums on campus and attended an avant-garde music program in a very old auditorium/lecture hall. One of the composers represented on the program was Terry Riley who wrote "aleatoric" or chance music where each player is given a pattern of notes which they can play randomly. It's fascinating to listen to the sonorities created by the organized confusion. The experience was enhanced by the juxtaposition of the very modern twentieth century music being performed on the stage of a room that was designed and built in a Victorian style for performances of music that would typically be heard in the late 1800s!

For no other reason other than my curiosity, I ventured into Boston, spending one evening wandering around in a notorious area of the city known as the "Combat Zone." It was supposed to be a dangerous place to be, but I was cautious and have always had the notion that I was a lucky person and that nothing bad would ever happen to me. So far, so good!

I also visited the historic restaurant known as Durgan Park, a hundred-year-old establishment famous for its chowders, apple pan dowdy, johnny cake, Indian puddings, New England boiled dinners and sharp-tongued wait staff. When you enter you are seated at a long plank table with a lot of strangers with whom you soon find yourself getting acquainted. I don't know if the décor has been up-graded by now, but at that time the lighting came from bare light bulbs. The food was hearty and delicious and I got my money's worth in food and entertainment.

I spent one weekend driving down to Stamford, Connecticut to meet and visit with Dr. Bernard Nemoitin. I had heard of the Nemoitins of Stamford as long as I could remember. They spelled their name slightly differently from ours, but there were so few families with our name that we were always convinced that they were relatives.

Dr. Nemoitin was just as curious as I was about a family connection. Dr. Bernard Nemoitin was not the first Nemoitin doctor in Stamford. His father, Jacob opened his office in the early 1900s and practiced medicine for fifty-six years, delivering thousands of babies. In addition to his medical practice he was an artist, a photographer and a poet. His son, Bernard, treated his patients in the same office that his father had used. It was an old house in a poorer neighborhood where many of his patients were immigrants. A delightful fact I learned about Bernard was that he was a singing actor who specialized in Gilbert and Sullivan operetta "patter songs" such as "The Captain of the Pinafore."

On another occasion I attended an outdoor concert of the Boston Pops Orchestra conducted by the colorful Arthur Fiedler on a splendid summer evening. The setting overlooking the Charles River with private yachts cruising by to the lilt of Strauss waltzes was a delight for everyone lucky enough to be there on that magical evening.

By the second weekend I was getting pretty homesick for my family. Those two weeks were the longest time I had ever been away from Sally and our kids. From time to time I had been thinking about driving all the way back to Quincy for a weekend. Sally was to be playing the lead in a play at the Quincy Community Little Theater and if I didn't make it back for the weekend coming up, I would miss it altogether. I cleared it with my profs and took off on my twenty hour drive, arriving in time for the curtain of *A Majority of One*. Sally was absolutely terrific in the female lead role that had been played by Gertrude Berg on Broadway and Rosalind Russell in the movie.

Sally starring in "A Majority of One"

The story is about a Jewish woman who meets a Japanese man on a cruise after World War II. They had both lost sons to that war, but find solace in one another through their mutual loss and eventually a romance develops. Sally used a subtle Yiddish accent so convincingly that a local company hired her to do their chicken soup commercial on the radio. She became the Dennis' Chicken Soup Lady. At the end of that theater season she won the award as the outstanding actress of that Quincy Community Theater season.

I returned to Harvard renewed and ready for the last two weeks. A frequent point of discussion in the classes was the fact that certain arts programs consistently lost money.

When that came up in a case study the for-profit professors seemed not to get it. They didn't understand how or why you should have an institution that is not profitable. Some of them had served on the boards of arts organizations, but none of them had ever actually run one. Near the beginning of the course there were some heated debates with the professors as we tried to get them to understand that not everything we produced could or should be commercially viable. We explained that without breaking new ground the arts become static and uninspired. There must be support for experimentation and commercial failure is part of the price tag.

We observed that gradually they shed some of their "I teach at Harvard so I'm smarter than you" arrogance. By the end of the course the professors were routinely interjecting into their cases sentences like, "…but there are certain artistic elements that must be considered." By the end of the session most of the students felt that the professors had learned as much as we had. That was fortunate, because the institute was to go on for several more years and the succeeding classes benefited.

On the last day of class we had a party at which the students entertained. Since I was the only man who had a beard, I was assigned to the spoofing of our bearded professor who had a certain routine that we all noticed. He would start out with full business attire. Gradually he would shed items as he got further into the case study. His suit coat, vest and tie would come off and finally he would roll up his shirt sleeves. I put a nonsense speech together and as I delivered it I started his famous clothes shedding act. The students cheered me on as I carried out the professor's strip routine and continued past it by removing my shirt, undershirt, shoes, socks and the belt to my pants, stopping at the crucial moment to shouts of "Take it off! Take it off!" from the class, which by that time had become a raucous mob!

Remember, though the students were all arts administrators, most of them had formerly been artists, actors, dancers and musicians. They were creative free spirits who knew how to have fun, and what fun we had on that last day!

As our final assignment we were asked to write an original case study, one that incorporated a specific area that we had studied during the course. I wrote up a case that involved the sale of season ticket subscriptions to symphony concerts wherein there was some difference of opinion about how the program was to be organized. After I returned home to Quincy I all but forgot the assignment I had turned in. Then, one day I received a letter from Harvard. The Institute staff informed me that my case had been selected to appear in a new case study book they planned to publish. However, the letter said that the only way they would use it was if they had my permission to do so and that I would not receive credit for having written it, nor should I expect any royalties. Naturally, I felt flattered that my case made the cut. It didn't matter to me about not getting the credit. I agreed to the terms and signed off on the legal forms they sent along.

Two months later I received a copy of the handsome newly published case study book. When I read my case as they had edited it I was very relieved that my name was not on it. Apparently the editor hadn't much knowledge or experience about the way symphony orchestras operate. He or she made certain changes in the facts that changed the situation in a way that made the case study invalid.

A question that I have asked of myself is what I got out of my Harvard experience. I believe I learned to look at problems in a new way that made it possible to see the big picture and understand the dynamics of the situation. The ability to see the big picture is vital to leading any organization successfully.

The other benefit was an eye-catching entry in my résumé.

Chutzpah!

According to Webster's New World Dictionary, chutzpah is a colloquial Yiddish word meaning "shameless audacity; impudence; brass." The example in this story fits the definition and carries it to the highest level.

The tale begins at the Mayflower Hotel on Connecticut Avenue in Washington, D.C. in the summer of 1972 and ends at the White House two days later. The American Council for the Arts (ACA) was holding its annual convention at that venerable D.C. hotel. During the second day, rumors began to spread that president Richard Nixon was going to speak to the convention the next day. This happened a full year before the "Watergate" events leading to Nixon's downfall. Being a lifetime FDR New Deal Democrat, I was no admirer of Nixon and I had a lot of company in that attitude among the convention delegates. But we realized that having the president, whoever he was, speak at our convention, was a very big deal. It would be the first time that any sitting president had spoken before an arts council organization and therefore of major historical importance.

The next day the convention bulletin confirmed it. We were to be in the hall by 2:45 p.m. with our convention badges as our admission. The security was tight. There were suddenly hordes of mysterious dark blue suited men on the premises. At precisely 3:00 p.m. the doors to the hall were closed. After an interval of ten seconds, the United States Marine Band, the "President's Own," marched into the room from a side entrance, halted, raised their horns and played the ruffles and flourishes that precede "Hail to the Chief." It was a thrilling "chills up your spine" moment to savor. It wasn't about Richard Nixon anymore. It was about the presidency, history, tradition, the greatness of America and being a part of it.

As "Hail to the Chief" began, the main entrance door flew open and Nixon, surrounded by the bluesuits, charged into the room and strode briskly up the stairs to the stage to great applause from an audience that simply couldn't help but get swept up in the significance of the moment.

Nixon launched into an enthusiastic speech in support of the arts and their importance to the nation. He reminded us that he derived great pleasure himself as a pianist. He displayed a surprising amount of charisma and personal charm and then capped it all off after a twelve-minute speech by inviting the entire convention to a reception at the White House to be hosted by his wife Pat the next day at 4:00 p.m. We found ourselves presenting the man many of us truly despised, with a thundering standing ovation as he left the room to the irresistible strains of Sousa's "Stars and Stripes Forever."

The next afternoon the convention came to a halt as we all prepared for a once in a once-in-a-lifetime event. Everyone dressed up for the occasion and some of the women went shopping that morning. As we entered the greatest home in America, the power of its historic significance captured us completely. It was a sunny day and the room where the reception was held with its huge windows was bright and cheery. Elegant tables were festooned with gorgeous flowers, delicious cakes, bonbons and petits fours in a riot of colors and flavors.

As we lined up for the personal greeting by Pat Nixon, the Navy Orchestra began to play in an adjacent room. After shaking hands with Mrs. Nixon, most of us strolled into the room where the orchestra was playing a series of Broadway show tunes including selections from *The Sound of Music*. As they began the inspiring strains of "Climb Every Mountain," a member of the audience stepped in front of the orchestra with full confidence and a rich mezzo soprano voice and sang the song beautifully to the gathered audience. The proper military conductor appeared flustered, but carried on valiantly. The orchestra members looked delighted and amused.

The singer was someone we all recognized. Her name was Madeline. She was a member of the convention staff who had come in from their offices in New York. Madeline had been very visible during the convention, helping at the registration desk and seemingly everywhere aiding with room arrangements. She was a large, warm and friendly young woman who was like so many others who go to New York seeking a show business or concert career, but settle for a job to pay the bills until the big break comes.

By the time she finished, nearly everyone at the reception stood surrounding the orchestra and admiring Madeline's singing. When the audience broke into a thunderous ovation, even the conductor joined in the applause for his impromptu vocalist. Afterward, some of us put the question to her and without hesitation when asked why she did it answered, "I wanted to be able to put it into my resume!"

I don't know whether Madeline ever made it in show business, but I know she had three essentials for success going for her: talent, chutzpah and a very impressive resume!

The Audition

As mentioned earlier, in 1972, as the Executive Director of the Quincy Society of Fine Arts, I had written a grant proposal that resulted in the formation of the *New Quincy Trio*. This consisted of a violinist, a cellist and a pianist. The trio performed in Quincy and throughout the area for one year. This is a story about one of the members.

Paul was a "nice Jewish boy from New York." In his mid-twenties, he'd been to Julliard and had a brand new Master's from Indiana University, having studied with the storied teacher of violin, Joseph Gingold. Paul was selected for the *New Quincy Trio* on the strength of all that, and an impressive audition tape of the Tchaikovsky violin concerto. In addition to his musical talents he possessed a sweet personal charm, wavy dark hair and a warm frequently present smile.

Paul was out of his element in Quincy, Illinois, this small, conservative town of less than 45,000, with no Jewish delis and no subways. He didn't and couldn't drive. We chauffeured him around a lot. He bummed rides from whomever to rehearsals, performances and even to go shopping. It was like that all autumn and on into the winter. His salary was modest, but expenses for rent and food were cheap compared to New York prices. By early spring he had saved up some money and became convinced that he needed "wheels."

Paul bought a decent looking used maroon Pontiac for which I suspected he paid too much money because of his auto inexperience. After some minor scrapes, he became fairly proficient driving through Quincy's slow moving lightly trafficked streets. I consoled him when he failed his first driving test, telling him that I had failed twice myself before getting my license. When he passed on his second try, Paul had the mistaken idea he was now ready for anything. He knew the basics all right, but lacked the experience. He was about to gain that experience, the hard way.

The *New Quincy Trio* was only a one-year thing, so it was natural that Paul would start to look for a position for the coming season and beyond. He phoned Arnold, an old friend who was a member of the St. Louis Symphony, and found out about auditions for a second violin section vacancy. Paul started practicing four hours a day and made an appointment to audition.

St. Louis is about a hundred miles south of Quincy on the other side of the Mississippi River. It took about three hours by car depending on the weather, traffic and your destination in the city. Sensing that his friends might try to dissuade him from making the trip alone because of his dubious driving skills and experience, he told no one where he was going on that early Wednesday morning in May.

Paul packed his violin and a snack or two, filled the Pontiac's tank with premium gas and after a quick breakfast, nervously started across the torturously narrow bridge over the Mississippi to West Quincy, Missouri on his way to Hannibal. It appeared from the maps he studied that the way to St. Louis was connected to Route 61 via a road through Hannibal.

The road was there all right, but Paul didn't realize that the dotted line on the map that was soon to come up meant that that part of the road was unpaved. He was cruising along at fifty-five miles-per-hour when he suddenly hit the rough gravel surface. The Pontiac vibrated crazily as he tried unsuccessfully to bring it under control. He was powerless to stop as he careened into the ditch on his left side of the road, his door coming to rest with a crunch on a sturdy rural mail post.

His heart pounding wildly, Paul, unable to get out of the driver's side door, climbed over the passenger seat and out of the right side door. After assessing the damage, which was miraculously confined only to the unopenable driver's side door, Paul sat down on a log by the side of the road. Realizing he was lucky to be unhurt, he waited until he could calm down a bit before trying to figure out what to do next.

After a wait of about twenty minutes, a farmer driving a small but powerful tractor came along and offered his help. Paul was soon on his way again continuing slowly—very slowly—down the gravel road. It took nearly an hour to reach paved State Route 61, a two-lane road that continued through several small towns and then on to the wide interstate highway that ran into and through St. Louis.

This was Paul's first experience driving on a fast moving interstate and he was beginning to relax and enjoy it when he noticed what appeared to be a big scrap of rusted metal dead ahead about fifty yards. A forty-foot tractor-trailer was to his right and two cars were to his left. There was no escape. He struck the object at full speed and immediately following the initial bang there was a loud *kerplunk, kerplunk, kerplunk.*

Looking desperately for an exit, Paul worked his way to the right lane taking the first exit ramp he spotted without noting where it would take him. Instead of leaving the highway and spilling into a St. Louis city street as expected, the ramp led to the left, up and over the interstate on to an ancient narrow bridge that, to his dismay, carried him and the Pontiac back over the Mississippi in the opposite direction from St. Louis. In fact, he was heading back to Illinois to the city of East St. Louis. As he came down the exit ramp to a street of abandoned boarded up buildings, Paul began to recall overhearing some conversations about East St. Louis being one of the most depressed and dangerous black ghettos in America!

Kerplunking his way through the scary scarred streets, Paul cautiously steered his way through some twenty blocks before he spotted a gas station with a mechanic on duty. He told the man what had happened and watched while the mechanic crawled under the car. After some minutes of banging and cursing, the mechanic emerged and declared the car now fixed and drivable.

After paying for the service, Paul phoned his friend Arnold. All of the delays had made him too late for his audition and Arnold said he would call the symphony office and let them know. He then invited Paul to lunch at his house and suggested that if Paul needed any work done on his violin, they could visit a violin maker/repairman that Arnold said was excellent. Paul was given directions on how to get out of East St. Louis and into downtown which he wrote down meticulously. He was told how to find the "Famous Barr" department store garage where he was to park. Arnold would pick him up in half an hour.

Paul arrived at the garage in twenty minutes. It was a multi-level affair with a ramp that spiraled up and up until Paul found himself on the fifth floor in a space just opposite the glass enclosure in front of the elevator door. Arnold was waiting when he stepped out on to the street and Paul felt a release of tension for the first time since he had left early that morning, which now seemed like a very long time ago. Paul recounted his misadventures in detail to his old friend. Arnold was appropriately sympathetic. After a light lunch they drove to "Hans, the Violin Maker's" cluttered shop. Paul asked if Hans would please re-hair his violin bow. Hans agreed and set to work immediately on the very fine bow which Paul had recently purchased for $1,500. Yes, good bows can cost that much and a great deal more!

While the work was being done, unknown to Paul who was watching Hans intently, Arnold phoned the symphony office. He spoke to the personnel manager, explaining what had happened to Paul and asked if there was any possibility that the committee could hear Paul later in the day. After putting Arnold on hold for a minute the manager said, "We had a cancellation. Bring him in at 3:45." Hans was asked to finish the bow as quickly as possible. He was done in ten minutes and placed a small pouch of rosin powder in the case along with the bow.

Paul paid and thanked him and hurried with Arnold to Powell Hall, the magnificently restored 1930s movie palace that has served as the home of the St. Louis Symphony for many years. They arrived with only five minutes to spare and Paul had no opportunity to warm-up but was to report to the stage as soon as his violin was out of the case. Paul plucked the strings to determine that the instrument was still in tune. He was very nervous as he stepped out onto the stage of the vast hall with its two thousand bright red plush seats. He thought to himself while he waited for the panel to tell him what they wanted to listen to "there is something wrong, but I don't know what." Then he thought, "Everything was wrong today, but what the hell, I'm lucky to have made it to the audition."

Just then, the concertmaster of the symphony greeted Paul warmly and asked what solo performance audition piece he had prepared. Paul thanked the panel for allowing him to play later in the day and announced that he would play the first movement of the Tchaikovsky violin concerto. The auditioners nodded their approval at the choice and eagerly awaited his performance. Paul, who by this time was beginning to feel a little more comfortable, put his violin under his chin, raised his bow and brought it down to the strings for the opening notes of the famous violin masterpiece.

Nothing! No sound! The panel members, as one, sat up in their seats as if straining to hear a very soft sound. But there was no sound. Paul's violin was silent. At that moment he realized what was wrong and there was no time to fix it. He put his violin down and faced the panel explaining that he had just had his bow re-haired and that the violin maker hadn't had the time to do the essential step of applying the rosin powder to the bow. He was asked if he had another bow. He had, but it was an inferior one that he retrieved with shaking hands. He quickly applied his rosin cake over the hairs and started to play.

Later I asked him how he felt he had performed. He said, "All things considered, pretty well."

"Then what happened?" I asked.

"They asked me to sight read," he replied.

"How did it go," I asked.

"Not too well" He answered.

"Was the music difficult?" I asked.

"No, I left my glasses in the car."

Arnold took Paul back to the Famous Barr garage. Paul had little experience backing up his Pontiac in small places. When he described what happened next, before he could finish I found myself saying "Oh no! I don't want to hear this!"

He reminded me that he had parked directly in front of the glass wall that enclosed the elevator door, a fact that I hadn't forgotten. His next words were, "It was surprising how little noise that glass wall made when it shattered!"

After cleaning the shards from his roof and trunk, he started down the long spiral ramp to the exit booth. According to Paul, the parking attendant used really foul language when he told him about the glass wall. He asked Paul to get out of his car to show his driver's license I.D. and insurance information, but he couldn't because the space on the right side was too narrow and, of course, the damaged left door couldn't be opened at all.

Paul didn't get the position in the St. Louis Symphony. He left for his home in New York at the beginning of the summer and I left for a job in California wondering where Paul was and what he was doing.

Thirty-five years later, I learned through the internet that he had taught violin at the prestigious Cleveland Institute of Music for several years, and that he now resides in Ashville, North Carolina where he teaches at Brevard College. He has gained a splendid reputation in that part of the country as a performer and violin teacher. A number of violinists have him listed as their teacher with great pride. That doesn't surprise me. Paul has the soul of a musician, and while he is a fine performer, he has the perfect personality to be an even better teacher.

I recently phoned him. He was both surprised and delighted to hear from me after all these years. But I promised myself in advance that when we spoke I would not dredge up memories of *The Audition*.

Our Weekend With Victor Borge

The Quincy Symphony had never put on a "pops" concert before. The season was usually four performances: early fall, late fall, winter, spring. The music was mostly standards—garden variety Mozart, Beethoven, Haydn, Tchaikovsky. Occasionally smaller fee soloists were hired.

But things were different now. Instead of a "fly-into–town-once-a-week" conductors, we had secured a grant from the Quincy Foundation for a resident conductor/composer. We had hired Thom Ritter George, "Ritter" as he preferred to be called. He was very bright and talented having earned a doctorate at age twenty-eight He was an accomplished violinist and had been an arranger for the U.S. Navy Band in Washington. Ritter was open to new ideas and so were some members of the symphony board of directors.

We were going to be raising money for a new acoustical shell for the stage of the Quincy Junior High auditorium. I knew what was to be discussed at the next board meeting and I was prepared. But when I said, "Let's hire Victor Borge to do a pops concert," some of the startled board members looked at me as though I needed some mental health adjustment. Others, including Ritter were delighted with the idea, even if they thought Borge's fee would surely be out of our league.

"It will cost $5,000." No reaction. "We scale the house," I continued. "The orchestra section tickets go for $10, the balcony $6 and $4. We budget $1,000 for publicity."

Then the comments came.

"Nobody ever paid more than $5 for a ticket to anything in this town before."

"Is Victor Borge really that well known around here?"

"What if we don't sell enough tickets?"

Then the tide turned as others said, "Victor Borge is terrific and the very best person we could get for a successful concert. The worst we could probably do is break even."

Finally one board member said, "I'll personally buy ten of those ten dollar tickets, but do I get to meet him?" That's when I knew it was really going to happen.

The publicity provided by the Quincy Herald Whig and the local TV and radio stations for the April 9, 1972 concert created an avalanche of excitement. It soon became apparent we were going to have a winner as phone orders started pouring in from places all over the region like Hannibal, Missouri, Keokuk, Iowa and Jacksonville, Illinois. We sold nearly all of the "unsalable" $10 seats and eventually realized a profit of over $5,000!

The orchestra had been working very hard on the pieces Borge was to conduct, one of which was the overture to Johann Strauss's *Die Fledermaus*. We secured the best piano available in town and had it tuned and adjusted to perfection. Everything was set for the arrival of our internationally famous celebrity artist.

As orchestra manger, it was my responsibility and, incidentally, my privilege to meet Mr. Borge when he arrived in town. He was booked at the Travelodge which was, at that time, the newest and best motel in town. Borge's entourage included his stage manager and Marilyn Mulvey, the beautiful and talented soprano who worked so expertly with the maestro and his humorous barbs.

I had arranged for interviews with Quincy's two TV Stations. The first was at WTAD with Hal Barton, a crusty-voiced old timer who preceded his Borge interview with the daily farmer's hog reports. Barton misread some of the copy I had provided for the introduction that led me to suspect he hadn't any idea who Borge was or what all the fuss was about. The chemistry between them from the start was zero. Barton began by asking a long convoluted and ill-advised question. Borge's response was one word: "No." Barton asked another long meandering question. Borge smiled and I thought he was going to let loose with a barrage of his famous wit when he nodded affirmatively and simply answered "Yes." It went downhill from there. Barton ended the interview early, and we were on our way across the way to Maggie Thomas's show at WGEM.

Maggie was a friend who was active in various arts organizations, and I was determined the interview would go better this time. I called her aside and described the public relations disaster at their rival station. I learned a lesson that day when she responded, "Long questions, short answers; short questions, long answers… not to worry." Maggie was masterful in charming Borge while drawing information out of him about his life as a concert artist/comedian, his family, his origins and some of his favorite routines. Borge became the Borge we expected—relaxed, charming, sophisticated, and funny.

On Sunday my wife Sally and I picked up Borge and Ms. Mulvey at 10:00 a.m. and headed east to the home of Betty Kircher, chairwoman of the symphony board. Borge appeared edgy. As we drove through and out of town on the two lane highway, I tried small talk about the town, the orchestra, Thom Ritter George, our unique conductor/composer-in-residence and the people who would be at the brunch. Borge was silent. After fifteen minutes of Western Illinois scenery of farm houses, corn and soybean fields and hog farms, Borge became impatient and downright irritable.

"Who is this Kircher woman and why is it necessary to drive halfway across Illinois to have brunch with her?" he demanded.

"Betty and Don Kircher are wonderful people," I assured him. "There are others you will enjoy meeting. It's not far now—maybe ten minutes."

There was another long silence. "You know, I have a rehearsal today and the concert tonight. Maybe we should go back," he growled.

"We're almost there," I replied. "I know Mrs. Kircher has been preparing for your visit and the others would be very disappointed."

I was getting worried we were going to have a very unpleasant situation on our hands. It appeared as though our guest was little more than an irascible prima donna! Marilyn Mulvey said something to Borge we couldn't hear, and just as he started to say something I announced, "We're here. It's the beautiful house on that hill with the fenced-in horse pasture behind it."

We made the introductions to our hosts, the conductor and his wife, and the other board members. When I introduced him to Ritter, Borge said, "I understand you are half and half-and-half conductor and composer. Does that mean you only conduct half an orchestra?" Without skipping a beat, Ritter's retort was, "Yes, but you see I only compose half symphonies, so it all balances out."

Trading quips continued and blossomed. The conversation with all present was warm and congenial. The serving table was set before a large picture window overlooking a meadow on a perfectly beautiful spring day. The brunch included delicately delicious crepes, excellent wine and wonderfully fresh fruits all served on fine bone china and crystal stemware. Borge was obviously enjoying himself and seemed in no hurry to leave. But soon it was time to head for the rehearsal.

Betty Kircher with Thom Ritter George

On the return trip it was very quiet in the car as we all savored the pleasure we had shared. Then Borge spoke. "I want to apologize for what I said on the drive out here. We had a wonderful time. Please thank Mrs. Kircher for me. You see," he continued, " shortly after leaving my home in St. Croix in the Bahamas on this concert tour, I suffered food poisoning and I have not been feeling very well. That brunch was the first time I enjoyed food on this tour. I have been very irritable at times. I hope you will forgive me."

From that moment on, Victor Borge's health and disposition couldn't have been better. The rehearsal went beautifully and he expressed his delight at the quality of the orchestra. The concert was a huge success artistically, financially and humorously. Borge performed some of his best known routines, but also sprang a few hilarious surprises. Afterward, he attended a reception, signed autographs and later sent a personal note in reply to an adoring fan letter from my son David.

Victor Borge died in his sleep in December of 2000 at the age of ninety-one, having brought music, joy and laughter to millions for more than seventy years. We were fortunate to have experienced one magical, but very human weekend with that extraordinary artist.

Twenty-fourth Season 1971-72

THE QUINCY SYMPHONY ORCHESTRA

Thom Ritter George, Music Director and Conductor

Sunday, April 9, 1972 - Quincy Junior High Aud., 8:15 P.M.

AN EVENING OF MUSIC AND MIRTH WITH

VICTOR BORGE

PROGRAM

Die Fledermaus Overture — Strauss

Romanze — Svendsen

Paul Statsky, violin

Medley of Broadway Show Tunes — Rodgers/Bernstein

-Intermission-

"For All We Know" — Karlin, Wilson and James

"Musetta's Waltz" from "La Boheme" — Puccini
"The Laughing Song" from "Die Fledermaus" — Strauss

Marylyn Mulvey, colorature soprano

Triumphal March on the Occasion of the
World's Columbian Exposition in Chicago — Glazounov

Orchestra Personnel additions: Second Violin,
Dr. Richard Cooper; Viola, James Franke,
Vivian Langellier, David Hermann; Cello,
Julie Ann Jennings; Bassoon, Dennis Beiermann;
Horn, Ed Bostley

QUINCY SYMPHONY ORCHESTRA FINAL CONCERT
OF THE 1971-72 SEASON, APRIL 26, 1972 - Verne Reynolds, Horn soloist

BONUS CONCERT, The New Quincy Trio, April 28, 1972

Life by the
San Francisco Bay

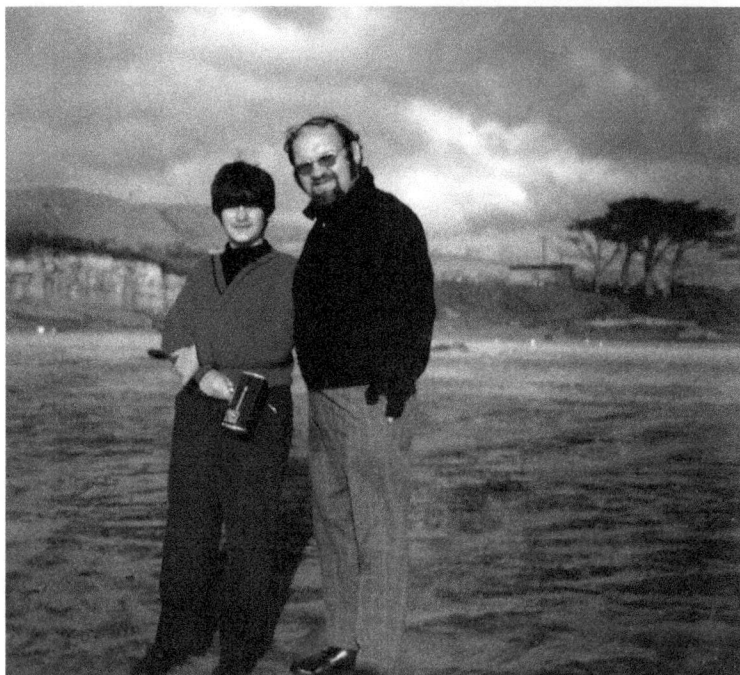

David and Bill on the beach
soon after moving to the Bay Area in 1972

How I Came To Be a Californian

I had been the Executive Director of the Quincy Society of Fine Arts in Quincy, Illinois, for nearly three years and though I was doing well enough in my job I had grown very unhappy. It was at the tail end of the wild '60s and two of our four children were actively rebelling by experimenting with drugs, pot and alternative life styles. They were driving us quite crazy. Some days I felt like I was going to really lose it and have a "nervous breakdown!" For a while I had developed the habit of visiting a bar near my office every day before going home and having two or three martinis. I would often drink with Don Nicholson, the city's mayor, who may have been an alcoholic. One day I took a hard look at myself and decided that I didn't need to add being an alcoholic to my problems.

I had also grown disenchanted with a fundamental aspect of my job or I should say jobs. In addition to being the executive director of the Quincy Society of Fine Arts, America's oldest community arts council, I was the manager of the Quincy Symphony, booking agent for the Quincy Civic Music Association and administrator of the Historical Society of Quincy and Adams County.

A large part of our funds came from the Quincy Foundation which was chaired by Mr. George Irwin. Mr. Irwin was also chairman of the Quincy Society of Fine Arts and heavily involved in all the other groups. He was generous with his and the foundation's money as long as everyone went along with all of his ideas and priorities. If he had an idea for a project he would call me, tell me his idea and ask me to write up a proposal and have it on his desk the next morning. Of course, it was always approved by the Foundation which he also controlled.

Little happened in the arts in Quincy if it wasn't backed by George Irwin. And while much of what he did was admirable, it didn't necessarily have anything to do with what the people of Quincy were interested in. To the outside world of the arts, Quincy appeared to be the epitome of what the arts should be like in a small city. But it was, in many ways, a bogus situation.

It had become important to me to know that I could function in a real environment where the community as a whole was setting the priorities and supporting the arts institutions. I began to look around for other opportunities in other places. The position of Executive Director of the San Mateo County Arts Council, as announced in the bulletin of the American Council for the Arts, was perhaps the most attractive arts council job offering in the entire country in 1972. The pay looked good and the location looked spectacular. I sent in a résumé and waited to see what would happen.

In the meantime, I had been contacted by the chairman of the board of the Memphis Symphony. Their music director, Vincent DeFrank, had guest conducted one of our concerts and we hit it off well. When their manager left, DeFrank recommended me for the job. I was invited to Memphis, wined and dined and given the grand tour. The situation was pretty good, but I turned it down because my heart was, at that time, much more into the very exciting arts council movement. Also, in the summer, the Memphis weather was even more stiflingly hot than it was in Quincy. In the back of my mind I still had the idea that I might be able to land that California job.

I had all but given up on the San Mateo position when in late June I received a letter telling me that, out of 105 applicants, I was one of four chosen to interview and that they would pay my air fare to California. I was surprised and excited because I had only been in the profession for three years.

One of the four to be interviewed was Ron Caya, a friend and colleague who was the director of the great Civic Arts Department of Walnut Creek, California. I was sure that since Ron had been in the field much longer and was a local person, he would certainly have the inside track on the job.

But I went ahead anyway and planned to give it my best effort. I knew that the reason I had been selected to interview was because I was the director of one of America's best known and oldest arts councils and also because I was president-elect of what is now known as the National Assembly of Local Arts Agencies.

The interview was held at the beautiful Beresford Recreation Center on Alameda de las Pulgas in San Mateo. Among the interviewers were Harold Atkinson, a well-known landscape architect and chairman of the San Mateo County Arts Council, the county schools art supervisor, Dick Sperisen, the director of the county historical society, Les Wilson, and Fenton McKenna, the head of fine arts at San Francisco State University.

The interview went pretty well even including that favorite question, "What is art?" But I had no idea whether or not I would actually land the job.

While in the area, I looked around and really liked what I saw. I took the opportunity to see the musical "The Rothchilds" starring Hal Linden at the Curran Theatre. I also went to the San Francisco Opera and saw *Die Meistersinger von Nuremberg*, my first Wagnerian opera, which was four and a half hours long!

I was told that there would be a quick decision since they wanted the person to start as soon as possible. So shortly after returning to Quincy I received a call from Ron Caya saying "Welcome to California." Apparently, I was correct in assuming that he would be the person to whom they would offer the job. But Ron was only using the offer to gain leverage in his own Walnut Creek position. When they asked him who of the applicants he would recommend, he said, "Bill Nemoyten", and that's how it happened.

I moved out to California, arriving by myself on August 1, 1972. I remember being enthralled with the incredible climate and writing home at the end of the month that I had just experienced the thirty-one most beautiful and perfect days in a row of my life. The sun shone every day. The temperature was in the 70s or low 80s and the humidity was always low. I used my spare time exploring the Peninsula and San Francisco, constantly finding new and exciting places. One of my favorites was the Bach Dancing and Dynamite Society in Half Moon Bay. My wife Sally and our two younger children joined me in the home I had purchased in Foster City in time for the beginning of school.

I consider myself a true Californian. I love this place. Our two older children eventually moved out to the Bay Area and they love it as well. I believe that in order to really appreciate what we have here you had to live somewhere else first. At this point I have lived nearly half of my life in the Bay Area. It's not just the weather that has enthralled me. It's the

Sally and Bill dancing
at the Bach Dancing and Dynamite Society
at their 25th Wedding Anniversary Party

beauty, the variety, the cultural life and, of course, the people.

If I had continued to live in Cleveland, my hometown, my life and that of our children and grandchildren would be very different. We would have been constricted by the expectations of my many cousins and aunts and uncles as well as our parents when they were living. We live much freer lives, with each person seeking what makes him or her feel happy and fulfilled. We all love the openness of this society and the acceptance of people of all races, religions and sexual orientations. Our move to California was the most important gift I ever gave to my family.

The San Mateo County Arts Council

Moving to California and Starting the Job

I rented a room in San Mateo and started looking for a new home. Somehow I hooked up with the Realtor, Bob Cahen. Bob was unusual, in that in addition to real estate, he was a highly skilled photographer with a great love of opera. He was, in fact, an official photographer for the San Francisco Opera and later became a close friend to Luciano Pavoratti. The best deals in houses were in Foster City. After consulting with Sally by phone, I purchased a four-bedroom, two-and-a-half-bath house on Gull Avenue for $45,000. We sold it ten years later for $189,000.

When I began the job, I of course knew what my salary would be, but I didn't know exactly what budget I had to work with. At my first meeting with Harold Atkinson, the chairman of the organization, I had a rude awakening. When I asked Harold about the budget, he said it was $100,000 and that sounded fine until I learned the figure was made up by a paid consultant. The Council actually only had $45,000. The consultant estimated they could raise $55,000 with some kind of a fund raising program. But the consultant was paid and gone and no longer in the picture. When I learned that, I told Atkinson that as far as I was concerned our budget was $45,000 from which the council had to pay my salary and that of my secretary. It also had to pay for office rental, phone, and utilities and for any programs we might sponsor.

Looking for an Office

Well, I wanted a challenge and I had it! Atkinson had set me up in a very expensive office on Borel Avenue in San Mateo. It was a prestigious address but too expensive and just one room for both me and my secretary. After about a month, I moved to a less expensive office in a stately old carriage house in Menlo Park. But it proved to be too isolated and distant from where most of my board members lived. So I looked for a better place. It was on the second floor of a commercial building on 25th Avenue in San Mateo. The rent was very affordable and the area was lively, with restaurants and shops of all kinds up and down the block. A local artist, Shirley Austin had her studio next door. I frequented the Crossroads Café, owned by the charming Betty Lokay who, since she had very limited seating, would introduce her customers to one another, getting them to happily share their tables. I met many new people that way.

The Sunshine Cottage

After about a year, we found out that a historic building called the Sunshine Cottage in San Mateo was to become available for rent. It had been used as an office by then Republican Congressman Pete McCloskey.

McCloskey, a decorated veteran who ran for president of the U.S. in

1972 and lost the nomination to Richard Nixon, was an anti-war candidate and later the author of the "Endangered Species Act." So it's not surprising to learn that he later switched to the Democratic Party.

We negotiated a good arrangement for the lease of the building and I inherited the congressman's office and impressive oak desk. The Sunshine Cottage had been built by Antoine Borel, a wealthy Swiss banker and land owner, as a wedding gift to his daughter and son-law. It had many windows and was indeed very sunny with a spacious welcoming front porch. Directly in front of the house, there were two large Sequoia Gigantia trees that provided dappled shade. We placed our secretary, and our Public Relations/Volunteer Coordinator, Joyce Golding, in the parlor. The living room and dining room areas eventually were made into a small art gallery.

The Sunshine Cottage
Watercolor by Rose Roskin

My office was in the back of the first floor behind sliding doors. The three bedrooms upstairs were rented out to artists in order to help pay our rent. The first artist to rent was Rose Roskin who became a great friend, a supporter of the Arts Council, a board member and later the chairperson.

During that first couple of years I spent a lot of time trying to convince artists of all kinds and all the established arts organizations that the San Mateo County Arts Council could help them to build audiences for their enterprises. I was also busy trying to raise money for our programs. We established two categories of membership in the Council; one was for individual donors and the other for organizations such as the Hillbarn Theater, The Peninsula Symphony, The Peninsula Ballet, etc.

Getting Support

I built a relationship with the San Mateo Foundation Director, Gladys Cretan, and her successor, Bill Somerville. Those resulted in several program grants. I also applied for California Arts Council and National Endowment for the Arts grants. We built a relationship with Hughes Airwest. The company had a large operation nearby. We installed an art exhibit in their lobby and later they sponsored an art exchange with artists of the state of Jalisco, Mexico which was curated by College of San Mateo faculty member,

Vince Rascon. At that time, color Xerox copies had just come into use. A local artist had developed a series of art works done on a color copy machine. I convinced the woman who owned a copy shop nearby to sponsor the show, which was a great success for both her and all of us.

More Programs

With a grant we hired Evelyn Leiske, a fantastic local pianist/organist who knew a great many singers and we began a series of noon time outdoor concerts in front of the Sunshine Cottage we called "Bach's Lunch." Workers from the Flour Company building and other area businesses brought their lunches and sat under the shade of the Sequoia trees and enjoyed the programs. On one occasion the amazing Evelyn put on a complete production of Gilbert and Sullivan's "Trial by Jury." Later, we expanded by doing programs in downtown Redwood City. One of the artists featured was tall, dark haired bass-baritone John Del Carlo, who a few years later became an international opera star, performing many times with the Metropolitan and San Francisco opera companies, most notably in the role of the title character in "Don Pasquale." The other very notable artist was a very young Wesla Whitfield who pleased our audiences with selections from the "Popular American Song Book." A few years later she was shot during an incident in San Francisco and became paralyzed from the waist down. But that didn't stop her. With her husband, great jazz pianist Mike Greensill, she has gone on to perform on Broadway, at Carnegie Hall, at the Whitehouse and countless times on TV and radio.

We Find a Carpenter

After we moved into the Sunshine Cottage, we looked for volunteers to help us fix the place up and make it more presentable to the public. One day a man in his early sixties came in and told us he was a retired carpenter and he would like to volunteer his services. His name was George Bachert and he was a terrific carpenter. One problem was that George only knew one way to build things. They had to be durable and lasting. So when we asked him to construct some light panels on which we could hang paintings, instead he built sturdy heavy walls. But he was great at repairing everything that needed work and he became an integral part of our Council family.

Then one day we had an unusual visitor. I don't recall his name, but remember that he was actually wearing a cape and had a mustache that gave him a somewhat sinister appearance. As he entered my office, he handed me his card. It had his name and the fact that he was a probation officer for the County of San Mateo. I learned from him that George Bachert was not a volunteer, but a person who had been directed to do community service by the court. George had gotten drunk in a bar in Burlingame and threatened people with a gun. I was asked by the probation officer how many hours George had put in and when I told him the number he wondered why

George was still coming around since he had, by that time, fulfilled his probation requirement. But George had found a home with us and spent the next four years helping with a myriad of projects.

Joyce Golding and the Peninsula Press Club

Joyce Golding came in to the Arts Council one day and ended up staying with us for the next six years. She began as a volunteer. Eventually we were able to find some money to pay her as a part-time employee, even though she worked full-time as our Public Relations Director/ Volunteer Coordinator. Joyce's husband, George, was a staff writer for the San Mateo Times and was very active in the Peninsula Press Club. It was Joyce's idea to have the Arts Council put on an annual Press Club party. We had artists do demonstrations and musicians perform and served wine and refreshments for the members of area newspapers. Joyce always managed to find volunteers to help out at those occasions. For one of them held at the Sunshine Cottage, she somehow lined up two young women named Hearst, one of them being Patricia, who two years later made the national headlines when she was kidnapped by the "Simbionese Liberation Party."

African Dance and My Knee

On one of the other Peninsula Press Club events, which were held in a hall in Burlingame, I had invited an exciting new dance company that had been organized in East Palo Alto by a man named Malonga Casquelourd. He had recently come from the Congo on some kind of an arrangement with Stanford University. I was very impressed with the job he had done with the young dancers and drummers, most of whom came from East Palo Alto which is in San Mateo County. They were our big feature for the event. As was their custom, after finishing their performance they came out to the audience and invited everyone to join them in their very vigorous dancing. When the tall female lead dancer in full African costume virtually pulled me out of my seat I could hardly refuse to participate. The energy created with the great drumming and wild dancing along with the drinks I had at the bar caused my inhibitions to leave me. I was to regret that in a day or two when my left knee started aching and swelled up. The doctor was surprised when I told him my injury had been was caused by my dancing with an African dance company. But he took note of that and when Worker's Compensation people first turned my benefit claim down, he verified that my claim was valid, since my participation was connected with my job. I used crutches for several weeks and eventually had to have surgery on that knee. Malonga Casquelourd's dance company went on to be one of the finest of its kind and eventually led to the establishment of the Malonga Casquelourd Center for the Arts in Oakland.

Politics

During my second year I became politically active in supporting state senator Arlen Gregorio's bill to increase the California Arts Council's budget to one million dollars. That was a paltry amount compared to New York and several other states. Up until that time the budget had been about $250,000 that was administered by a group of political appointee arts dilettantes as their little plaything. Many arts organizations got their members to write letters to their state senators. We worked very hard on that campaign and Gregorio's bill passed. He told me that the then Governor Ronald Reagan, who had the unrealistic and uninformed idea that all arts should be profitable and self-sustaining, was reluctant to sign the bill, but grudgingly did so because of the tremendous support it had received from the public.

I also had to learn the San Mateo County political game as well because we received what was called a "subvention" from the Board of Supervisors each year. That meant that we had to keep convincing them that what we were doing was valuable and important work for the county. I met with each of the supervisors and kept inviting them to events we were sponsoring. I also encouraged our board members to keep in contact with them. One of the supervisors was former Forty-niners football star, Hall of Famer, Bob St. Clair, known as the "Geek" because of his eccentricities when he played the sport. At the time he was a supervisor, I was hosting a weekly half hour show on a small local cable TV station in San Carlos. Each week I would interview artists, actors, dancers and musicians on the program. On one of those programs I had invited the director of the Nairobi Cultural Center of East Palo Alto. He was an extremely militant black man. Right from the beginning he used the opportunity to attack me as well as the San Mateo County Arts Council. When I asked him what he thought the Council could do for his organization he suggested that we should turn all of our money over to him. The interview was a disaster! Later that same evening there was a reception at the beautiful, but now defunct Borel Restaurant. Bob St. Clair was there. When he saw me he laughed and said, "Bill, that guy really gave you a hard time, didn't he?" I replied, "Bob, I can't believe you watched that program. I had begun to believe that no one ever watched it!"

The Crisis

The San Mateo County Arts Council chairman, Harold Atkinson, was a widely respected and influential landscape architect. We had been working harmoniously for several months when suddenly he began to propose new ideas that would change the direction we were moving into so very successfully. We met for lunch one day and Harold declared his opposition to the new programs we were developing.

We were in the process of establishing a fine little art gallery in the building we occupied and were making plans for satellite galleries in other locations in the county. We had begun a series of "Brown Bag" lunch concerts featuring local performers. We were publishing and distributing a monthly arts events calendar to promote the efforts of all the existing arts groups. But Harold had decided that we were going in the wrong direction and that our only role should be as an arts planning organization and that we should be spending our time planning the development of arts facilities for some future date. I respectfully disagreed.

I had come to California from Quincy, Illinois where I had, for the past three years, run a very successful classic community arts council. When I came out to California, the leadership of the San Mateo Arts Council knew my record of accomplishment and I thought we had an understanding of

Arts Council Chief Survives Ouster Try

William Nemoyten still has his job today after a group of directors tried Thursday to brush him off as executive director of the San Mateo County Arts Council.

Instead, the 45-year-old Nemoyten won a vote of confidence from a majority of directors following a nearly two-hour closed-door executive session.

Council Chairman Harold Atkinson would only say that the "vote of confidence" was not unanimous. The issue, he said, was the direction of the council and Nemoyten's involvement with it.

"Go have Bill explain it to you," Atkinson said.

But last week the San Mateo planning consultant said that there was a certain amount of dissatisfaction with Nemoyten but that "publicity could hurt the council."

A group of artists and representatives from many art organizations in the county supported Nemoyten in writing and personal appearance Thursday.

Some of them maintained

William Nemoyten
Wins Battle

a vigil in the old converted house in which the arts council calls home in San Mateo.

According to Nemoyten, the main issue appeared to be whether the two-year-old council becomes one of a countywide "super planning agency vs. a people, active-oriented organization. I'm for the latter."

And by the vote of confidence, it appears the majority

of the 21-member council is also.

Edward W. Pliska, a municipal court judge told the council behind closed doors that whereas "Harold (Atkinson) says it's not personalities. I think it is. I haven't seen this in other organizations. Everybody on the arts council has their own axe to grind and want to do it their way."

Pliska urged the council "to make a decision and lets get together."

His comments and those made by some other councilmen were heard because the council did not shut the doors to its closed hearing until 30-minutes after it had begun.

Another council member, Elio Fontana of Colma, was concerned that "somewhere along the line someone has gone to the Board of Supervisors criticizing Nemoyten. Some are talking to the county manager; the bickering is getting to a high level."

Another council member **(See Page 2, Column 5)**

what I was supposed to be doing. Now, suddenly, the chairman wanted to do something quite different. I had my suspicions relative to how that came about. I had agreed to take on an intern who had been studying arts administration at Golden Gate University. His teacher was very much into arts planning and not into running arts councils. The intern, who was a local man, who probably had applied for my job, appears to have decided he would go about getting it by undermining me and what I had been doing. He secretly set up meetings with Atkinson and went about convincing him that we were going in the wrong direction. He also befriended my office secretary and worked with her to undermine me.

Finally it all came to a head. A special meeting of the board was called. Harold Atkinson laid out his ideas and then I spoke. I first pointed out what we had accomplished in a very short time. I then made the point that we were a very small new organization in a very large county and that it would take some time to build up the credibility we would need to be taken seriously by the power structure of the county. I stated that eventually we would be in a position to become an effective arts planning organization, but right now we must develop as many programs as we can to serve a wide audience in all the arts.

After I spoke and before the board went into "executive closed session" to consider whether or not I was to be fired, several members of the arts community spoke and gave their opinions to the board. Then several of us went upstairs and waited for the results of the vote. I was fairly confident. I knew I had many friends on the board with whom I had worked closely ever since I arrived in town. But I also knew that there were a few people who had resented the fact that a non-Californian had been selected for my position.

After an agonizing hour, the meeting ended. The vice chairman of the council came over to tell me that the board voted in my favor. I was relieved and elated until I learned that as a result of the vote, Harold Atkinson, the chairman and co-founder of the organization had announced his resignation. I truly liked and respected Harold and felt sad about losing him as a friend and board member.

The story of what had happened that evening appeared on the front page of the San

(Continued from Page 1)

said it should be understood that some (city or group) art councils are complaining that they aren't getting money.

And a woman added that the "gripes are with the by-laws, which are set by the council, not the executive director."

Atkinson said during the closed-door session that there are "questions on whether policy is being followed that isn't set by the council."

Meanwhile, Nemoyten explained to The Times what he believed his critics' points were, and his responses to them.

"Some believed that I have set policy or made decisions which are contrary to the benefitting arts organizations, but the fact is that the council sets policy," he said.

Nemoyten said another point was an allegation that he and the council were going in opposite directions. "But I stated that the records of the council prove all policies are set by them."

He also conceded that money has been a difficulty. San Mateo County's Board of Supervisors has allocated $78,000, compared to $500,000 for San Francisco's Arts Council.

During Nemoyten's 19 months as director, the arts council has opened a new headquarters at Borel Estate in San Mateo, opened the "corridor gallery" at the County Courthouse, started publication of a county-wide inventory of artists, and arts group, promoted several musicales and dance groups, supported an East Palo Alto Negro art teacher's classes for minority groups, and a variety of services and assistance to a number of arts groups.

Mateo Times the next day. The undermining intern didn't come around anymore and the secretary who he had enlisted left after a few weeks.

The Twin Pines Manor and New Programs

Over the next five years we expanded our budget from $45,000 to $300,000. We moved to the Twin Pines Manor in Belmont and restored that badly neglected and vandalized building, making it into a place for artist's studios, our offices and the best public art gallery in the county. We developed new art galleries at the San Mateo County Government Center in Redwood City, Hughes Airwest's office building in San Mateo and in Daly City's City Hall.

With funds from the "Comprehensive Employment Training Acts" fund, we hired several artists who painted murals all over the county. We also hired a graphic artist who created promotional materials for all the arts organizations that requested her services and a weaver who created a huge woven replica of San Mateo County's seal which adorns the Supervisor's chambers. A sculptor fashioned a seven-foot high abstract sculpture of Venetian marble that stands outside the county Government office building. We organized poetry readings at the Twin Pines manor and published a small book of poetry.

A Failed Experiment

At the time of the American Bicentennial in 1976 a lot of money was available for a wide variety of programs, one of which was for multi-cultural arts endeavors. We came up with the idea of a "Multi-Cultural Task Force" which was to be made up of a project director and five artists of differing ethnicity. The idea was for them to put together some kind of a show and take it on tour around the county to community centers and schools. First I advertised for a director. The most interesting candidate and the person I hired for the job was Jose Antonio Burciaga whom we all called Tony. When Tony applied and showed me his resume I was intrigued. He had worked for the CIA. He explained that as a graphic artist his job was to organize aerial photos taken by spy planes in a way that could be studied by the staff. Tony assembled the Multi-cultural Task Force and went about trying to create an effective program, but it never worked very well and when it was over we knew it was a failure. Our board was not happy, but I explained to them that an integral part of engaging in the arts with new untried programs is the possibility of failure just as it is with any experiment. Jose Antonio Burciaga, who was a proud Chicano poet and artist, in the next several years after his arts council stint, wrote a great deal of poetry and became extremely well known in the Chicano community. After cancer led to an untimely death, I heard about him on the public radio station and that there would be a memorial service for him at a theater in San Francisco's Mission District. I tried to attend it, but the line of people to get into the theatre went around the block and the parking was impossible.

One very memorable program was when we had arranged for the Asian American Dance Company to perform in San Bruno for their local group called "Art Rise." We learned that Wendy Yoshimura was a member of the dance company, and though she was under indictment for her part in the Simbianese Liberation Army incident involving Patricia Hearst, she would be performing with the group on that night. Here I have to confess that I leaked the story to the press through Joyce Golding. I knew it would stir up some controversy. But the benefit would be that more people would know there was such a thing as the San Mateo County Arts Council. I further justified it with the customary claim that in America "you are innocent until proven guilty." What I didn't bargain for was how terribly upset some of the leaders of Art Rise would be. I was told later that some poor woman nearly had a nervous breakdown over it.

In 1978 I wrote a grant request that resulted in the formation of the Twin Pines String Quartet and the Twin Pines Woodwind Quintet. We were able to enlist excellently talented young musicians who performed in schools and other venues throughout the county.

During the American Bicentennial year we produced a film about the history of San Mateo County (see the following story about the film) which was narrated by our most famous citizen, Bing Crosby. There were many other programs and projects, some of which succeeded and some of which did not. But it all came to a screeching halt for me when Proposition 13 passed in 1978 and nearly all of our administrative funding was gone overnight. I had no choice but to resign and move on to the next part of my life.

I had a contract for another year, but chose not to enforce it because it would bankrupt the Council. I reasoned that with some good volunteers it might be possible to keep going until things changed for the better. Also, though there was virtually no money for administration, there was still program money available. One of our board members, Nancy Jalonen, a wealthy resident of Hillsborough who was very dedicated to the Council and well-connected in the community expressed interest in volunteering to do the job. Though I didn't always agree with some of her ideas about the arts, I felt that she was the kind of person that simply would not let the Arts Council die. I endorsed Nancy as the new volunteer director and she did an excellent job. A few years later the council was able to hire a very fine new executive director and the organization lasted for 30 years until sadly the board and director were not able to raise the funds to operate it anymore. But the Twin Pines Manor and its wonderful gallery were taken over by the Belmont Arts Council and has become a great asset to the community.

Post Script

In April of 2012 I attended an art exhibit at the gallery and learned that the City of Belmont had decided that the Twin Pines Manor was now so attractive that they were going to evict the artists and close the gallery. They intend to turn the building into some kind of meeting and party center as a source of income to the city. The city fathers have forgotten about how the fine old building was rescued by the San Mateo County Arts Council and the value of a fine center for the arts in their community. Perhaps the writing the writing of this story will keep all of that alive for some future researcher.

The Bicentennial Film
That Almost Wasn't

This occurred around 1975 when I was in my fourth year as Executive Director of the San Mateo County Arts Council. The Bicentennial of the United States was coming up the following year and there were all sorts of programming opportunities being announced for the celebration of the two-hundredth anniversary of the signing of the Declaration of Independence, and the funds to carry them out. One of the projects our board wanted to undertake was a film about the history of San Mateo County.

It sounded like a good idea at the time, but several months later I regretted going along with it. One of our new board members, who I will call Eve, when hearing it was to be a film, thrust herself into the position of heading the project because her claim to fame had been that she was, in her youth, in Hollywood movie chorus lines. Somehow that impressed our board members who were influenced by Eve's beauty and apparent wealth enough to downplay her actual experience in producing a film.

A couple of weeks after the meeting she announced that she had found the perfect director. His name was Al Dote. We were told that he was a musician and was somehow associated with Clint Eastwood and that he was the perfect man to make our film. Later I learned that he was a piano player in a cocktail lounge and claimed to be a friend of Clint Eastwood who lives in Carmel, California. But Eve was stalwart in supporting Dote for the position and we could only wait and see how he went about his task. I was impressed with the credentials of the cameraman he engaged so that part looked OK.

But when I asked how the film was coming along I didn't get very satisfactory answers from either Dote or Eve. In the meantime, our Bicentennial money was being spent at an alarming rate. I pressed them about their next shoot and was invited to witness it. It was for a scene that was supposed to take place in a tavern during Gold Rush days. They had assembled a large group of people in a local bar that was closed that evening. Dote didn't seem to have a clue about the fact that the room was all wrong for the historical period.

The actors were dressed in a wild assortment of costumes that covered a hundred years of styles, almost none in the correct period. They apparently had been given no instructions about what to wear.

After about an hour of general confusion, the filming began. Everything, and I mean absolutely everything, was incredibly amateurish; the script, the acting, the staging, the lighting, the set and most of all, the direction or lack thereof.

After witnessing the fiasco, I knew I would have to "blow the whistle" on the project. I also knew that meant an unpleasant confrontation with Eve, a formidable woman not to be trifled with. But I also knew that I couldn't let the project go forward and have such a travesty put before the public in the name of the arts council.

I called our chairman and told him what was happening. He called a special meeting of our board and I reported what I had seen and my recommendation to cut our losses and abort the project. Eve was livid, but the board trusted my judgment and was ready to scrap the project and return the remaining money to the county. Eve resigned from the board and stormed out of the room. Then, another board member, Ruth Kraenzel offered to look over what had been done and see if she could save the project. Ruth was, in fact, much better qualified to handle it. She was on the staff of KCSM and was well connected with a lot of resources.

Ruth went to work immediately and discovered that one scene was well done because it had been handled by Robert Brauns, the director at the Hillbarn Theater in Foster City. She wrote a working script and continued to use the fine cameraman that had originally been engaged. When she had a good deal of it together, she phoned me with the best piece of news I had received in months. She had secured the volunteer services of the most famous person living in San Mateo County at the time to read part of the narration. It was Bing Crosby! She sent him the script and he taped his part and that's all there was to it. The rest was provided by a local radio announcer.

When the film, which was entitled *From Sail To Satellite* was completed, we arranged for a gala opening at the Hillbarn Theater and then turned the film over to the San Mateo County Historical Society which has shown it to thousands of visitors. It still resides there today.

I will always feel indebted to Ruth Kraenzel for what she did. Many years later, I left the arts council and Ruth and her husband Jim moved to Groveland, California. We relived those exciting days when my wife and I visited Groveland and stayed in the Hotel Charlotte which was owned by the Kraenzels.

The Discovery

The call I made to Sally that summer in 1975 was one I will never forget. I was on a trip across the country by car from Quincy, Illinois to our home in Foster City, California. I had gone to Illinois to help our older son, Mark, move to California. I was calling just to check to see how things were going at home.

When Sally answered I immediately sensed some tension in her voice, even though she started out just inquiring about how the trip was going and when we expected to reach California. Then she said, "Bill, there is something I have to tell you. I was cleaning David's room and there was a letter open on top of his dresser. I couldn't help reading it. It was just sitting there as though he wanted it to be read. Bill, I think David is gay!"

The breath went out of me for a moment and at first I didn't say anything. Then, though I said, "Are you sure?" there was a part of me that wasn't totally surprised.

There were many signs over the years, but I knew I simply didn't want to think about them, add them up, and reach a conclusion that was unacceptable. David was, after all, a very masculine looking young man. Like any parent, I had a different life in mind for David—he would grow up, go to college, marry, and have children. I knew very little about homosexuality and what it was all about. The only hint of it in our family was that my mother told me about a cousin of mine who had a son she said was "different." In the coming years I was to get a very thorough education on the subject.

Sally answered my question with more certainty than she had expressed at first. She said, "Yes, I'm sure. We'll talk to him together when you get back home."

As we drove home across the wide barren stretches of Nevada, I had a lot of time to think about David, certain incidents in his life and his behavior. I remembered the way, as a child, when we visited my mother's home in Cleveland, instead of going out and playing ball, he preferred to sit in the kitchen and talk to Sally, my mother and his sisters. Although he had a sturdy build, he had little interest in the athletic things boys do. Instead, he loved to act and appeared in children's theater plays, in which he excelled. When he was twelve or thirteen, David suddenly became interested in the old movie star Mae West, putting her picture on the wall of his bedroom and even writing to her. Later I learned that she was a great favorite of gay men.

From an early age, David had temper tantrums on a scale that surpassed any of his siblings and were very upsetting to our whole family. When we lived in Quincy, we became so concerned that we took him to see our friend, Dr. Manfred Kydan, a psychiatrist and the head of the local mental health clinic. He met with and counseled David a few times when David was eleven, and though it seemed to help a little, the good doctor didn't have a clue as to what was really causing David's inner turmoil which had apparently troubled him from a very early age.

David recently told me that he remembers having homosexual feelings as a very young child. He told me that one time when he was playing with some of the neighbor children they were playing "cannibals" and Bobby, an older boy from across the street was chasing him. David told me that when Bobby said, "When I catch you I'm going to eat you!" he was both frightened and thrilled.

I was having a lot of turmoil myself on that trip home and was going through what most parents probably would—questioning how this could have happened.

"Did we do something wrong?"

"Did we treat David differently from his older heterosexual brother?"

I needed to talk to someone who could help me understand. I phoned my Cousin Annette's husband, Hal Shulman. Hal had a doctorate in psychology and was the head of the Mental Health Clinic in Champaign, Illinois. We were good friends, but I had never before discussed a personal problem with him, so it felt awkward to broach the subject. There was another reason why it was awkward. Hal and Annette's 18 year old son, Danny, had recently been diagnosed with an inoperable brain tumor. Whatever the problem we had about our son certainly paled in comparison with what they were going through.

I'll always be grateful to Hal for his response to my question. He told me that throughout the human and animal kingdom there have always been homosexuals. A certain percentage of the population has always been gay or lesbian. And most importantly he explained to me that being so was not a choice for each individual, but a fact that they must either come to terms with or live a very unhappy life. He also assured me that Sally and I had no blame to shoulder. He advised me to learn to accept David as a gay person.

Sally, who by her very nature was a master of the concept of unconditional love, especially toward her children, made the adjustment much more quickly than I did. We met with David and he was, of course, relieved to be able to come "out of the closet" to his family. Eventually we began to meet some of his gay friends and one particular person—a tall, handsome, wonderful young man named Mark Hotchkiss became practically a member

David Nemoyten with Mark Hotchkiss in recent years

of our family.

Over the years we met more and more of David's gay and lesbian friends. David moved to the Castro and later into San Francisco's Hayes Valley.

When the AIDS epidemic spread through the city we were very concerned about David's gay life style. He thankfully never contracted HIV but did develop Hepatitis C for which he has been successfully treated. However, he was deeply affected by the illnesses and deaths of many of his friends and acquaintances during the years before the current treatments were developed.

Sally and I learned to totally accept David and his gay and lesbian friends and then discovered that many of them envied David and his relationship with us because we were so accepting and so many of them had been estranged from their families. We heard many sad stories of their rejection by their parents that were heart breaking and sometimes tragic.

Once when I was at Mad Magda's Russian Tea Room and Café, David's business, I asked him about a woman customer who I realized was actually a man. He/she was trying to look like Barbara Streisand judging by the hairstyle worn. David, who seemed to know a great deal about everyone in the neighborhood, told me that that person's father was a doctor who simply couldn't accept the fact that his son was gay. He insisted on sending his son for all kinds of treatments to change him. The result was that the young man had lost touch with reality and who he was. David told me that he had seen that poor soul come into the cafe on several occasions as different characters, a totally lost and confused person.

After trying several other things, David had opened up his own cafe in San Francisco on Hayes near Laguna. "Mad Magda" was a drag character he had developed for certain gay public events like the Gay Freedom Day Parade. He made Mad Magda's into a very unique institution. It was a place where artists and writers liked to hang out. Magda's had interesting food, Tarot card readers and always unique art on the walls. From time to time, for special occasions he presented various entertainers and very unusual and even bizarre acts like "Juan, the Snake Dancer" who danced with a huge python wrapped around his writhing body.

Mad Magda is not amused.

One thing I particularly admired David for was that on certain holidays like Christmas he would close the café to the public but have a party for his many gay, lesbian and transsexual friends who had no families with whom to spend that evening. After Sally died and I married Barbara, she was just as accepting of David as Sally had been. We had both become attuned to the rhythms of the lifestyle to the point where we often have no problem recognizing a man who was once a women and visa versa.

Bill on the PFLAG float
at 2005 San Francisco LGBT Pride Parade

Mad Magda's lasted for eight years before David had to close because of rising costs and debts. But it was in some ways a very magical eight years that the people who frequented the café will never forget. Today, David has an excellent position with the California Academy of Sciences as an event coordinator and we are very proud of him.

We recently saw the powerful film "Milk" with Sean Penn playing the part of slain former San Francisco Supervisor Harvey Milk. It was seeing that film and the unfortunate passage of Proposition 8 that prompted me to write this story.

Getting in Touch

To the best of my memory, this happened around 1977. It was a splendidly warm and sunny day as we began our drive through the beautifully forested areas that surround Los Gatos, California. I had just asked Doris a question. Doris, an artist and a poet, was a woman in her early fifties. She possessed an earthy and joyful kind of charm and was an attractive woman who dressed simply and wore very little makeup. I had driven down to Los Gatos in connection with my role as an officer in the Association of California Arts Councils. Doris was supposed to be familiarizing me with the Los Gatos art scene. I asked her a simple question. It evoked a very surprising reply. I asked Doris where she would like to go on that beautiful day and what she would like to show me. After a pause, during which she seemed to be cautiously thinking about her answer, she asked me, "How would you feel about taking off all your clothes and getting into a hot tub with a bunch of strangers?"

Apparently Doris was prepared to show me more than the Los Gatos art scene. When I considered Doris's question, two thoughts came to mind. The first was that no woman had ever asked me a question like that before, and the second was that it seemed extremely unlikely that any woman would ever ask me a question like that again!

Then I remembered a certain time in my life that had occurred several years before when I had a painful illness that tortured me day and night. It was an illness that my doctors had been unable to diagnose correctly for several weeks. The neurologist had scared the hell out of me by declaring, after a brief examination, and without actually running any tests, that I had a malignant or a non-malignant tumor on my spine. It turned out to be a very erroneous diagnosis. I eventually had a complete recovery after wearing a back brace for two years. But during those dark days in my hospital bed, when I didn't know whether or not my life would soon be over, I promised myself that if I recovered, I would live a fuller, richer, more exciting life. When I knew the end was approaching, I didn't want to have any regrets about what I hadn't had the spirit of adventure to experience during my lifetime.

Realizing this was my opportunity to partake of one of those famous Bay Area activities that I had heard, read and dreamed about but never experienced, the next words out of my mouth were, "Which way do we go?"

Doris grinned, nodded her approval, and directed me to Route 17 up into the Santa Cruz Mountains and on to an exit that seemed half hidden. We wound up and down some narrow roads until she said, "Turn off here. This is the way. The place is called Getting in Touch."

As we worked our way steeply downhill along a road through a thickly forested area, we entered a mysteriously hidden valley. I felt my nervousness and excitement building, but I also began to wonder what I'd gotten myself into. Would I be able to go through with it? I have always been very self-conscious and never felt that I had a great physique by any stretch of the imagination.

Now we were approaching a rustic two-story lodge that was splendidly designed to fit into the surrounding environment. I didn't see anyone around, but after we parked in the small lot where there were about a dozen cars, I heard voices coming from the other side of the lodge. We climbed the stairs to the second floor into an airy, sunny room that had a fireplace and a few chairs casually scattered around. There was a hallway with some rooms off to the side. Doris told me that they were massage rooms, but it was required that the doors must be kept open at all times since sexual activity was prohibited on the grounds except in a group of cabins on the nearby hillside provided for overnight guests.

When we entered an adjoining hallway Doris, speaking in an almost business-like tone said, "Just hang your clothes here on these hooks." Then she nonchalantly proceeded to remove her blouse and bra. Her nonchalance helped put me at ease and I started to disrobe. When we were both ready and heading for the door to the outside deck, I felt my face redden as I thought, *Well, here go*! We stepped out into the bright sunlight to a group of a dozen or so nude sunbathers, mostly female, in varying ages, shapes and sizes. Many of them greeted Doris very warmly. She was obviously a regular. I was still a bit nervous but the natural accepting attitude of everyone soon began to work its magic on me.

Doris motioned for me to follow her and we climbed down a flight of wooden steps to the grassy field behind the lodge. Walking outside on grass in my bare feet feeling the sun all over me was a strange sensation that would take some getting used to. Directly in front of us was a large hot tub, not built down into the ground, but sitting up on top of the grass. There was a ladder to get into it and Doris quickly climbed it. I followed as she entered the steaming tub and went over to each person who gave her a warm liquidy hug.

She then announced that she had brought her friend Bill along and said, "Bill, I'd like you to meet my good friend Gladys." Gladys was an imposing figure. About three inches taller than I am, Gladys was, I'd estimate about 285 pounds of ample tanned fleshy nakedness, with enormous breasts and hips. I soon discovered that she was also an extremely friendly woman because, when I came in range of her to say hello, she smiled broadly, grabbed me and gave me a hug which was record-breaking on several levels! Doris laughed with delight at the scene and then introduced me to Bob, a hairy beast like me who insisted on following Gladys' example by giving me his own wet fleshy hug of welcome. Believe me, that was another truly unique experience!

After being hugged by the other three women in the tub, I began to realize why they called the place "Getting in Touch." There was a lot of conversation that went on for quite a while. You know, the kind of stuff that seven naked people usually talk about in a hot tub.

I was now beginning to relax and more importantly, reach a comfort level that surprised me. I think I was really beginning to "get it," that is, to understand what this whole "clothing optional" business was all about. The more you saw of the naked body, the less the nakedness meant. The sexual part became less of an issue between the genders. There was, inherent in the experience, a total acceptance of the idea that the body is only the wrapping on the package and not the essence of the person. There was, of course, also the whole matter of expunging the embarrassment and shame of being seen naked by others. Seeing how comfortable and accepting everyone else was enabled me to be comfortable as well, and in a way, completely liberated from ordinary conventions. From what I could tell, these people were neither exhibitionists nor voyeurs. Neither were they hedonists. They were ordinary men and women, for the most part highly educated professionals, who found "Getting in Touch" to be filling a special need in their lives.

The conversation was momentarily interrupted when suddenly everyone turned their heads as a slender, attractive young woman came jogging past the hot tub heading toward the volley ball game that was taking place about 50 yards away. She was the only woman I saw there that day who was wearing anything. She had on a dark green bikini bottom and somehow that made her look very sexy!

After a while Doris asked if I would like to see more of the grounds. We left the hot tub and passed by the volleyball court where a spirited game with lots of epidermal jiggling was taking place. I don't know why, but volleyball is apparently a recreational requirement in places like "Getting in Touch."

The hot sun quickly dried our bodies as we headed toward a lush and riotously colorful flower garden on a winding narrow trail that then circled back through a cool pine forest. We sat down on a thankfully smooth log for a few minutes, just to enjoy the scene. I knew then that this would be the closest in my life that I would ever come to feeling like I was in the Garden of Eden. Thankfully there were no snakes around, and neither were there any apple trees. We then returned to the lodge, dressed and re-entered the real world.

It may surprise you to learn that when I returned home later that evening I shared the experiences I had at "Getting in Touch" that day with my wife, Sally, who was a remarkably understanding and open-minded person. Nevertheless, when I asked her if she would like to visit the place with me sometime soon, she declined. I visited there one more time and shortly afterward learned that Getting in Touch had closed. The place was no more, but I had a beautiful memory that would last me a lifetime and provide me with what I hope would be a good story to tell.

Adventures on the Ahoy Vay

My pal, Harvey, called up one evening right as I was ready to start on the thick, nicely broiled lamb chops that Sally had made for me. His opening was his usual term of endearment, "What's happening schmuck?"

I said, "Nothing schmuck, why are you calling me at dinner time?"

"I've got some news. I bought a boat. It's a twenty-seven-foot Chris Craft power cruiser that sleeps four. It's in berth twenty-nine at Coyote Point Marina. You wanna be my partner?"

Harvey with Bill
Notice where Harvey's fingers are...typical!

My response was, "Harvey, are you nuts? What do you need a boat for? No, I can't afford it. Don't you remember the old saying, a boat is a hole in the water that you pour money into? So when do we get to see this yacht of yours?"

Harvey talked to Lillian for a minute or so and then got back on the line. "How about Saturday at four?" and then he said, "I really didn't expect you to be a partner, but I need a first mate. Do you want to apply for the job?"

"We'll see, but you're not going to suck me in on this deal. Sally and I will be there on Saturday."

Now it's Saturday and we're at berth twenty-nine. There's the Chris Craft. It's kind of old, but has beautiful varnished wood and classic lines and appears to be in good shape. Harvey and Lillian came out of the cabin and we exchanged greetings and kisses. Harvey said, "Do you want the grand tour?"

I said, "Sure." So he showed us the sleeping berths, the galley and the head. We were impressed and frankly excited about the idea of some kind of sea adventure.

Lillian said we've been trying to think of a name for it. "Any suggestions?"

We kicked around several ideas like "Harvey's Folly," "Lil's Thrill" and things like that, but nothing stuck. Then, being facetious, I offered "how about the Ahoy Vay?" Everyone laughed and then it was quiet for a minute or two. First Lillian, then Sally, then Harvey nodded. They all looked at me. I told them I was just kidding, but asked, "Do you really like the idea?"

Lillian offered "It's nautical, it's Jewish and it sounds like fun, so why not?" And that was that.

The next time we went to the marina we found the beautifully lettered "Ahoy Vay" at berth twenty-nine and Harvey presented us with "Ahoy Vay" lettered caps. The name turned out to be a little too prophetic. Yes, the ahoy part was nautical, however the part that was derived from the expression "Oy Vay," which means something like "woe is me" in Yiddish proved to be the case several times in the years to come. But there was also lots of fun and adventure.

We realized that neither of us knew anything about operating a power boat so Harvey and I decided to take some "power squadron classes" offered at San Mateo High in the evening. We stuck it out for about four of the eight classes, just enough to learn the basic safety rules that would keep us from killing ourselves or anyone else.

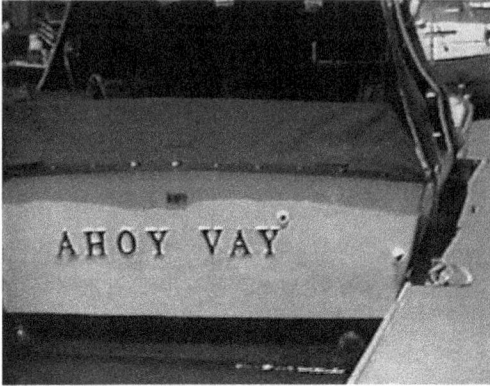
The Ahoy Vay

We began to take short trips out into the bay. The first thing we learned was how much larger the bay looks from the water and the second was how strong the wind, waves and currents can be. The Ahoy Vay was a single screw power boat. That means it only had one propeller, which further means it was very hard for an inexperienced helmsman to handle when the bay was rough, and sometimes damned near impossible to maneuver into our dock without hitting something. In fact, we managed to knock a few dents and one large hole on the hull, fortunately all above the water line.

One day we navigated our way to the Redwood City Marina, managed to dock the boat without a problem and stopped for a snack at a marina restaurant. We headed back at about 3:00 and began to pull into berth twenty-nine at Coyote Point at around 5:30. Harvey was at the wheel and as we approached the dock I took my usual place on the bow and prepared to step onto the dock and tie the boat up. As we drew closer I stepped to the edge of the bow and prepared to jump onto the dock. I jumped and realized too late that I had misjudged the distance.

I still remember my exact thoughts in the ensuing moments. They were, *Oh shit, I missed the dock! The bay water isn't as cold as I thought it would be! There go my glasses! Got to get back to the surface!* The next thing that happened was that as I emerged from the water I felt a very strong arm wrapping a rope under my arms and pulling me up and out of the water. I also saw that whoever the person was, held his other hand out to keep the forward moving Ahoy Vay from trapping me against the dock. The stranger helped me up onto the dock and asked me if I was OK. Other than being terribly embarrassed, cold and soaking wet, and missing my much needed glasses, I was in remarkably good shape thanks to the stranger and I told him how much I appreciated what he had done.

This was the odd thing about what happened that day. Did you ever notice that when you look out at a marina you seldom see anyone around? We had never seen my rescuer before and he was the only person around anywhere on the marina at the time. Not only that, but he was working on his boat just a few feet away on the other side of the narrow dock, saw what had happened and immediately knew exactly what to do.

Harvey had not seen me go into the bay. He just didn't know where I was. When he came out from behind the wheel and found out what had happened he turned a shocking shade of white and appeared to be in much worse shape than I was. I thought he would have a heart attack, but he finally calmed down. I was able to dry off in the boat and find some clothing. I never saw the mysterious stranger again, and never misjudged the distance to another dock.

A month later we decided to move the Ahoy Vay to the calmer waters of Discovery Bay on the Delta near Brentwood. I got a new pair of glasses because "Charlie the Tuna" was wearing mine.

The official Ahoy Vay patch

Peninsula Temple Beth El

Temple Beth El is located on a splendid street in San Mateo with the delicious sounding (in English) name Alameda de las Pulgas. I learned early on that the name in Spanish means the not so delicious "Avenue of the Fleas," a name that goes back historically to the time when the Spanish owned all of California and fleas infested that agricultural land. Reform Temple Beth El had about 600 family members in 1972. It was led by the founding rabbi, Sanford Rosen, who was born in Cleveland and trained at the Hebrew Union College in Cincinnati. We attended some services when our family first arrived in the area and soon joined and became active members. We attended Shabbat services and celebrated the Jewish Holidays there. David and Susan went to the religious school.

When my job at the San Mateo County Arts Council evaporated as a result of Proposition 13, for the first time in my life I found myself in a line at the Employment Development Department. I was wondering what I would do next, but very determined that I must find a job in the area. I loved the Bay Area and our beautiful Foster City home. And by that time all of our kids were living nearby. Had I pursued it I probably could have found an arts council job elsewhere in the country, but that became a last resort strategy.

Perfect Timing

This is another example of perfect timing, something that happened several times in my life. The long time administrator of Temple Beth El had retired a few months before and the temple had hired a replacement that wasn't up to handling the job. Sally and I had joined a temple chavurah (group of friends), two members of which were on the temple board of directors. When they learned I was looking for a job they encouraged me to apply to the temple. At first I balked at the idea. After all, I thought, "What do I know about running a Temple?" But they continued to press me to apply. I made some inquiries, thought it over and realized that the job was not that different from what I had been doing. The temple was a non–profit organization with a membership, an office staff, a facility to manage and a program of events. The Rabbi was like the artistic director. I applied and got the job just before the High Holidays in September of 1978.

There was plenty to do with logistics to handle for High Holiday services where nearly a thousand people attended. There was usually a flood of new members to enroll in a very short period of time. And, of course, I had to get familiar with the staff which included Rabbi Rosen and Cantor Epstein, the office receptionist, the Rabbi's secretary, the bookkeeper, the live-in custodian, the maintenance man and the Sunday school teachers. There was also the board of directors, the Temple Brotherhood, the Sisterhood and the Fifty Plus Club which was made up mostly of people eighty-plus in age. And then there was the building and grounds; the beautiful synagogue was designed to emulate Noah's Ark. There was the social hall which was connected to the synagogue, the kitchen, the Fireside room for small events, the gift shop run by the sisterhood, the library, the school, the play area for the students and the parking lot.

The Staff

I worked from 9:00 a.m. to 5:00 p.m. each day and usually attended every Shabbat and every holiday service. In addition, I attended all board meetings. Early on I learned many things that I didn't know as a member. Rabbi Rosen and Cantor Epstein didn't get along well at all. Rosen, after so many years, was definitely suffering from "burn out." He would often come into his office in the morning, check his mail and any messages he might have received and then would disappear for most of the day. He was an impressive figure at services and conducted them with great cool dignity. Herb Epstein, on the other hand, was warm and spontaneous. He had a good, but not great voice, was a fine musician and knew the liturgy extremely well. Herb was not well organized. Rabbi Rosen would make requests of what music he wanted and Herb would just do whatever he felt like doing. Their relationship made for stressful times.

During my first four years I sometimes had the feeling that everyone was depending on me to hold things together, but a lot of the credit should have gone to Selma Holtzberg, our incredible bookkeeper who had been with the temple for about thirty years and knew virtually all the members. She was a person with a great well of information about everything and everyone. There was a small apartment for the live-in custodian in the rear of the building. When the long time custodian left I hired a Vietnamese man named Hiu Hong. His English was poor, but he was a very intelligent man and had been a successful businessman in his native land. When he left I saw it as an opportunity to help out a Russian Jewish émigré. Several hundred Russians had come to San Francisco in recent times. The agency that helped them get jobs sent me a young man who called himself Ross Lauren. In Russia he had been a metallurgist. He was very well educated and had a large library of books he had brought with him. We became quite friendly. I found out that his name in Russia was actually Rostoslav Lipschitz. I asked him how he happened to become Ross Lauren. His answer was, "You know the designer Ralph Lauren? He also was Lipschitz!" Since Ross was a very well educated man, a voracious reader and quite fluent in English I had the idea that the Temple members would be happy to associate with him and perhaps befriend him and invite him to their homes. But that never happened and he led a very lonely life while working for us. That was pretty disillusioning to me. In reflecting on it I see that though Ross was an interesting and educated person, he was, in the minds of the members, after all, just their custodian. While he was with us I met one of his Russian friends who was a cab driver. About a year after Ross had left the Temple I saw his friend in his cab on the street outside Saul's Delicatessen in Berkeley. He share with me that his old friend now lived in New York, was happily married and also happily employed as a metallurgist. That made my day!

Bringing the Arts to the Temple

I brought my experience and expertise in the field of the arts to the Temple. We held art auctions of Jewish art and were given some fine works by the auction company. I persuaded a generous member of the congregation, Ozzie Osharow, to purchase a beautiful set of lithographs that depicted scenes from the Hagadah by famed Israeli artist Schlomo Katz. When he saw that we were building an art collection, temple member, retired Rear Admiral Herschel Goldberg donated a folio of fine prints that we framed and put into

Temple Brotherhood Show
Bill is obviously the star!

the Fireside Room. We also put on a talent show in which I played some trombone and Sally was the co-narrator. I wasn't involved in scheduling guest speakers, but recall many fine ones and particularly an appearance by Leon Uris, famed author of "Mila 18", "Armageddon", "Battle Cry" and 'Exodus" among many others. He was there on a book tour with his third wife, the photographer Jill Peabody. We have a treasured book autographed by Uris.

The Temple is Threatened

Certain negative events stand out in my mind. A week before one of our major holidays we received an anonymous anti-Semitic threatening letter warning that something bad would happen at the temple on that holiday. We contacted the police who went to work on the case immediately. We decided to ignore the warning and went ahead with the service as planned, making certain we had plenty of security. All went well. A few weeks later the police identified the person who sent the letter. I was to testify, but the trial ended early with some kind of plea bargain, so I lost my one chance to be a "witness for the prosecution."

A Great Tragedy

The other event was perhaps the worst one to have ever taken place involving active members of the congregation. As I recall it happened in 1983 right around the time of Rosh Hashanah. We awoke that morning to the news that two members of Temple Beth El, Dr. Robert Glasgal, an orthodontist and his wife Sondra had been bludgeoned to death. Their son Russell was missing and arrested three days later. He was put on trial twice and acquitted because the evidence was all circumstantial. Russell eventually shared one third of his parent's four million dollar estate with his two siblings. His uncle, brother of Sondra, told me he was absolutely convinced that Russell was indeed guilty. Our daughter Sue knew Russell who was in her confirmation class. He was a very good looking and clever young man who had developed a little magic act. Getting away with murder, however, was his top "trick.."

A "Fellow in Temple Administration"

Almost from the very beginning of my work at the Temple I had become active in the National Association of Temple Administrators. I attended meetings with Bay Area administrators and also went to the national conventions. On one occasion I was invited to make a presentation about the use of computers, something that was just beginning to happen in religious institutions. I also wrote a humorous story that was published in the NATA newsletter. During my fourth year in, 1982, I applied to take the examination enabling me to earn the certificate that would entitle me to be called a "Fellow in Temple Administration." I learned that not many who earned that title had been in the field for such a short time.

Stormy Times at the Temple

My years at the Temple were stormy ones. First there was a move to offer early retirement to Cantor Herbert Epstein. I liked and always got along with Herb, who was a good cantor. But he wasn't capable of performing his other duties. He was a failure as an educator and couldn't even handle preparing kids for their Bar and Bat Mitzvahs. As the years went by he kept defining his role in smaller terms while expecting a larger salary. When he was forced out, a group of Temple members who were very fond of him were very upset and some of them quit the temple.

Rosen Out, Rubinstein In

Then the board authorized temple president Joyce Share to offer early retirement to Rabbi Rosen. Much to the relief of the board, Rabbi Rosen agreed that it was time for him to retire and a deal was worked out. Following that, the board launched a nationwide search for a new Rabbi. They selected Peter Rubinstein, a great Rabbi from White Plains, New York. Even though Peter and I got along well, I sensed that it would soon be the time for me to move along. He wanted to change the congregation into one that was more involved in volunteering their help, but the members had become accustomed to the idea of "letting Bill handle it." A new board president was elected and began attacking the temple staff in ways that were unjustified. At one meeting while everyone else was quiet I challenged him. It was then that I realized that we could have had a battle that would be harmful to the temple. I was confident that I had many allies who would take my side, but I didn't want it to ever come to such a confrontation.

A Great Honor

Our family was closely entwined with temple life and on December. 2, 1984, Sally and I were honored at the annual State of Israel Bonds dinner with the Ben Gurion Award. Much to our surprise and delight we were told that more Israel bonds were sold that night than had ever been sold at the event before. The Ben Gurion plaque on my wall is one of my most treasured possessions.

Several months before, I had been deeply involved in establishing our own Jewish Cemetery at Skylawn Memorial Park. It is known as "Gan Hazikaron" (Hebrew for "Garden of Remembrance"). It was and still is the only Jewish cemetery on the Peninsula. Working with the general manager, Randy Storer, I learned about the possibility of starting a new business. After several meetings with Storer and a lot of soul searching I resigned from the Temple at the end of 1984 and went into a business venture that I was hopeful would garner me and my family some serious money for the first time in our lives.

A Visit from Mr. Platt

The office secretary rang my phone and announced that a Mr. Platt would like to see me. I was very busy that day and annoyed at the intrusion, but managed to hide my annoyance when I welcomed Mr. Platt into my small administrator's office at Peninsula Temple Beth El in San Mateo.

I opened with, "What can I do for you Mr. Platt?" He replied with, "I want you should help me arrange for funerals and a cemetery for me and my wife, who's not doing so good right now." Mr. Platt was an elderly man, short in stature and of average build. He had a pleasant face, very fair skin and very little hair. He spoke clearly enough, but with a heavy Yiddish accent that I placed as derived from Eastern Europe. In some ways he reminded me of my late father Jacob, who was born in Russia.

"Mr. Platt, I'd like to help you, but I don't believe you are a member of our congregation." He thought about what I said for a few moments and replied enthusiastically, "But I belong to the country club right next door and every year I donate to the Jewish Welfare Fund."

"That's very nice Mr. Platt, but it doesn't help this congregation and I must use my time to serve our members." He nodded that he understood and then said, "I tell you what I do. I make a donation of a thousand dollars to the Rabbi's Fund." After getting over that surprise announcement I said, "Mr. Platt, you have my undivided attention!" After all, I reasoned, a thousand dollars was more than a regular temple member's yearly dues donation and Rabbi Rosen would be most grateful for such a donation.

Mr. Platt and I met the following week when we visited a local mortuary and then went up the hill to Skylawn Memorial Park. At that time, Mr. Platt explained further why he was seeking my help. I was a appalled to learn that his children, who lived on the Peninsula, had told him they wanted their parent's funeral and burial in the San Mateo area because they felt it would just be too much trouble for them to have to go to Sinai Chapel, the Jewish Mortuary in San Francisco and to have to visit a cemetery in Colma.

The visit to the mortuary was taken care of in short order. He selected two caskets and agreed to a specific schedule of services that the funeral director set up in his file for future use. I arranged for a cemetery salesman to show us around Skylawn, a beautiful cemetery high on the coastal range with spectacular views.

As we drove through the expansive grounds, the salesman tried to find out what preference Mr. Platt had by asking him several questions. "Do you belong to the Masons? How about the Elks or the Lions? Are you a veteran?" There were several more questions, but Mr. Platt answered in the negative to all of them. Finally, after an interval of silence Mr. Platt asked very earnestly, "You got a section for Pinochle players?" We all laughed at the tension breaking humor.

Finally I interjected myself into the conversation and asked, "What kind of a place would suit you best, Mr. Platt?" He responded, "I want a place with a view! From my house in Hillsborough I got a beautiful view of the bay." Bouncing off of his earlier humorous question I asked, "Would you like a periscope installed?" He smiled and said, "That's a good idea!" The salesman looked perplexed.

Mr. Platt didn't get his periscope, but he did settle for a burial site on a hill with a very nice view. I set up a file labeled "Platt" so that I, or any future Temple Beth El administrator would be alerted to the arrangements we made.

A few weeks later I encountered Mr. Platt walking in downtown Burlingame. It turns out we were both heading to "Brothers", a Jewish style deli/restaurant that had been established by two Jewish brothers. When after 20 years in the business the brothers sold the restaurant to a Chinese family, they spent a considerable time training the new owners in the intricacies of handling bagels, lox, matzo balls, corned beef, pastrami, kosher dills, knishes and blintzes. They did a fine job, and as far as I know "Brothers" is still going strong with a large Jewish clientele.

I was delighted when he asked me to join him for lunch. There was something about Mr. Platt that drew me to him. I believe it was the way he reminded me of my father and some of my uncles. I wanted to know more about him. After we ordered I asked him what his native country was and when he came to the U.S. I learned he was born in Poland and came here as a teenager. He worked hard in a plant that made paper boxes and then went into business for himself. I inquired about what kind of boxes he made and to whom he sold them. After chomping on a kosher pickle he said, "Mostly fancy gift boxes I sold to Macy's, I Magnin's, Emporium and Capwells." He then told me he had sold his business to United Paper Box Company twenty years ago and had been retired ever since.

There is a postscript to this story. Mr. Platt was so pleased with my services that after he wrote out his one thousand dollar check to the Rabbi's discretionary fund, he wrote another $500 check to me, personally. I wasn't sure I should accept it. No one had ever offered me a gratuity and I wasn't aware of any temple policy on such a thing. When I hesitated, Mr. Platt insisted, so I took the check but didn't expect to cash it until I was satisfied that it was OK to do so.

I phoned another older, more experienced temple administrator I knew who had an F.T.A. after his name, indicating that he was a "Fellow in Temple Administration." When I laid out the story of Mr. Platt to him, he congratulated me and gave his official OK for me to do whatever I wanted with the money.

I left Temple Beth El a year or two later hoping that my successors followed through for the, at least to me, unforgettable Mr. Platt.

ONGAI SHABBAT = CALORIES = POUNDS
OR, THE ADMINISTRATOR'S GUIDE TO COMBATING OBESITY

William Nemoyten, Executive Director, Peninsula Temple, Beth El, San Mateo, California. 1981.

I have always had a weight problem. Since becoming a Temple Administrator I have begun to realize that my job is more hazardous to a person with a case of acute sweet tooth than if one worked at Winchell's Donuts or Baskin and Robbins. During one recent and typical weekend there were no less than six assorted events (including a Bar Mitzvah — the dieter's nemesis) during which I could have easily added at least two inches of girth to my already well padded mid-section. In fact, by comparison, working at a Cheesecake Bakery would be a snap. There you would have to pay for what you consumed or be forced to covertly sneak your snacks. But as a guest or participant at most temple events, the bountiful feast is always free and there is invariably a *balabosta* waiting for your words of approval after testing her latest mega-calorie creation. At last year's Israel Independence Day celebration, in a moment of temporary insanity, I agreed to serve as a judge in the Noodle Kugel contest. Have you ever attempted to taste and objectively judge the relative merits of 18 kugels at one sitting with the creators looking over your shoulder?!?

Recently my mirror, scale, subtle and not so subtle comments from friends and family (when added to a certain pervasive discomfort with my clothing) combined to motivate me to examine my wayward course. After all, was I not the proud recipient of a Gold Weight Watchers International Lapel Pin for achieving my ideal weight goal in 1978? I determined to become a, pardon the expression, "born again Weight Watcher". So I developed the following strategies that I freely share with those who are beset with the same tantalizing temptations.

1. Prepare yourself psychologically — you know what lies ahead. You have identified the enemy and can do combat armed with the knowledge of what a blintz with sour cream, two stuffed mushrooms, a finger knish and two pieces of mandel broit can do to your image.

Decide ahead of time what, if anything, you are planning to eat. As Administrator you have the privilege of reconnoitering the kitchen in advance without arousing suspicion. Think fruit! An apple takes time to eat, keeps your mouth busy and is fairly filling.

2. Avoid alchohol — Besides the large number of calories, even in a harmless appearing glass of chablis, there is the lowering of inhibition factor to consider. A time tested strategy is to head straight for the bar and order a soda with a twist which is sipped slowly enough to last the duration of the ordeal.

3. Eat a large and filling, but dietetic meal, just before you attend the more challenging event. Enough salad and diet soda will tire your jaws and fill your tummy. Did you know, by the way, that the act of chewing celery actually consumes calories?!?

4. Monitor your weight regularly. Your scale will not lie. Any deviation will reveal itself immediately and you will be put on notice to return to your righteous ways.

5. A little exercise wouldn't hurt! Administration is one of the world's most sedentary jobs. Find excuses to get up and walk around. Inspect the premises frequently — avoiding the kitchen. If you can, take up jogging or racketball. Whatever you do, try to get more of your body moving more of the time. Walking is the best exercise for the more mature adult. I make resolutions about how many miles I am going to walk each week. (It is usually raining on the day when I am all psyched up to start my program!)

A closing comment . . . In those moments when temptation becomes nearly unbearable, think about fitting the latest fashions on your trim, slim body; think about living a long and healthy life — being in good enough shape to enjoy your great grandchildren; and, finally, if all else fails — consult the Rabbi on the use of an appropriate prayer. Good luck. ∎

Cartoons courtesy of Ellen B. Nemoyten, daughter & critic.

Advice for Temple Administrators
published in the newsletter of the National Association of Temple Administrators

They're Dying To Do Business With Me!

I had spent most of my life as a teacher or working for non-profit organizations and now I was going to try something totally different. There were lots of guys out there who were making a lot of money—way more than me—who I didn't think were any smarter than me. This seemed like a good time in my life to see if I could make some serious money for the first time. By serious, I mean I had six figures in mind.

This was going to be a dramatic veering off of the path my life had taken up until that moment. After many years working in the pleasant fields of education, the arts, arts administration and religious administration, I was about to get myself involved with the decidedly less pleasant field of death.

I wasn't a complete novice in the field. For the past six years I had been the administrator of Peninsula Temple Beth El in San Mateo, a reform Jewish synagogue with about 600 member families. Part of my duties was to sell cemetery lots, crypts and cremation niches to our members at the Hills of Eternity Cemetery in Colma.

When we decided to establish the first Jewish Cemetery on the grounds of Skylawn Memorial Park, I became involved with their manager, Randy Storer, who interested me in the idea of going into a partnership with him in a new business.

I learned from Randy that most cemeteries will not buy back properties from their owners, or if they will, for pennies on the dollar. The idea was not for us to buy properties, but to list them and get notarized legal permission from the owners to sell the properties. They would be graves, crypts and niches which could be worth anywhere from one-hundred to five thousand dollars or more.

I was to research the value of each property and sign an agreement with the owner indicating how much they could expect to receive. We would sell the properties at discounted prices in order to draw customers.

We knew that lots of folks wasted their money running ads in their local papers, very rarely getting any response. To get listings all we had to do was scan the area papers and contact the people who placed the ads. We could also let all the cemeteries and mortuaries know about our service. They received many inquiries about properties that people wanted to sell and were more than happy to have a place to refer them.

We decided to call the business BACP Brokers, Inc. (which stood for Bay Area Cemetery Property Brokers). There were to be four stockholders; Randy and his wife Wendy Storer and my wife Sally and me. I was designated as the president of the corporation. We even issued stock certificates. Boy, was I impressed with what we were doing!

The next thing I had to do was to obtain a cemetery broker's license. Usually you are expected to first get a cemetery salesman's license and spend a

232

few years as a salesman before you can apply for a broker's license. Then there was the test on California cemetery law to pass. I studied the booklet issued by the state and then recorded the whole thing on tapes that I played in my car everywhere I went for about six weeks. Next, I made an appointment to appear before the State Cemetery Board, which would be meeting in San Diego, to request that they waive the salesman requirement and allow me to take the broker's test. They took into consideration my work at the temple and granted the waiver. Finally, I went to Sacramento to take the broker's test which I passed with little trouble.

In a relatively short period of time we managed to accumulate about 200 properties spread around the Bay Area in about 20 cemeteries. At our peak we had about 700 properties in our inventory.

Most sales were about the same in the matter of procedure, but there were certain exceptions that stand out in memory. A woman phoned me one day with a particularly unusual request.

She said, "My father died last week. He had a specific request as to how he wanted to be buried. I want to know if I can carry out his wishes. Can you help me?"

I replied that I would do my best to help her and then I asked, "How did he want to be buried?" I confess her reply stopped me in my tracks.

She said, "He wants to be buried in a standing up position, so that he will be all set to ascend to heaven!"

I thought that apparently, he figured he already had a reservation.

While I was sympathetic to her predicament, I had to advise her that I was familiar with the California cemetery laws and that, as far as I knew, there was no provision for such a burial in a public cemetery. Actually, she seemed relieved to learn the news. I then proceeded to tell her about an arrangement that would come as close as possible to meeting her father's request.

I happened to have just received a listing for a crypt in an outdoor mausoleum at Oakmont Memorial Park that was close to where the woman lived. It was in the very top seventh level, and the cemetery is high atop a hill in Lafayette. I explained that her father's body would have no one above him and the location was one of the closest to heaven you could find in the Bay Area. We met later that day and she bought the crypt.

Sometime later I received a phone call from a very emotional man who had a very decidedly African American accent. He tearfully sobbed, "My mama died and I gotta do somethin 'bout her body. I wonder can I put her in one a them drawer things so I can roll her out and look at her once in a while? I sure do love my mama and I'm gonna miss her!"

As tactfully as I could, I explained that such an arrangement could not be made at any cemetery. Apparently the man had no idea what happens to the body after we die and I didn't feel that this was the moment to educate him about natural decay. Having remembered a listing I had at Rolling Hills in

El Sobrante, a cemetery which is very popular with many Oakland African Americans, I suggested we meet there later that day. When he arrived, I showed him an available crypt I had in an outdoor mausoleum right around the corner from the cemetery office. It was at the third level. I explained that I had made arrangements with the cemetery for him to borrow a chair any time he visited so he could sit down next to the crypt anytime he wanted to and touch the outside of it, knowing that his mother was just on the other side of that thin stone wall. He was comforted with that idea and bought the crypt.

Though I spent a lot of time in cemeteries and mortuaries, I had nothing directly to do with dead bodies or particularly tragic deaths with two exceptions. The first occurred in a mortuary in Walnut Creek. I was talking to one of the morticians on the lower floor of the building near where the bodies were prepared. The door to the room where another mortician was working was ajar. The naked body of a man lay on the cold sterile metal table in the center of the room. Out of the corner of my eye, I saw the mortician pick up a hose with a sharp metal tip and jab into the cadaver's stomach in order to empty the body fluids into the drain in the floor. I skipped lunch that day.

The most tragic event that I heard of didn't involve me in any way, but I was made aware of it by a cemetery salesman I was dealing with. He told me that one of his colleagues was making arrangements for the burial of a ten-year-old boy who had drowned while on a trip with his divorced father and his father's girlfriend. The boy's mother was in the office and the scene was as hard, angry and heartbreaking as could be imagined.

My favorite memory had to do with the sale of a very fine and expensive indoor mausoleum crypt at Oak Hill Cemetery in San Jose. The seller called me several times to express how anxious he was for me to find a buyer.

I was pleased when I found someone who was able to pay the $4,500 asking price. I called the seller to tell him the good news—that I would be meeting the client the next morning at 10:00 a.m. He told me he wanted to meet me at the cemetery so he could get the check immediately after the sale.

I admit that I thought that he wanted to do so because he didn't trust me. I tried to assure him that he would receive his check as soon as possible, but he insisted on meeting me at Oak Hill. He arrived the next morning just after I completed the transaction with the buyer. When I presented him with his check, he thanked me with great enthusiasm and then said, "There is something I want to show you." He reached in his pocket and pulled out a small framed photo and said, "The check for that crypt will now make it possible for us to adopt this beautiful child." At that moment I realized more than ever before what an important service I was performing.

A number of factors contributed to my abandoning the business. The main problem was caused by the fact that a very large cemetery conglomerate called S.C.I. from Texas was buying up many of the cemeteries and mortuaries I had dealt with and they were freezing me out. But, truthfully, having given up my dream of a six-figure salary, I wanted to get out of this unhappy profession. A year after the business closed I was back teaching music.

Exotica Erotica

This is an X-rated story for adult eyes only. If you are burdened with Victorian sensibilities, proceed with caution.

The year was 1985. Halloween was coming up soon. I had been dating Barbara Levy who would later become my wife. Barbara is a remarkable woman with a remarkably open mind who appeared to be "up for anything." For several years as Halloween approached I had noticed the always tantalizingly enticing ads in the Chronicle touting the naughtiness of the annual "Exotic Erotic Ball." When I asked Barbara if she would like to check out the ball with me, she confessed that she was also very curious about what went on there.

Costumes were expected. I had my mind on one I'd seen in a local shop. It was something I had always fantasized about trying on some day. I was recalling seeing "King Kong" and those funny scary movies with Abbott and Costello and the "Three Stooges" when I was a kid. It was a gorilla costume, but not just any gorilla costume. This was a serious gorilla with a huge magnificently ferocious looking head and a full and robustly hairy body.

Bill with Barbara Levy

I was please by how I looked after I donned the costume but I knew it was not necessarily appropriate for the erotic part of the ball's theme. So I visited the local adult bookstore and came up with the perfect enhancement. It was a huge dildo! Barbara assisted me by pinning it on my costume. We had decided to come as "King Kong" and Fay Wray, perhaps hinting at their strangely erotic relationship. She wore a silky black nightgown and constructed a four-foot cardboard "Empire State Building" which she strapped to her body. We invited our friends David Hardy, an artist, and his wife Sally, who owned a gourmet cake bakery to join us, and off we went.

There appeared to be thousands of revelers at the huge venue who lost their normal inhibitions for the night with the help of alcohol, drugs and the atmosphere created by the party organizers. Many areas were dimly lit. There were bands playing in several of the rooms and some dazzling light shows going on. Barbara soon got rid of her cumbersome "Empire State Building" so we could dance.

Our costumes were hardly noticed compared to many that we saw, from the most elaborate, imaginative and glamorous to the most minimal. Some women, but more often men, appeared in nothing at all except perhaps a mask, or shoes, or things like a little white cotton ball glued to their butts. The major activity was people watching people and we were no exception. There was so much to see!

In the main room a costume contest was being held on the stage. The finalists had been chosen and the audience applause was being measured for the selection of a winner. The finalists were:

1) A six pack of Coca Cola with expertly painted human sized cans with the legs of the wearers protruding from the bottoms of the cans which were fastened together.

2) A "Mr. Nasty": A costumed man with a massive ugly head mask and a tongue that was so long it rolled out onto the floor.

3) A gorgeous woman with a spectacular figure whose naked body was elaborately painted as an American flag with the stars strategically placed.

4) A large black man who was wearing a dress, a wig and a costume that looked startlingly similar to the famous picture of "Aunt Jemima" on the pancake flour boxes and syrup bottles. When she appeared, the crowd suddenly took up the chant "Aunt Jemima, Aunt Jemima, Aunt Jemima," over and over as she continuously lifted her sagging bosom. Somehow in the midst of all the decadence, the wholesomeness of Aunt Jemima struck a responsive chord with the throng, and so, the least exotically, erotically costumed person won the first prize!

It was getting late and we had lost track of our friends. I had gone to look for them and had left Barbara near the entrance to wait for us. While I was gone, a short man, also wearing a gorilla costume approached her. He leaned in toward her and asked, "What's your sign, baby?" "Closed," she replied. He was trying to "break the ice" with her when she saw us coming and said, "Here comes your big brother!" The man turned around to face the erect dildo enhanced "King Kong" and immediately took off for parts unknown.

That was the one and only time we ever attended the Exotic Erotic Ball. But like other occasions in our lives when we have dared to step across new thresholds, we have benefitted with memories that have returned to amuse and tickle us.

Returning to Teaching

I was fifty-nine when I closed BACP Brokers. It was time to look around and determine what I would do next. I had been out of the arts administration field for ten years and though I felt I could still succeed in that realm, there were few local opportunities available. It had to be local because I was once again determined not to leave the Bay Area.

I answered an ad for a manager of San Francisco's amazingly long-running musical, "Beach Blanket Babylon," a show I had enjoyed many times. I knew I didn't quite have the right background for the job so I was neither surprised nor disappointed when I didn't get it.

Doing temple administration again didn't appeal to me. I realized that the job I was best suited for was teaching music and Barbara encouraged me to pursue that course. Even though I hadn't taught for twenty years, I was nearly always engaged in musical activities. By that time, my son Mark had been teaching music for several years. When I told him I was looking into returning to teaching after a twenty year interval he said, "Dad, are you sure you want to do that? Teaching these days here in California is not like it was when you taught in Ohio twenty years ago." I told him that I was aware of that, but just to satisfy myself about how things were actually different, I decided to visit a high school band rehearsal. I arranged to visit the James Logan High School band in Union City. The kids looked a lot different than my students at Woodridge High where almost everyone was very white. The Logan kids were typical for Bay Area schools and included all races and backgrounds: African Americans, Hispanics, Filipinos, other Pacific Islanders, Indians and a few Caucasians. Other than the diversity, it looked to me like teaching music was still just teaching music.

The "CBEST"

In order to teach in California I would have to secure a teaching certificate. That would require passing the "CBEST" or California Basic Educational Skills Test which included a segment on Algebra, a subject I had last stumbled through forty years before and one in which I had never excelled. There is absolutely no use for algebra in teaching kids to play instruments, so why would that be a requirement? It was just another one of those arbitrary things that officials think up. The result could be kids being taught to play instruments by an incompetent music teacher who is, however, a whiz at algebra! Before I had a chance to become discouraged about my chances of passing the test, Barbara came to the rescue and said she would tutor me. I also signed up to take a special course designed to assist teachers scheduled to take the CBEST. I took the test at California State University Hayward and got the results a couple of weeks later. I had passed the algebra with a score of seventy-three and all the other sections with much safer margins. I learned later that most older teachers had to take the test several times before passing it.

I Become a String Teacher

I began my job search hoping to find something close to home. I was fearful that my age, the fact that I hadn't taught for twenty years, and the need to pay me more than a beginning teacher because of my years of experience might make it impossible to find anyone who would hire me. I had a good interview in nearby San Leandro and provided them with some excellent references. I had all but given up when two weeks before the 1988-89 school year was to begin I received a call from the personnel director at San Leandro offering me a job as a string teacher at John Muir Junior High School and three elementary schools. Although I had made it clear that I was best qualified to teach band instruments, they were offering me a job at a fairly decent salary to teach mostly beginning violin players! I had grown up playing in school orchestras and my daughter Jo was an accomplished violinist. I had accompanied her to her lessons with a great teacher for several years. I had taken an excellent course in string methods in college and felt confident about teaching strings though I was a terrible violin player. So I said to the personnel director, "You want me to teach strings? I'll teach strings."

During that year I became very adept at tuning violins and cellos. My classes made good progress. For our spring concert I composed a simple piece for beginning strings I called "The San Leandro Easy Rock." We had a functioning string program and I had a job teaching strings for another year if I wanted it. But near the end of the school year I learned that Mark Boyd, the band director, was interested in getting into administrative work and was applying for jobs. Barbara and I were planning on taking an extended trip to Israel and Europe the summer of 1989. I contacted the head of my department and Ann Farias, the principle of John Muir and requested formally to be considered for the band job if Boyd left, and also suggested that they then hire a string specialist if I was assigned to the band. At the end of the summer I learned that Boyd had indeed left the system, I was to get his job and that they had hired Paul Zawilski to teach strings. Paul was not a string specialist, but a terrific pianist and singer and had a little experience on the string bass. He did a great job and was a wonderful colleague.

Building the Band at John Muir

John Muir was at that time in the last year of being a junior high and would become a middle school with grades six through eight the following year. Boyd had taken the band to CMEA Festivals each year, mostly getting "Excellent" and "Good" ratings, but never "Superior." Several years before under the direction of Gordon Mewes, John Muir had a fantastic jazz band that had received top honors at the Reno Jazz Festival. The jazz band library, music stands, a fine bass guitar and powerful amplifier/speaker were all in the band room but hadn't been utilized for years. The band room at John Muir was an excellent facility: a very large room with built-in risers, it had an office, practice rooms and a large music library. There were percussion instruments, tubas, baritones, French horns, a bass clarinet, an oboe, a bassoon and a baritone sax. I looked the situation over and seeing the potential started to work on strategies to build the program to a level that would match its potential.

We had all those fine instruments but no one to play them. I put a notice on the chalk board: "Wanted, Players for the following instruments…" I also explained to the students that we would never sound the way a band should sound without those instruments. None of the students responded when I first made my pitch, but over the next couple of weeks three of four came to me privately and told me they wanted to try those instruments and they all stuck with them. Some of our instruments were badly in need of repair, but I was told the school board had not allocated any money for repair of instruments. When inventorying the instruments I was surprised to discover a huge ancient bass saxophone, an instrument that is obsolete as far as concert bands are concerned. I learned that there was another bass sax in storage at the board of education storage facility. At the next staff meeting I proposed that we sell those instruments and use the funds to make badly needed repairs on other ones. Red tape, as always, reared its ugly head and I was told the school board would have to publicly declare the saxes as surplus and open them up for bids before we could do anything else. We did so and thankfully the required time passed quickly without a claim being made. I sold each sax for $1,800, so we had $3,600 for repairs!

To create more interest in the band I held auditions for student conductors. I also had tryouts and encouraged challenges within the sections of the band. I got permission to take the Muir band on a tour of the elementary schools and the principle of Monroe school who played the sax joined us for the program. I formed a band boosters club of parents who put on a pot luck band banquet at the end of the year. I found some money to purchase a group of trophies and plaques to honor the better student musicians. I also organized a jazz band that met after school. Lee Saltnes, one of the school guidance counselors, who played guitar, joined the band and helped with the school owned bass guitar and amplifier. Justin Griffin, a great drummer, transferred into the school and knew how to make the band really rock! Among the pieces we played were "Louie, Louie" and "Stand By Me." One memorable noon hour we played for the students and they enthusiastically danced to our music. We were also the only middle school jazz band to be invited to perform at a concert of area high school jazz bands held at Arroyo High School in nearby San Lorenzo.

I took the concert band to the CMEA festival in 1990 and we received three II's. In 1991 we received II's and a I. In 1992 it was the same, but I knew we were improving each year. In 1993 we received two I's and one II. That is a Superior rating, the first one for John Muir in perhaps twenty years, and as far as I know there have been no others since then. In some ways that accomplishment was more satisfying than the top ratings my groups had received in Ohio many years before. The ethnic backgrounds of my students

John Muir Band
Bill is standing on the right.

were very diverse and Muir was located in a lower income neighborhood. Only one member of the Muir band took private lessons. Many of the kids owned inferior instruments. Some couldn't practice because they were being shuttled back and forth between the homes of divorced parents. Those factors were not present back at Woodridge High.

I Retire

By the end of the school year, my fifth in San Leandro, I was totally exhausted. I had accomplished many of my goals and had even been cited for my good work at a meeting of all of the teachers in the district. I found out the hard way how things were different than they had been twenty years before. Yes, that it was possible to get good results, but it took much harder work to succeed. It was more difficult to get and hold the attention of the students and to motivate them to work harder. I turned in my resignation, but before leaving I attended a board of education meeting where I learned that the board had decided to eliminate the elementary school instrumental music program. I found myself making a plea in vain to the board just as Richard Dreyfuss had done in the movie "Mr. Holland's Opus." That summer, because of a lack of funds, they laid off Paul Zawilski because he had the least seniority in the music staff. He was, in my opinion, one of the most effective and talented teachers in the system. But because in public education, seniority takes preference over excellence, a great teacher was cast aside. Paul went on to a brilliant career in other school systems.

The Peninsula Pops Orchestra

Before school ended in 1989 and Barbara and I set off on our great summer trip to Israel, Egypt, Greece, Austria, Germany and England I had applied for a part-time job as conductor of the newly forming Peninsula Pops Orchestra which was to be sponsored by Foothill College in Los Altos Hills. The idea for the orchestra had come from a man named Fred Achelis. Fred was a saxophone player and an arranger of music and had substantial financial means. He approached the college offering to act as orchestra manager and to purchase the music if the college would list the orchestra as a course and employ the conductor. Once again, I found myself in the right place at the right time. When we returned from our trip in August I was certain that the orchestra had found a conductor while I was away and I was correct. However, that person had received another job offer out of state and just a week before and the orchestra was back to looking for a conductor who could start in a couple of weeks. I interviewed with Fred Achelis and Terry Summa, the Foothill College band director and got the job! It involved Saturday morning rehearsals at the college and a few programs in the community. About twenty people of various ages and musical levels showed up for the first rehearsal. Some were "rusty musicians", that is, people who had played well at one time but hadn't played for a while, sometimes as long as ten or more years. We started with some fairly easy music from Broadway shows, film scores, novelties and light classics, increasing the difficulty as the orchestra improved and grew in size. We performed pieces like Ravel's Pavanne, Strauss's Pizzicato Polka and Brahm's Hungarian Dance Number Five.

Mary and I Surprise the Orchestra

At the second or third rehearsal I had a very pleasant surprise when a violinist named Mary Driscoll showed up. Mary taught string classes in the Palo Alto schools, but she was also a fine coloratura soprano. I had known her in that capacity about fifteen years earlier when she was a featured singer in the San Mateo County Arts Council's lunchtime concert programs. After a warm greeting I called Mary aside and asked her if she knew the Sigmund Romberg operetta songs we were going to play that day. She said she did, so I proposed that without an introduction to the orchestra she should put her violin down, stand up and sing the songs she knew, and sing she did to everyone's delight and surprise. The songs were those sentimental old Nelson Eddy and Jeanette MacDonald selections such as "Softly, as in a Morning Sunrise", "One Alone", and "Lover Come Back to Me." From that point on she was featured in most of our concerts.

During the four years I conducted the orchestra we developed a very congenial group of people who came from diverse backgrounds and professions who just loved making music and sharing it with others in the community. We performed once at the Stanford Mall and another time at the Saint Anthony's Dining Room in Menlo Park. We also performed at retirement homes and mobile home parks. When I retired from teaching in 1993 I resigned as conductor of the orchestra because Barbara and I had decided to start to take long trips in our motorhome beginning with a trip to Alaska. It was at that time that Fred Achelis and I agreed to hand the baton over to Kim Venass. Kim had a different vision for the orchestra. He set about changing the repertoire entirely into light pops, did a fine job of programming and promotion, brought in some professional players, built a financial structure and changed the name to the California Pops Orchestra. It took a young man with a lot of talent and ambition to do what he has done with the orchestra and I salute him! Check out the California Pops Orchestra website and you'll see what I mean!

The Peninsula Pops Orchestra
Bill is on the bottom right with the baton.

Adventures in
"Retirement"

Bill and Barbara on their travels

Behind the Iron Curtain

We had decided to take a boat ride down the Danube River to Budapest. This was in 1989 when Hungary was still a communist country, so we had to go to the Hungarian Consulate in Vienna to get visas for everyone. There was a long line to wait in and the process seemed extremely cumbersome and unnecessary for a weekend excursion, but as we understood it, that was to be expected from a communist bureaucracy.

All my life I had heard the expression "the beautiful blue Danube" in connection with Johann Strauss Jr's *Blue Danube Waltz*. So, of course, I had a picture in my mind of what it would be like. What a letdown! To begin with, the boat we were booked on was one of those small advanced design vessels that rose up on top of the water when the engines were revved up. It spewed smelly fumes as it sped at a breakneck speed down the river past loading docks, polluting smoke stacks and big freighters. It took an hour of loud engine roaring before we reached a more rural area and the scenery left some impression of what the Danube riverside country may have looked like a century earlier when the famous waltz was penned.

We arrived in Budapest late that afternoon and immediately headed for the official government agency that certifies places where you can stay, that is, if you wish to be in someplace other than an expensive downtown hotel. As we waited in line to go into the office, we were approached by a man and a woman in a cab who asked us if we were looking for a place to rent. We said yes and we had a party of four. The woman told us she had a very good place to rent and we could have it for one hundred dollars American money for three nights. She said they would take us to the place and bring us back if we didn't like it. Other than thinking that we might get kidnapped for ransom, it sounded like a good deal and the woman looked and sounded honest.

We all piled into the little car, a Russian made Lada, and drove to what we were beginning to think must have been the outskirts of Pest. Remember, Buda is on one side of the Danube and Pest on the other. We arrived at a large dreary looking apartment house that hadn't won any architectural awards. Our apartment was on the second floor. It was small but clean. The décor looked like thrift store rejects. It had a small kitchen and just enough room to work for us for three nights, so we signed on.

The next day we decided to go to one of the central shopping areas, I think it was called the "Utsa." We proceeded to the "amazing" corner where we were told you could find a cab any hour of the day or night. None of the drivers spoke any English. Most of them drove those Russian Ladas, cars styled and equipped like American cars were twenty years earlier. The fee for all four of us was two dollars. That was the standard price for any location in Buda or Pest, no matter the distance.

On that day we drew a very friendly but slightly crazy driver who gave us a ride that was somewhere between thrilling and terrifying as he surged through the narrow old streets at top speed barely missing cyclists, pedestrians and parked cars by inches. When we arrived at our destination we explored the area, noting that the most popular place seemed to be the newly opened MacDonald's restaurant which was located in a prime spot and had a long line waiting to get in. Besides the fast food, another attraction was the fact that it was the only place in the area with a public restroom.

Ellie Cohen, our musician friend and I spotted a sheet music store where we found a modest inventory of piano and instrumental music, all at incredible prices because as a communist country, at that time, they did not recognize international copyrights. The music cost about a third of what it would at home. Ellie bought about one hundred dollars' worth of piano music for thirty dollars and I bought thirty dollars' worth of trombone music for ten dollars.

The Money Changer

In the meantime Barbara, who was doing some window shopping nearby, stopped at a corner where there were three banks posting the current exchange rate for Hungarian forints on their windows. They were all around 140 per one American dollar. As she stood trying to decide which bank to go into, a short, non-descript middle aged man, wearing a very ordinary brown suite sidled up to her. One of the few Hungarians who spoke any English at any time during our stay, he uttered softly to her the words, "You want change money? I give good deal. Much better than bank." Barbara nodded. The man reached into his pocket and pulled out a wad of Hungarian paper money. The man asked, "How much you want change?"

Barbara hesitated, then said, "One hundred dollars."

The man quickly stuffed the money back into his pocket and gestured with his head for Barbara to follow him as he walked a short distance around the corner, out of site of the banks. She followed him. He pulled the wad of bills out again and quickly but carefully counted out one 170 forints and gave them to Barbara. She then handed him a one hundred dollar bill and the man disappeared quickly.

Later when we all had gathered Barbara excitedly told us about the terrific rate she had gotten. That evening at dinner, our other travelling companion Barbara Goren, asked Barbara Nemoyten if she would please change some money for her tomorrow when we returned to the Utsa. Barbara agreed, and the next day returned to the same spot where she had stood the day before while we explored more of the area, Barbara began looking for the short, non-descript man in the ordinary brown suit. She stood for a while in the same spot and then moved around a bit, but no one approached her. Finally, she spotted a non-descript middle-aged man in an ordinary brown suite who she was sure was the same man. As he approached she smiled at him. He smiled back. She smiled at him some more. He smiled back some more. She then gestured for him to follow her, which he gladly did. It was when they had turned the corner out of site of the main street and he came closer to her that she realized he was not the man she was looking for and that his interest was in exchanging something, but it wasn't money. She beat a hasty retreat and apparently learned her lesson. All future money exchanges were at the bank.

The Challenge of Going Shopping

Later that day when we returned to our apartment, the ladies sent me out to see if I could find some breakfast cereal and milk. There was a small shopping area across the street just behind our building. On my way to find the market I noticed a long line of people standing silently in front of a store. They all had containers in their hands, plastic buckets and glass jars of varying sizes. I was very curious and investigated. It turned out to be an ice cream store! Apparently, the ice cream store actually having ice cream to sell was a special event. I took my place at the end of the line and when my turn came I motioned that I had no container, so they provided one for me, for which I assume they charged me. When it came to choosing the flavors, since I couldn't read or understand any Hungarian I merely pointed to the ones that looked good to me. When it was time to pay I put some money on the counter and accepted the change with no idea as to how much it cost or if I was receiving the correct change. When I returned to the apartment the ladies were surprised and delighted, but I still had to go on my cereal hunt.

The market I was looking for was a little way past the ice cream store. The sight of the merchandise was a mild shock. There were no recognizable brands, no Kellog's Corn Flakes, no Post Cereals. The packaging was mostly yellow boxes with black lettering—all in Hungarian! I looked for boxes about the size of U.S. cereal boxes and shook a few of them to see if they had cereal acoustics. I picked what I thought was the most likely one and then looked for the milk. That was easier, but also surprising because there were no cartons or bottles. The milk is sold in plastic bags. Later I discovered that that was standard in many European countries.

When I returned to the apartment and put the box on the table I declared, "I'm really not sure what I brought you, it might be dog food, it might be candy or it might be breakfast cereal." It turned out to be corn puffs.

One of the saddest, most pathetic sights we saw in Budapest was at an open air farmer's market. At one end of the market there was a line of about ten men and women, some shabbily dressed, all of them quiet and with somber expressions. They stood shoulder to shoulder, facing any possible passerby. Each person had a household item they were trying to sell. One carried a bent umbrella. Another had some parts of a coffee pot and incredibly one man held up a single boot! In a society with so little in the way of consumer goods apparently anything even marginally usable had some value. But a single boot?!

Almost Marooned in Buda

Everywhere in that communist country we saw examples of people trying to make money by one enterprise or another that wasn't controlled by the state. It began with those people who by-passed the government tourist agency by intercepting us before we went into their office. The money changer was another example as was the group of people selling their household castoffs.

Another example we experienced occurred when we took a cab to Buda one night to see a delightful Hungarian folk dance program. After the concert, which was in a hall located in a mostly residential neighborhood, we looked around for a cab. Then we noticed that there was a man out on the sidewalk hailing cabs for people. We lined up to get a cab but when our turn came he ignored us. Almost everyone was gone and we were worrying about how we would get home when Barbara Goren said, "Of course! Why didn't we think of it? We've got to tip him!"

It was great news when Hungary was freed from communist rule a few years later and became a democracy. Most Americans who have traveled widely seem to have the same thought that I did upon my return home. That is, that while our system of government is far from perfect, it is the best, to date, that the human mind has been able to devise.

The Family Secret

This happened in 1990 when I was sixty-two years old. We had arrived in Woodland Hills, California the previous day at the home of Joe and Charlotte Lubman, old family friends. Before our trip I had called to ask if it would be convenient for us to stop by on our way to San Diego. Charlotte answered that not only would it be OK, but that there was something she wanted to talk to me about. That sounded strange since I hadn't seen her in years and there were no loose ends I could think of involving that last time we saw each other. Barbara and the rest of our party were in the house finishing breakfast when I took Charlotte out to see our newly acquired motor home.

After I showed her around she said, "There is something important that I want to tell you and I'll get right to it. I'm your half-sister."

I wasn't sure that I had heard her correctly, but before I could say anything, she continued.

"Here's what happened. Your father, Jacob Nemoyten, was impotent. Your mother desperately wanted to have a child. My father, Alex Gottlober, who you know was an artist and a sign painter and a bit of a Lothario, was only too happy to oblige. And so I am your half-sister. Everyone in the family was sworn to secrecy but since all of the people who were involved in our parent's generation have passed away, I've decided that you must be told. As you know, my brothers Hy and Abe have been gone for several years and I want to claim you as my kid brother."

Charlotte, who was nine years older than I, was surprised when I said to her, "It had occurred to me. I always thought that I didn't look anything like my father. I would try to think of who I did look like and the person who I always came up with was your father. But it was always more in the nature of a day-dreaming fantasy. This is, of course, a big shock to me. It will take a while for me to sort everything out."

Shirley with Gottlobers
Standing far right is Uncle Hy
Seated left is Charlotte, far right is Shirley
Mary on the floor

Alex Gottlober with Hy as a toddler

When we returned to the house, Barbara told me that I looked as though I had just seen a ghost. I shared the story with everyone, and they were astonished by it. I wasn't one hundred percent certain that the story was true, so the next thing I did was to phone my aunt Pearl in Cleveland. Aunt Pearl was the older of my mother's two younger sisters and had kept a close relationship with my family since my mother's death four years earlier.

I related the story to her. There was a long pause on the telephone. Then she blurted out the question, "Who told you that rumor?" In that instant I knew that my life had truly changed. Aunt Pearl knew something. There was no doubt about that. But I don't think she knew the whole story since my mother had an older sister named Jennie, deceased a few years before, with whom she much more likely would have shared such a secret.

Over the next several weeks and months, many riddles about my earlier life were answered. Why was it that I was the only one of all my cousins who had no brothers or sisters? I now knew that my father's inability to make a decent living was not the only reason for my mother's unhappiness. Unless he was simply a cold and grouchy old man, I began to understand why my paternal grandfather, who lived on the first floor of our two family house, was never very warm or friendly to my mother and was so indifferent to me.

When I was twelve, Hy Gottlober, who was recently divorced, moved into our house as a boarder along with his ten-year-old son, Louis. I didn't know it at the time but Hy was my half-brother. Being an only child I was delighted to have Lou's company, even if I had to share my tiny room with him.

Hy, who could be a very disagreeable guy sometimes with other people, was always kind and caring to me, treating me as if I were another son of his. Hy, like his father, was also an artist and a sign painter. He seemed to be unusually curious as to

Abraham Ber Gottlober

whether I had both a talent for and an interest in art. He bought me oil paints and gave me a few lessons, but by that time I was too deeply into my music to turn to art. One thing that I remember being particularly strange was how he

Bill with Lou having fun in the park

would tell me with such pride about his great-grandfather, Abraham Ber Gottlober, who was a famous Jewish writer in 19th century Russia and that there was an article and photo about him in the Encyclopedia Judaica. I couldn't figure out why Hy was so anxious for me to know about the man.

One funny thing happened after the big revelation. I phoned Louis in Cleveland and told him the story. He told me he was not entirely surprised. Then I said, "Do you remember how we used to wrestle when we were kids and I was so much bigger than you that I would get on top of you and use that curious expression 'Say uncle'? Well I was your uncle, wasn't I?"

So what about my father? He was the man who raised me. It wasn't Alex. Jacob did the best he could. I know that and I realize that his was a very unusual and special kind of love. And what of my mother? In those days the women all stayed home while the men worked. The women were expected to have children and take care of them. I believe my mother could see no purpose to her life if she didn't have at least one child to take care of. In those days there was no artificial insemination available. If you wanted a child you had but one choice. Being a religious and moral person, she

Jacob Nemoyten with baby Bill

must have had an enormous inner conflict about what she did. One of the saddest parts of this story is that during the last years of her life when she was suffering terribly from a crippling stroke she often declared, "God is punishing me!" We would try to assure her that she was always a good person and that there was no reason for God to punish her. But in that matter she always seemed inconsolable.

There is a great gift that this knowledge of my true parentage gave me about myself. Without even knowing my true heritage, I naturally gravitated to a life in the arts and, in a way; it helped me to make sense of my whole life.

Bill and his biological father, Alex Gottlober

Jack Nemoyten in 1965

RV-ing in Ohio

The Dream Catcher

In January of 1990, Barbara and I went to the RV Show and Sale at the Alameda County Fairgrounds to check out the latest models and dream about owning one of those great big beautiful houses on wheels. Late on Sunday, the last day of the show, we spotted what appeared to be the perfect motor home for us.

It was a twenty-four-and-a-half-foot Jamboree Rallye, cream colored with blue trim. It had handsome light colored woodwork (an absolute requirement for Barbara), lots of windows, sleeping for up to five, a refrigerator, freezer, propane stove, microwave, nice bathroom with a shower, place to hook up cable TV and lots of other amenities. It was built on a Ford

The Dream Catcher
Bill and Barbara's well-traveled motor home

truck chassis and had power steering, cruise control, and a fine radio/tape deck. We were so excited about it that we made an offer one half hour before the show was to close, not thinking that it would be anywhere near enough to be considered. The salesman came back after meeting with his boss and we struck a deal.

After we took a few short trips we settled on a name. We called it "Dream Catcher" after the Native American willow hoops with their spider web weaving. Good dreams are captured in the web of life and carried with them, but the evil in their dreams escapes through the hole in the center and is no longer a part of them. Our "Dream Catcher" turned out to be everything we had hoped for and more.

It is now fifteen years and 150,000 miles later.

We have been to forty-five of the fifty states, including Alaska, and to seven Canadian provinces. We've had countless adventures and misadventures. The following are some of the many such episodes.

The Ohio Canal

We had set out on a trip around Ohio during the summer, of course. When we reached Xenia in southwest Ohio, a town near Dayton, we learned that they offered rides in a replica of the canal boats that traveled the old Ohio Canal. We could take a ride on a small portion of the canal that was still in existence. The ride was such a pleasant surprise that in my mind I can still relive its special qualities.

The canals were relatively narrow and bordered on either side by high soil embankments. It was vital that the boats keep to a speed of no more than four miles per hour so that the wake from the boat did not wash up on and erode the banks. The boats had no motors, but were towed by mules plodding along the "towpath" at a surprisingly long distance from the boat.

The ride was totally silent and totally smooth. The scenery was the lush verdant banks on both sides. It was as close as I have ever felt to finding myself living in a bygone world where life was slower, simpler and quiet. The captain of the boat pointed out many aspects of how the boats operated, about the cargo they carried and their significance to the growth of Ohio commerce. He also pointed out the fact that although we were being pulled by a team of two horses that day, the old canal boats were always pulled by mules. The reason was startling to me. Apparently, horses, as long as they are being driven to pull, will keep going until they drop dead. Mules, when they are tired, will simply stop. The expression "stubborn as a mule" took on a new meaning.

Indian Mounds

Most people know very little about Indian Mounds. For a long time I felt that Barbara knew too much about them. Barbara has such a passion for Indian Mounds that I once jokingly said that if we had to visit one more Indian Mound I would dig a hole in one and put her in it! But her love of the mounds gradually made an impression on me. We have now visited a total of at least two-dozen mounds in Illinois, Alabama, Georgia, Louisiana, Wisconsin, Missouri, Tennessee, Florida and most notably, Ohio. What I discovered is that the more mounds you visit, the more you gain a perspective of their function and the amazing varieties of forms they take.

Southern Ohio has one of the premier mounds in the entire world. It's called the "Great Serpent Mound." Nearly a quarter of a mile long and averaging only three feet in height, it is an earthen sculpture of a giant serpent uncoiling. On our visit I climbed to the top of the observation tower that affords a dramatic view of the serpent. In that moment I came to realize what a truly remarkable achievement that construction was as were many others we have seen.

Surprising Flowers

We continued our trip and a few nights later found ourselves in a campground near the town of Peebles, Ohio in a far southern part of the state. As we were pulling into our campsite, an older gentleman came by to greet us and said something we didn't quite comprehend. He said, "We'd like to invite you to come over around 7:30 and see the show." We thanked him and went about our business, connecting the RV to water and electricity and then had our dinner.

At 7:20, the man knocked on our door and said, "You best come on over now or you'll miss the show." I said I'd be right there and followed him. Barbara said she'd be over in a few minutes.

Our neighbors were living in a small mobile home that was permanently set down on the ground. It had some plantings around it including some flowers and shrubs. The man and his wife were standing and looking at a large plant that was covered with pale yellow buds. Suddenly the man said, "I think the show is starting. Look there on the left." One of the buds started to shudder, gently at first, then a little stronger until it began to shake as the bud opened up wider and wider revealing a beautiful pale yellow flower. It continued to open as other buds began the same procedure, shuddering and shaking and opening up.

Frankly, I was astounded as I inquired, "What kind of flowers are those?" They said they didn't know what they were called, but they sure enjoyed them. I said, "Wow! I'll be right back!" and ran over to our rig to get Barbara.

I told her what I'd just seen and she said, "I'll be right there, but first I want to grab our flower book."

When I returned to the site about half the buds had opened and more were popping out all over. Barbara followed a few seconds later. She looked at the flowers for a moment or two and then read from her book, "They're called Hooker's Evening Primrose. The buds open as the sun is going down and shortly afterward they are visited by Humming Bird Moths."

Just then, as if responding to a director's cue, the largest moth we had ever seen entered from "stage left" and went about the business of visiting the newly opened buds. We all watched entranced for a long time. Then Barbara broke the silence with, "They're called Hooker's because they only come out at night!"

Looking for a Campground

After having breakfast the next morning in the town of Peebles, we headed northwest toward Chillicothe where there are more mounds and a summer outdoor pageant called "Tecumseh" after the famous Indian chief. We decided to see the show that night and were looking for a place nearby to camp. A park ranger looked at one of her maps and suggested that we try the "Redbud Creek Campground" which was supposed to be about five miles away on a country road for which she gave us very vague directions.

We drove to the area and shortly got completely lost because the few street signs we found were set on strange angles so that you couldn't really be certain that you were on the right road. It was a very hot day. We wandered around for quite a while until Barbara became extremely frustrated and suggested that if I didn't stop and ask someone for directions she was going to get out and walk. She has a thing about men not wanting to ask for directions and one of her favorite lines is, "Do you know why the Hebrew people wandered in the desert for forty years? Because Moses wouldn't ask for directions!"

Being rural country roads there was no one to ask for a long time. Finally, Barbara spotted an old woman by the side of the road who was apparently looking for discarded aluminum cans and was placing them in a large plastic bag that she dragged along. Despite the intense heat of the day the woman was wearing a faded wine colored sweater. Of course, I stopped the RV as directed. The woman was on the right side of the road, so it was up to Barbara to keep us from wandering further "in the desert."

Barbara leaned out the window saying, "Pardon me ma'm, but can you tell us how to get to the Red Bud Creek Campground?"

The woman put her plastic bag down and climbed up the small embankment and leaned on Barbara's door. This is what she said and just the way she said it. "Ahm from round here, but ah don't know nothin bout no campground. There's a old man down the road a-ways. You ask him. He knows evrythin!"

Barbara thanked the woman and we continued down the same road until we spied "the old man who knows ervythin."

He was also dragging along a big plastic bag, but was on my side of the road. I stopped and called to him. "Pardon me, mister. Can you tell us how to get to the Red Bud Creek Campground?"

He put down his bag, took out a hanky and wiped his brow, then trudged over to the RV. His face had that sunken-in look of a person who has no teeth and forgot to wear his dentures. I don't think I'll ever forget what he said to us as he flashed his toothless smile and pointed up in the direction in which we were headed. "Ya ga ba glob ba jamb ramba shu loppa gaber lay hay."

My hearing had been failing recently, so I said, "Would you mind repeating that?"

He nodded agreeably and emphatically stated, "a go da mala to anwata do lerdo, OK?"

Being completely befuddled, for some stupid reason I turned to Barbara and asked, "Barbara, did you get that?" She looked at me as though I had totally lost my mind. I thanked the toothless bagman and proceeded in the direction that he had pointed with little hope in my heart.

The road grew narrower and the scenery changed from farmland to woods. We had given up hope of finding traces of civilization when there it was, the rustic sign, our Holy Grail, "Red Bud Creek Camp Ground." We entered and drove around a bit, but saw no other motor homes, trailers or campers. We finally spotted what looked like an office. I went in and when I returned had the disheartening news for Barbara. "Red Bud Creek" was a private church camp.

Somehow we found our way back to the main highway and to the Amphitheater where "Tecumseh" was presented nightly all summer. Tecumseh, who was born in 1768 in the area near Piqua, Ohio was a chief of the Shawnee tribe. He was famous for his work to unite other Indian tribes to oppose white expansion into the west in the early 1800s. Adorned with a large cast, thrilling music and lots of battle scenes, it was a wonderful surprise. Set in the outdoors, the show used the natural land as a stage set. When it finally became dark enough to begin, Chief Tecumseh, in full Shawnee Indian dress on a magnificent white horse, came riding toward the audience from across the field. Other Indians rode in yelling war cries from both sides of the audience grandstand. Sitting to our right was an eight year old boy. He got so excited when he saw the Indians that he took out a sling shot and was just about to use it when his father grabbed the loaded weapon! The show was pretty spectacular and we enjoyed it thoroughly.

Our Ohio experiences were only a fraction of the story of our adventures during the 21 years travelling in our "Dream Catcher."

Give Me a Brake

We sold our 24 foot Jamboree Rallye motorhome in late 2011 after enjoying 21 years of fun and adventure over 130,000 miles in 45 U.S. States, including Alaska and six Canadian provinces. This story is about the most memorably terrifying experience we had during that time.

Bill at the top

We had left Jasper Provincial Park in British Columbia a few hours earlier and were heading southwest when we encountered a very long downhill grade. The scenery had been spectacular and Barbara and I were happily chatting about how much we were both enjoying the trip, having no idea about what lay ahead for us a few miles down the narrow two lane highway. It was unusually busy with many cars, trucks, and tractor-trailers. We were sandwiched between two enormous behemoths of the highways as we plunged down the mountain. It became necessary to constantly apply my brakes as we rolled on and on in what was feeling like an endless downward journey.

The huge rig behind me was right on my tail. I could see the scowling face of the burly truck driver in my rear view mirror. He appeared frustrated to be stuck behind another damned "mom-and-pop" motor home. It looked like, if he could, he would crush us like bugs on his windshield. I tried to put some space between us, but because the road was getting steeper, I had to instead, pump my brakes more and more. And still the road continued its descent. We drove down and down, mile after mile, continuously braking to keep control. At that point I wasn't concerned for our safety because, after all, I had driven safely for thousands of miles over many mountains and felt very confident about my driving skills.

And then it happened—the one most terrifying feeling that a driver can experience other than an impending head-on collision. I applied my foot to the brake and it went down to the floor, followed quickly by that horrific sinking feeling in the pit of my stomach. I tried it again with the same result.

"Yes," I told myself. "My God, I've lost my brakes!!" Immediately and terrifyingly it felt like we were going much faster.

Then the conversation with myself continued in rapid bursts of terror:

Turn off the motor! No don't do that! You'll lose your power steering. Turn on your emergency lights! What the hell good will that do?!

In milliseconds, these thoughts:

We're rolling down this mountain road in five tons of steel and fiberglass with all of our stuff. If I can't somehow stop I'll have three alternatives; 1) Pass the truck in front of me on the left, most likely into a head-on collision, killing us and them, whomever they might be; 2) Crash into the rear of the big truck we're bearing down on causing a pile-up of several cars and trucks and road kill mayhem; 3) Turn off on the right shoulder, lose control and tumble headlong down into the canyon below.

What a set of choices! The firing squad, the electric chair or the noose!

Stop and think. Yes, I know what to do. Turn off the overdrive. Shift down to second gear, then to first gear. Then the parking brake. It didn't hold. Try the foot brakes again. Nothing!

We slowed down just enough so that the guy behind us looked like he would go nuts. But thankfully we had put some distance between the motorhome and the truck in front of us. Then I asked myself if I had remembered to turn off our propane tank. If I hadn't and we crashed, we could be incinerated in a huge ball of flame—not my first choice for checking out of the game. Suddenly we were coming to something other than mountain scenery. Flying by on our left we saw the "Radium Hot Springs" spa. Now there would be more vehicles on the road. Just what we needed! I don't remember what Barbara was doing at the time, but it was probably whatever an atheist does that substitutes for prayer.

And then, suddenly, deliverance! We saw it and felt it—the bottom of the hill at last. We were leveling off and slowed some more. Then, thankfully, a long stretch of flat grassy land appeared on the left side of the road. After two cars passed, I cut across the median strip, continued to roll another 200 yards, slowing gradually and finally (incredibly!) coming to a stop just before a rude introduction to a substantial unmovable pine tree. Barbara and I looked at one another and sat in silence except for the sound of our heart beats pounding for several minutes. Our trip would continue, as would our lives!

So what had happened? Applying them so many times in rapid succession had caused the brakes to over-heat, vaporizing the brake fluid. I was able to find a phone and call the good old "Good Sam Club." And, as they had done many times before and after, we were rescued.

Barbara, "Shopper Extraordinaire"

On August 12, 2003 Barbara earned her M.S or "Master of Shopping" degree, magna cum laude, and she has the receipt to prove it. But more about that later. Reaching the apex of such an art form leaves me breathless with admiration because I have observed that it takes years of research, hard work and persistence for accomplishments of the magnitude that Barbara has achieved.

I learned that her motivation to not only succeed, but to excel in the realm of shopping, was derived from being a member of a family that struggled through the great depression. It was later reinforced by her years as a single divorced mother of three on a very limited budget.

First comes the diligent daily scanning of the newspapers and the comparison of prices and discounts. Then there are the important issues of what items are needed and how they will match and coordinate with the existing inventory on hand.

Next comes the decision of which establishment will be targeted. It is usually Macy's, Target, Walmart or Kmart. However, an exception is occasionally made for outlet center stores such as the Nordstrom Rack in San Leandro, or farther away at outlet centers in Napa, Gilroy and beyond at Jones New York or Liz Claiborne.

When Barbara arrives at the designated target she is truly "in the trenches." She surveys the racks for certain attractive items at substantial discount prices. With a practiced eye and the nimble fingers of her very tiny hands she riffles through the racks at full speed looking for a unique treasure that has very specific requirements. First, the size must be right. Then comes the price. Well actually, that's not always true. Sometimes if the price is fantastically low, she will buy the item if it's too large, take it home, and spend hours altering it.

Many times, if she is really crazy for an item but the price is too high in her opinion, she will make a mental note of its price and location. Then two weeks later she'll look for the same item to see if it is still there and has been reduced in price, which is often the case. This is where her master shopper's instinct kicks in. If she has a hunch it will still be there in two more weeks at a further reduced price she takes the gamble, leaves and returns again two weeks later.

Using what I named her "Barbaraic System," I have seen her actually purchase a beautiful four-hundred dollar jacket for forty dollars after returning to inspect it for reductions four times. My admiration for her achievement was unbounded!

But the compulsion for bargains can have its downside. One time during her newspaper scan she spotted the grand opening of new Food Max in Oakland that was to begin at 3:00 a.m. the next morning. They were giving out a free carton of a dozen eggs just for coming into the store and Foster Farm Chickens were being sold for twenty-nine cents a pound, on a first come, first served basis. There were many other incredible buys listed in the full-page ad. I thought she was kidding when she said she wanted to check it out. We went to bed at 11:00, but at 2:15 a.m. I found out she was deadly serious and that if I didn't get up she'd be heading for an unfamiliar, dangerous part of Oakland at 3:00 a.m. all alone.

I dragged myself out of bed and, while making unseemly comments under my breath, threw on some clothing. Off we went. She advised me to think of it as "just another wonderful new adventure." We wandered around in the dark for a while looking for the designated street. Suddenly we came to a brightly lit parking lot jammed with cars. As we drove closer, we saw a line of people waiting to get into the store. It stretched around the corner with the end out of sight, lost somewhere in the darkness.

We sat there for a while in silence just marveling at the number of people who had shown up at three o'clock in the morning. Then I said, "You know, there must be a lot of people who need free eggs and twenty-nine cents a pound chickens much more than we do." Barbara nodded and we headed home, stopping for an early morning snack at Denny's. If I spot another similar ad in a paper before she does, it usually mysteriously disappears.

It was on a routine visit to Macy's at Hillsdale Mall in San Mateo that Barbara earned her degree. There was a big sale on that day and the store was jammed. She was checking out various sale items when she spotted and picked up two attractive hand bags. One of them was a Ralph Lauren designed red cloth handbag with a price tag of $69.95, the other an off-white leather bag with no price tag. Barbara got into the long line at the nearest cash register and waited twenty minutes for service.

She asked the clerk, or as they are now called, the "associate," to check the prices. The associate put the label up to the scanner. The leather bag was $280 marked down to $140 Barbara said, "A good markdown, but not good enough." The associate then scanned the Ralph Lauren, hesitated for a moment, looked questioningly at the screen and ran the tag through the scanner again and then said, "This item is marked down to one cent." It was very noisy in the area and Barbara, who is beginning to lose her hearing was incredulous and asked the associate to please repeat what she had said a little louder. "The price for this purse is one cent," she said, loud enough for all in the immediate area to hear. For a moment there was a hushed silence in the line of women behind Barbara, then came shouts of "Where did you get that"? "Are there anymore"? One of the women even tried to grab the bag out of Barbara's hand saying, "That's just what I was looking for"!

But she didn't have a prayer! Barbara's grip was ironclad. While several women got out of the line and headed for the table of handbags, Barbara calmly said, "I'll take it," dug down into her purse, pulled out a shiny penny and handed it to the associate who rang it up. She brought the receipt home and framed it.

It is, after all, a trophy, a testimonial, a document that freezes and commemorates a special moment in time that will live on in the legends and folk tales of the great shoppers for all time!

A Visit to Marvin Picollo

On May 7, 2006 Barbara and I loaded up the car, our 2000 Toyota Echo, with our "thirteen horns from around the world," seven days' worth of clothing, extra pillows and a cooler with drinks and snacks. We were heading for Reno to perform in the schools and libraries of Washoe County, Nevada. This was our second stint in Reno. We had done eight shows from the 5th to the 8th of April, all sponsored by the Pioneer Center for the Performing Arts. In addition to our fee, we were "comped" at Cal-Neva's Nevadan Hotel just like the "high rollers" who gambled at their casino across the street.

We had performed at three libraries on Monday and Tuesday. Our first assignment on Wednesday was a school on the south side of Reno called Marvin Picollo. We were told by someone that the name was pronounced "pick-OHLOW with the accent on the OHLOW and not like the diminutive flute. After a short ride down Route 395 we turned off to some roads in a rural area, arriving at a modest cluster of old school buildings.

Shortly after we started to unload our instruments and equipment a happy and very pleasant looking thirty-something woman greeted us. Her name was Diane Bell. She was the music teacher and I don't think I'll ever forget her! Diane told us that several children would be coming into the multi-purpose room for the performance in wheel chairs and that this was, in fact, no ordinary school. It was a school for children and adults ages five through twenty-one with very special needs. This was a total surprise to us. Our contact person at the Pioneer Center had not mentioned it. When hearing the news I said to Diane "You are obviously the kind of person who likes a challenge and so are we." Barbara and I have performed at a small school for blind children in Alamo and also at a school for kids with learning problems in Scottsdale, Arizona.

But I soon discovered that the challenge here would be at an altogether different level. As the students began to enter I was confronted by one of my greatest personal challenges as a performer. The older I get the more I have begun to allow my emotions their expression. I began to feel, and was trying desperately to suppress a welling of tears and keep my composure. Barbara and I witnessed a growing audience of youngsters severely wounded by an array of maladies, psychological, physical and emotional, some walking, some in wheels chairs, some with various leg braces and some with caretakers supporting them all crowding into the room and surrounding us on three sides. Sitting at our feet on a rubber mat was a group of teenagers, some probably brain damaged, and a young man with Down's syndrome. Seated on the left in the back was a boy that had been wheeled on a chair specially adapted to support his head which appeared to be permanently hanging to one side. I don't think he could move his head at all! To our right was an assortment of older teens and young adults, some in wheelchairs, some with odd tortured movements and many accompanied by adult aids. I noted a large boy in the rear who periodically lifted his arms and simultaneously opened his mouth letting out a roaring sound that appeared to be totally involuntary, most likely Tourette's syndrome.

Barbara looked over at me and pointed to the wheelchair she was sitting in. She has a bad arthritic condition and can only walk short distances comfortably. I understood that she was indicating that the presence of her wheel chair would help us connect with our audience.

As we scanned the room that would eventually be filled with nearly 160 student/patients plus a substantial number of teachers and other staff, my head was filling with these thoughts: *Bill, you are a performer. Once you begin to perform you know you'll be OK, won't you? Every one of these kids has a family, a father and a mother, siblings and grandparents who had their hopes and dreams for a bright future for these precious lives when each of them came into this world. This place is filled with the afflicted bodies and minds of those who will never fulfill those hopes and dreams. Barbara and I are so fortunate. Between us we have thirteen mostly healthy children and grandchildren.*

And more kept arriving. Now it's two of those nursery school carts that each carries five or six small children, all tightly belted in place...more heartbreak!

The room was noisy, as I knew it would be. I was glad I asked for a microphone. I have usually been successful in holding the attention of my school audiences, even up to nearly 500 at a time. But this was different. Many of these kids would not be capable of controlling themselves. We were almost ready to start when an aid pushed in a big contraption, the like of which we had never seen before. It was apparently designed to hold its occupant, a ten or eleven-year-old boy, in an upright, standing position. Heaven help me, this poor child couldn't even sit down!

Now it was time to start the show. Diane, joyfully, as she seemed to do everything, introduced me to this audience, my greatest challenge. Diane's joyfulness was infectious. If she could be that way here in this place every day, I knew I could perform at my highest level for these kids on this day. I launched into my conch shell opening and told the story I usually begin my show with. As I went along, with Barbara's help, and despite the noisiness of some in the audience we began to sense that we were making connections.

We always make a point of it to look at the faces of both the children and the teachers. After a while many were clapping along with the music and there were laughs of delight. I was concentrating very hard on just how I would present each instrument and tried to edit my show on the spot to what I thought would work for this unique audience. One high point was when the Down's syndrome young man in front came up with the right answer to a question I asked. He was cheered by his classmates.

All through the show Diane stood in the back of the room beaming with delight while keeping an eye out for any problems that might arise. As the show ended she thanked us enthusiastically and we received another round of applause. As the audience was leaving, an older woman leading a boy of about seventeen came up to me. The woman asked me if it would be OK with me if the boy could feel the Alpine Horn to learn how long it was by touch. What was startling was that the boy's pale blue eyes were very large, very wide open and totally blind. The woman guided his hand down to the end of the twelve-foot-three-inch horn. As he slowly and carefully moved his hand up the ridged surface, a grin formed on his face. By the time he reached the mouthpiece at the other end he was smiling broadly. The woman then said that she had never seen him enjoy anything as much as he had enjoyed our show.

As we packed our instruments away I thanked Diane for the inspiration she gave me with her joyful, positive attitude. I'm certain we will never forget her or our hour at Marvin Picollo.

Name Dropping

When I look back on my life I find it hard to believe that I have come in contact with so many very famous people one way or another, either by seeing them in person, shaking hands with them, meeting them, or in a few cases, working closely with them. I was neither famous nor wealthy, just an ordinary person who was in certain special places at opportune times. What follows is a list of those famous names and a description of how our paths crossed or in more cynical language "shameless, blatant name dropping."

ACTORS

Gregory and Charlton

Many of the famous people that I saw up close and sometimes in a personal way came about as a result of my profession as an arts administrator. At the first national convention that I attended with my wife, Sally, I recall saying to her at the banquet, "If you turn around slowly, you'll see that Charlton Heston and Gregory Peck are sitting at the table behind us!" Incidentally, I was surprised to see that Gregory Peck was a lot taller than Heston. And as far as I am concerned, as a human being he always stood taller than Heston, the notorious apologist for the National Rifle Association. Sally and I were both thrilled by that encounter.

Otto

Especially memorable was a regional arts council meeting where the publicity announced that the famous actor/director Otto Preminger was to be the main speaker. Preminger was the distinguished director of forty films including classics like "The Man with the Golden Arm" and "Laura." At the banquet the person who was introducing Preminger went on endlessly with a long and boring speech of introduction. When he finally turned the mike over forty minutes later to Preminger, he stood up, thanked the introducer, thanked the arts council for the invitation to the meeting, then said in his distinctive Austrian accent "No one told me I was to make a speech, so I am not going to make a speech," and he sat down, and that was that.

Kitty

I was at a reception in New York in connection with the American Council for the Arts in a darkened penthouse room with lots of windows overlooking the twinkling lights of Manhattan. The room had the look of the kind of glamorous setting of a cocktail party in one of those black and white movies of the 1930s.

As I moved about the room I noticed a number of people gathered around an attractive, elegantly dressed dark haired woman who I quickly recognized as the legendary Kitty Carlisle Hart. Taking

advantage of a moment when she wasn't otherwise occupied I walked up to her and introduced myself and we chatted for a few moments.

I must confess that meeting her was extremely exciting. She was one of a small number of people whom I've met in my life who I could really call charismatic. Here was a person who had spent a lifetime in the spotlight as a singer and actress on Broadway and in Hollywood. She had been the female lead in *A Night at the Opera* with the Marx Brothers. She starred on *To Tell The Truth?* in the early days of TV and for many years served with distinction as the chairperson of the New York State Council on the Arts. The Hart part of her name was because she was married to the famous playwright Moss Hart, who with George S. Kaufman wrote the popular plays *You Can't Take it With You* and *The Man Who Came To Dinner*.

Miss Hart, born in 1910, incredibly, appeared at the Plush Room of the York Hotel in San Francisco at age ninety!

POLITICIANS

Franklin

The first one was President Franklin Delano Roosevelt, a man who almost had God status to our family. He had come to Cleveland in the 1936, probably on the campaign trail. I was eight years old. FDR's motorcade drove down Euclid Avenue on the way to Cleveland's public square. I saw him pass below from of one of the second floor windows of the Andre-Schwartz-Singer Company. My uncle Harry was the Singer. It was a thrill to see the great man at the time and it still thrills me to think of it.

Hubert

The next national figure was vice president Hubert Horatio Humphrey. He was on the campaign trail in Akron, Ohio in 1964. As he walked down Market Street with his caravan and Secret Service agents he moved out to the barriers where we were standing. I put my hand out and he shook it.

Dick

Then came Richard Nixon, who next to George W. was my least favorite president. I was at a national convention of the American Council for the Arts at the Mayflower Hotel in D.C. (see the story Chutzpah!) He was a surprise guest speaker and following his speech he invited all the attendees of the convention to a reception at the White House the next day. While there, I shook first lady Pat Nixon's hand in the reception line.

CLASSICAL MUSICIANS

Leopold

There are many musicians on my list. I'll start with famed conductor Leopold Stokowski. I was attending the Midwest Band and Orchestra Clinic in Chicago and decided to skip that evening's program so I could hear the great Chicago Symphony. The guest conductor was to be Leopold Stokowski of "Fantasia" fame. The lights came down at Chicago Symphony Hall and we held our breath in anticipation of the entrance of the great maestro.

He entered the stage walking very slowly, a bent over, frail old man. It appeared that he was almost too weak to make it to the front of the stage, but he did, and then slowly climbed the podium. He held on to the brass rail, as if to steady himself, as he bowed to the thunderous applause and started to turn slowly toward the orchestra. When he was half turned around he suddenly went into "high gear." He threw his right hand out giving a forceful and energetic downbeat and off the orchestra went on the speedy and brilliant overture to the "Bartered Bride" of Smetana. It was as if the music was a flash of lightning that had instantly charged the man's battery. His conducting was fast, crisp and, as always, supremely expressive. He continued through the rest of the challenging program in the same mode. And then when it ended and the music had stopped, he bowed slowly, almost painfully and turned back into the frail old man as he made his way into the wings.

George

In the story "Trombone" in the section called *The Western University Band*, I confessed how I found a "secret passage" from a room in Severance Hall, the home of the Cleveland Orchestra. At the time I was working as a librarian for the Western Reserve University band that rehearsed in a room on the third floor. The passage led to the upper balcony where I hid and observed George Szell rehearse his ensemble to perfection for many hours. The Hungarian born, Austrian raised Szell conducted the orchestra for twenty-four years, raising it to world-class status.

Beverly

Speaking of Beverly Sills reminds me that I saw her perform with the Cleveland Orchestra at several of their pops concerts many years before she became an "overnight success" at the Metropolitan Opera in New York. She was beautiful, glamorous, sexy, and a sensational singer who was a favorite of pops conductor Louis Lane. Lane was also the conductor of the Akron Symphony when I was their manager.

Eugene

During my year as manager of the Akron Symphony I once received an invitation to a concert by the Philadelphia Orchestra, sponsored by nearby Kent State University. I was also invited to attend a reception for Eugene Ormandy following the concert. I introduced myself to the maestro and then went about socializing. At one point in the evening, Ormandy was surrounded by several admirers, had enjoyed a few drinks and became expansive in talking about various musicians. Someone in the group asked him about Beverly Sills, the reigning coloratura soprano of that time. Ormandy, with a broad smile on his face, disdainfully declared, "Miss Sills is a lovely and talented singer. But she will never again appear with the Philadelphia Orchestra because she broke a contract with me to go and sing in an opera."

Leonard

During that same year I was invited to a concert by the Youngstown Symphony. Their soloist that evening was the superb cellist, Leonard Rose. I was invited back stage after the concert to meet Rose, one of my musical heroes. He was a warm and gracious man. One of my favorite records was of Rose performing the Schumann Cello Concerto.

Luciano

One of my treasured possessions is a record album of Luciano Pavarotti's music signed by him to "Bill and Sally." However, we did not actually meet him. We only heard him with the San Francisco Symphony along with thousands of others at the Golden Gate Park Band Shell. The album was a gift from my real estate agent, Bob Cahen. For the past forty years, he has photographed his friend Luciano and many other opera stars.

Placido

The other great tenor of our time was and still is Placido Domingo. It was our privilege to enjoy his splendid performance in The Tales of Hoffmann at the San Francisco Opera several years ago.

Maria

In the early 1970s my son, David, who was later to study with Met Opera singer, Blanche Thebom, asked if I would like to join him when he went to hear the legendary diva Maria Callas and the great tenor Giuseppe DeStefano in their "Farewell" concert tour. The evening was memorable on many counts. Though the voices were no longer at their prime, the musicianship, the drama and the emotion were superb and there was a real "love fest" with the opera-wise San Francisco audience.

Marilyn

In the story *Yellow Cadillac Convertible*, I described how Marilyn Horne, one of the greatest mezzo-sopranos of the 20th century, happened to be the first famous artist that I worked with as manager of the Akron Symphony. That was in 1968 and she was not well known as yet by the general public. Two years later she created a sensation with her Metropolitan Opera debut in "Carmen" which was conducted by Leonard Bernstein. She was a delight to work with—friendly, warm, with a great sense of humor and a vocal technique that was nothing less than dazzling.

When I lived in Illinois I made a point of it to see her perform in Bellini's opera "Norma" in which she sang a famous duet with Dame Joan Sutherland.

Frederica

Every year for the past fifteen years I have performed in a brass quartet for Christmas and Easter services at Saint Joseph's Basilica in Alameda. I was told that the great soprano Frederica Van Stade lives in Alameda, and is a member of that Catholic church, and that from time to time actually comes in and performs there. It is highly unusual for internationally famous artists of her stature to do such a thing and I don't think I believed such a gesture was possible. About five years ago I was proven wrong. Not only did she sing beautifully during the service, but she brought along a wonderful young tenor who was a protégé of hers and also sang. After the service she graciously came up into the choir loft to meet the members of the quartet and to tell us how much she enjoyed our performance.

Isaac

The first time a saw Isaac Stern was when I was going to college. He had just gotten on the bus in front of Severance Hall, the home of the Cleveland Orchestra. He was about thirty years old and already world famous. Of course, he was in Cleveland to appear with the orchestra. Stern, who was born in 1920, had an amazing sixty-year career during which he recorded a great deal of music, discovered such artists as Izhak Perlman, Yo Yo Ma and Pinchas Zukerman and almost single-handedly saved Carnegie Hall from the wrecker's ball. He was one of the most gifted and beloved artists of the 20th century.

Victor

I've included a fairly long story about a weekend when I was manager of the Quincy Symphony and we had Victor Borge as our guest soloist. I chauffeured Borge around town, arranged his schedule and got to spend several hours with the great pianist/humorist. The story explains that Borge was at first very irritable and difficult to work with because, as we found out, he had contracted a case of food poisoning at the beginning of his tour and simply wasn't feeling well. I was proud to report that the Quincy people were such good hosts that he made a quick recovery, performed beautifully and left town feeling great.

JAZZ MUSICIANS

Louis

More of this story is in the section called "Accompanying a Jazz Great" in the story "Trombone." I was playing with Buddy Murray's Orchestra, a local big band in Cleveland in 1950 for the homecoming dance at Western Reserve University. The dance organizer announced that there would be a famous guest artist appearance at midnight. A few minutes after midnight, in walked the world's most famous jazz musician, Louis "Satchmo" Armstrong. He came up to the bandstand, turned to us and in his famous gravelly voice asked, "Can you cats play Basin Street Blues?"

We obliged. He sang and we all had a memory that would last a lifetime.

Oscar

One of my favorite jazz pianists was the incredibly talented Oscar Peterson, one of the true giants of jazz. My wife Sally and I were staying at the Barbizon Plaza Hotel in New York and noted that Peterson was appearing nearby at the famous Plaza Hotel right off Central Park. Peterson is a very large black man with huge hands that seem to be all over the keyboard at once. We had an extra bonus that evening on top of our enjoyment of the music. The great Carmen McCrae, a terrific singer with a unique sound was in the audience a table or two away. She was there to catch Peterson's act and was obviously enjoying it immensely.

Coleman

It was Christmas Eve in New York. Sally and I had flown to the "Big Apple" with my cousin Don and his wife Ruth to see some Broadway shows and visit the great museums. We had no plans for that evening. The Times had a notice about an all-star jazz jam session that would be taking place at some hall later that evening. The place was in an out-of-the-way location on the second floor of an old building. As we entered the lobby we were surprised that hardly anyone was around. It was a cold and snowy night.

We found the check room for our coats and that's when I spotted him.

It was the legendary tenor sax man, Coleman Hawkins. His recording of "Body and Soul" and other great jazz standards influenced a whole generation of tenor sax jazz improvisers. He'd performed with Fletcher Henderson's band, with Louis Armstrong and all the greats of that period. And here he was on a frosty night in New York, about to perform in an obscure hall with an audience of no more than a couple dozen people.

We talked a bit and he said, "I feel sorry for the guy who put this together. He's gonna lose his shirt tonight, that is, if we get paid."

I asked him if he thought they might call it off since there wasn't much of an audience. He replied, "No chance! We got together some great horns tonight. Wait till you hear these cats blow!" And blow they did. I heard some of the greatest jazz of my life that evening.

Benny

I saw Benny Goodman, "The King of Swing," sometime in the 1960s in an appearance he made with what was probably his last tour with a band. He was in his late '60s and still the master of the clarinet. The band did his regular stuff like his theme song, *Let's Dance*, *Don't Be That Way*, *Honeysuckle Rose* and, of course, the piece that put his greatest band on the map when he performed *Sing, Sing, Sing* at Carnegie Hall in 1938 with Gene Krupa on drums and Harry James on trumpet. Goodman was, as usual, very laid back in his manner, almost sounding as if he was bored, but the band was great and so was his playing. Men who played with him over the years well remember the famous "Goodman stare," a frightening look that he would level on a player who wasn't up to his high standards.

In addition to his musicianship, which was superb in both jazz and classical music, I will always honor his pioneering work in breaking the color line when he refused to take engagements at places where they wouldn't allow black musicians—notably, the members of his quartet, Teddy Wilson, pianist and Lionel Hampton, vibraphone.

COMEDIANS

Henny

Sally and I had gotten tickets to the Mike Douglas Show which was broadcast from downtown Cleveland during the '50s. On that day, the special guest was the "king of the one liners," Henny Youngman. Henny was a very large man with a very pleasant smile who looked like he was always having as much fun as his audiences. He told some of his famous jokes then came over to the first row where we were seated and patted Sally's head. I don't remember what he said at the time, but it was very funny, of that I'm certain.

Here are a few of his classic one liners:

A man goes to a psychiatrist. The doctor says, "You're crazy."

The man says, "I want a second opinion!"

"Okay, you're ugly too!"

A doctor gave a man six months to live. The man couldn't pay his bill, so he gave him another six months.

Doctor says, "You'll live to be sixty!"

"I am sixty!"

"See, what did I tell you?"

Totie

Sometime in the '60s, I was booked to play in a band that was opening and backing up a show featuring plump comedienne, Totie Fields. Totie, who had appeared on the Ed Sullivan show forty times, was famous for her self-deprecating humor. One of her famous lines was "I've been on a diet for two weeks and all I've lost is fourteen days."

Totie was a lot of fun to work with and it was a very enjoyable experience. The show room was at a new hotel called the "Yankee Clipper." It was located on the main highway between Cleveland and Akron but actually not close to either

TOTIE FIELDS

Totie Field's autograph
Bill, Thanks for a great job. Totie Fields

one and essentially out in the country. One night Totie was complaining about this place "in the middle of nowhere, where you can't even get a bagel!" The next day I went to Lou and Hy's Deli in Akron and bought a bag of bagels for her, proudly presenting them to her in the hotel restaurant prior to the show. She looked them over and disdainfully said, "You call these bagels? I want some water bagels, the kind that become as hard as cement if you don't eat them in two days!"

Totie had a great but short career because of health problems. Her left leg was amputated when surgery failed to remove a blood clot. To the astonishment of her fans, soon afterward she starred in an HBO special, seated in a wheel chair. She died of a heart attack in 1978 at the age of forty-eight.

LOCAL CELEBRITIES

Sally

Shortly after I arrived in California to begin my job as executive director of the San Mateo County Arts Council, I began to make contacts with the other arts council directors in the bay area. One of the first people I met was Sheila Considine, director of the Sausalito Arts Center and the organizer of the Annual Sausalito Arts Festival which has become a huge bay area event in recent years. Sheila was a colorful local character. She was single then, but had been married to the son of the well-known sports commentator, Bob Considine. She seemed to know everyone in town.

She invited me to come to Sausalito to see the impressive arts center that she had set up in an old school building. Afterwards we went to dinner at Sally Stanford's famous Valhalla Restaurant in the old house with the red light in the window. The restaurant was situated on the water with a spectacular view of San Francisco. The legendary former madam, who would, four years later at the age of seventy-two become mayor of Sausalito, greeted Sheila warmly as we entered. She was, as usual, seated in her large old fashioned barber shop chair at the end of the bar. Sheila introduced me to Sally who instructed the waiter to give us a great table at the window where we enjoyed the incomparable view, the excellent food and a fine bottle of wine. As we finished, the waiter retrieved our bill and said, "Compliments of Miss Stanford."

I had many exciting new experiences when I first arrived in the bay area, but being treated to a gourmet dinner by a famous bordello madam was going to be very hard to top!

Herb

Somewhere around 1995 Barbara and I were at Davies Symphony Hall to see a concert by the San Francisco Symphony. During the intermission I went to the men's restroom on the street level floor. While at the urinal I couldn't help but notice that one of San Francisco's most famous people was occupying the stall next to me. It was the always dapper Chronicle writer Herb Caen. When I returned to my seat I turned to Barbara and said, "Guess who I've been hanging out with?"

Louise

Speaking of Davies Symphony Hall reminds me that when I was director of the San Mateo County Arts Council, one of our board members managed to get Louise K. Davies to join our board of directors. The hall was named for her because of her generous contributions. She attended two of our meetings, fell asleep during the second meeting, and we never saw her again.

Francis

Article first published in "Advance," newsletter of the Association of Concert Bands

When we learned that the Saint Helena Community Band would be a participant in the Golden Gate Park Band Festival, I saw the possibility of a unique way to promote the 2010 Festival if we could get the famous director of "The Godfather" epic and many other films, Francis Ford Coppola, to agree to do a radio interview.

A story about Coppola appeared in the press in 2007 that caught my attention. It told how F.F. Coppola had played the tuba in his high school band and was a member of a very musical family. As a young and up-coming maker of movies he once told the fabled dancer Fred Astaire about how he loved to play the tuba in his school band. He related that he had to play a beat up dented old school instrument that was so bad that one time some of the students had made a fire in it! He had always dreamt of someday owning his own instrument. Astaire was so impressed by his enthusiasm for the instrument that when the movie they were working on ended, Coppola found the gift of a shiny new top-of-the-line Miraphone tuba in his office.

For many years Coppola was too busy working on his movies and later on his wineries to be able to play in a band. When he finally had time to devote to it he decided that since there was no community band in Saint Helena, California, the site of his family home, he would have to start one.

The conductor selected was a man named Michael Mendelson and in a short time the band was a reality, with Coppola happily joining the tuba section when his still hectic schedule allowed it. After only being organized for three years the band had attracted many fine musicians in the area and was selected to participate in the "Let's Do It Again in 2010" Golden Gate Park Band Festival. One of the selections performed by the band was the Saint Helena Community Band March composed by Carmine Coppola, Francis' father.

I had been in contact with conductor Mendelson since the band began, so when I learned that his band would be in this year's Festival I asked him to contact Coppola to find out if he would be willing to help us promote the Festival with a radio interview. We exchanged a few emails and just when I had my doubts about any kind of response, I was shocked one morning when I picked up the phone. Francis Ford Coppola was on line. I explained that the Festival was very popular with the bands and the audiences, but that we needed help to get the size audience that the event deserved. He was very sympathetic and offered to help. In fact, he was warm, friendly and easy to talk to.

After the call I reflected on the fact that I had just had a conversation with the man who directed Marlon Brando, Al Pacino, Robert Duvall and a host of other famous actors. Coppola put me in touch with his assistant and we linked her up with station KGO, the ABC affiliate in San Francisco. They arranged for a ten minute radio interview on the Tuesday morning before the event which covered several subjects including a great boost for the Golden Gate Park Band Festival.

Coppola himself was not able to participate, but the Saint Helena Community Band, the newest and smallest to appear at the Festival gave an admirable performance.

An Homage to School Band Directors

Article first published in "Advance," newsletter of the Association of Concert Bands.

A few years ago I received an invitation to attend my 50th High School Class reunion. It would involve a trip across the country at substantial expense and would be time consuming at a busy time for me. I thought about it for a while but hadn't made up my mind. About three weeks before the event, I was contacted by one of the organizers. She urged me to come and then said, "I know you were in the school band. You'll be interested to know that Joe Lanese, your band director, is planning on coming."

That was the clincher. I knew I had to go. It brought back a flood of happy memories, the strongest one being my affection and respect for the person who inspired me to pursue and enjoy music for a lifetime. I went to that reunion and spent several precious moments reliving those happy memories with Joe—in his eighties and still enjoying life with his wife of over sixty years.

Reunion with Joe Lanese
Bill front row left, Joe is next to him.
The rest are all former Glenville band and orchestra members.

Any musician who has continued to play and enjoy his or her band experience into adulthood will remember the school band directors who taught, motivated and inspired them. Each of ours is a unique personal story that began in an elementary, middle or high school, in a tiny rural village or in a big city. The teacher might have been fresh out of college or a thirty-year veteran. Surprisingly, the quality of the band that first ignited the flame might have been anywhere from superb to very mediocre.

Exactly what occurs that turns certain students on to a life-long love of the experience of playing in a band is a mystery. Some persons may first be attracted by the fascinating array of beautiful instruments and others by the power of the music itself. Some are seeking a group in which they can feel a special intimate bond with their fellow musicians, but nearly everyone will tell you that the greatest influence came from their school band director.

Stop and think about what it takes to be a successful school band director:

- a working knowledge of all the instruments, often even including how to make on-the-spot repairs
- familiarity with both the standard literature and the latest compositions
- skill in directing concert and marching bands, orchestras and jazz ensembles
- ability to control large groups of hyper students, all of whom are holding powerful noise makers in their hands
- in many schools they must be able to train their students in the intricacies of the marching band (half-time shows or street parades or often both!)
- be excellent communicators with their students, the school staff, parents and their community
- know how to raise money and how to handle it
- they must have skill on the computer with graphics, music writing programs, marching band maneuver charting, instrument inventories, music libraries and many other areas.

In addition, many band directors are also fine instrumentalists who somehow also find time to play with or conduct local amateur and professional groups and maintain a schedule of private students. All in all a daunting job description!

Let's take some time to reflect on how our school band directors influenced our lives and gave us the priceless gift of the love of playing music. If your band director is still around, send a letter or an email or phone him or her and let them know that you are still playing and enjoying making music and thank them for their gift to you.

My band and orchestra director, Joe Lanese, taught at Glenville High School and West Tech High School and other schools in Cleveland in the '40s and '50s and later served as Supervisor of Instrumental Music for the Cleveland Public Schools.

As a postscript I decided to take my own advice and tried to locate Joe Lanese again. He wasn't to be found anywhere in the Cleveland area and I expected the worst. Then I called an old colleague who promised to do some digging for info about Joe. The next day I had the news. Joe is now ninety, in good health, and had moved with his wife to the warmer climate of Columbia, South Carolina. He lived to be ninety-four.

I found his phone number on the internet and phoned him. We had a wonderful conversation with reminiscences of old times and caught up on whatever information we had of former classmates. He told me how much he appreciated hearing from me and definitely *made my day!*

How I Became "The Hornman"

Sometimes when I start unloading my car and getting ready for a performance, I ask myself, "What in the world possessed me to put this crazy thing together?"

Then, when I start the show and see the looks of surprise and delight on the faces of my audience, I am filled with that feeling of wonder that only performers can really understand—that special connection with the audience where they seem to be saying, "We're glad you are here. You have brought us something wonderful!"

For several years I have been performing a unique show. I call it "The Hornman." In it I perform on fifteen different horns from around the world. If you've read this book up to here, you know that I have played the trombone since I was twelve. So where and how the other fourteen horns came about is the subject of this story.

The Trombone and the Baritone

I had been playing the trombone for six years when I entered Western Reserve University as a music education major. The university band had a strong trombone section and a weak baritone horn section. I knew that the instruments were similar so I asked if I could check out a school owned instrument. I pretty much taught myself how to play it in a couple of weeks. That makes it sound like I'm some kind of genius, but it really is one of the easiest instrument switches. The parts are both in the bass clef, the mouthpiece is virtually the same as a trombone's and each fingering corresponds to a particular slide position.

Trombone

That switch was key to many of the other ones I was to do in the future because I began to develop some dexterity in my fingering technique.

The Trumpet and the Bugle

The next thing I added was the trumpet. During most of the fall of 1952 I was teaching beginning trumpet students at the Higbee Department Store Music Center on Cleveland's Public Square. After a few weeks I reasoned that if I played along with my beginning students I might be able to develop myself into a combination trombone/trumpet player in time. There were student trumpets available for me to use. After a year or so I bought a professional trumpet of my own. By 1955 I was playing both trumpet and trombone with the Chic Tesmer Band in Peninsula, Ohio. I already owned an old bugle (which uses a trumpet mouthpiece) that would later be used in the show.

The Shofars from Israel

My next acquisition was the shofar, the ritual horn used mainly during the Jewish High Holidays. That occurred several years later when we had moved to California. On a trip to Jerusalem with my wife, Sally, I picked out a fine Yemenite shofar which was to be presented to Temple Beth El by the confirmation class. Around that same time, Cantor Epstein, who had sounded the shofar in

Bill playing the shofar
for Rosh Hashanah services

the past, had retired. The temple was in need of someone new to do that job at Rosh Hashanah services and I was ready. Several years later, on another trip to Israel, I bought my own fine shofar and put it in the show.

The Conch Shell from Florida

During the 1990s Barbara and I were traveling the country in our RV. On a trip through Florida we stopped at the "Sea Shell Factory" in Fort Myers where I selected an excellent conch shell that was prepared as a horn by having one of the points cut off in exactly the right place. The mouth positions I had developed playing several other horns made it relatively easy for me to play the conch shell. I also began to develop a story to tell about a mythical conch shell on a mythical island. That's around the time I started to think I could add two or three more horns and put together a show of some kind.

The Alp Horns: Lake Louise and Pottstown, Pennsylvania

On another RV trip, this time to Canada, we stopped at the incredibly beautiful Lake Louise in Alberta. When we opened our RV door we heard what sounded like a giant French horn playing a song that floated beautifully over the nearby mountains. We investigated and found a lederhosen-costumed musician playing a huge Alp Horn at the rear entrance to the Chateau where the tourists arrived. As they got off their busses, the delighted and surprised travelers dropped money into the bell of the 12 foot horn. I spoke to the musician and learned a little about the Alp Horn, soon becoming convinced that if I had such a horn I could learn to play it. Not only that, but if I had such a horn it would be the clincher in making my Hornman show

The Alp Horn

idea a winner.

Barbara said to me in that special way that made me know she meant business, "We've got to get one of those for you!"

For the next two or three years we thought about the Alp Horn and did some investigation, but the price for such an instrument imported from Europe was prohibitive. Then on another RV trip, on the recommendation of my son Mark, we stopped in Pottstown, Pennsylvania to visit the "Trumpet Museum." I spoke to the director of the museum and he let me try to play one of their Alp Horns. He then told me where I could find out about some new American made fiberglass Alp Horns that were less expensive than the traditional European wooden ones. I phoned the distributor, Morris Secon, a French horn player in the Rochester Philharmonic Orchestra and he arranged to have an Alp Horn drop-shipped to my niece's home in Richmond, Virginia, our next scheduled stop. I was very pleased with the instrument, but struggled mightily for the next two years to try to play it well enough so I could perform on it competently. I finally mastered it and it did indeed become the clincher in making my show a success.

The Tuba in San Francisco

I borrowed a baritone, tuba and French horn from John Muir Middle School in San Leandro, California where I formerly taught. Then I began rigorous practice on those instruments. But I wanted my own horns—ones that played well enough and looked better than the dented older school instruments. Barbara, who possesses enormous tenacity, continuously scanned the newspapers for ads about tubas, French horns and baritones. That was happening in the pre

Tuba

E-Bay and Craiglist days. Finally, after many months, she spotted an ad for a tuba on sale in San Francisco. It turned out to be a Chinese made tuba I had never heard of, but tubas can run into many thousands of dollars, new or used. I paid less than a thousand dollars for it and it has served me well for almost 20 years.

A French Horn in Naples Florida

We had taken our show to Naples, Florida to do school concerts and also performed with the outstanding Naples Concert Band for an audience of 6,000. I was still using that old school French horn. I tried a new resource and called some local pawn shops. One, to my surprise, said they had one but didn't know who had made it. I should mention here that most musicians are very aware of what companies make the best and worst instruments. When I arrived at the pawn shop, I was delighted to discover the name "H.N. White Company" etched into the bell but barely readable because of the number of coats of lacquer that had been applied over it. It was a fine old King instrument, made in my hometown of Cleveland. We negotiated a reasonable price and had one more horn.

An Unusual Euphonium in Las Vegas

On our way home from Naples, we camped at "Circus, Circus" in Las Vegas. I reasoned that Vegas was a place where there would certainly be a lot of well-stocked pawn shops for obvious reasons. I began calling them to see if anyone had a baritone horn or a euphonium for sale. After calling 20 or so, most of whom had no idea what I was talking about, I gave up on that source. Then it occurred to me that the musicians union might be worth checking out. Sure enough, a member wanted to sell his euphonium. When I phoned the contact person he gave me this sad story: *"A friend of mine came here with his band from Germany to play some concerts. But while he was here he lost all his money in the casinos. I bought his euphonium so he*

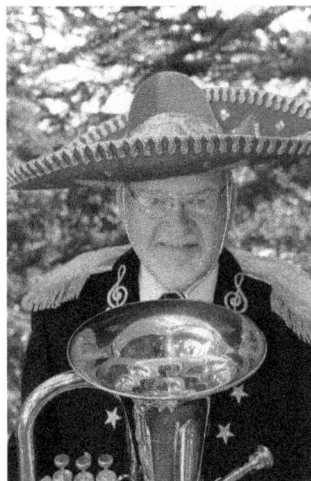
Euphonium with Sombrero!

would have money for a ticket back home and I don't play the euphonium. That's why I'm selling it." The horn turned out to be an Amati four rotary valve European oval style euphonium made in the Czech Republic. It is an unusual horn that has added a special panache to my collection.

The Dijeridu in Australia

In 1993 we visited Barbara's son and his family, who lived in Canberra, Australia then. I took my trombone along and got to play with the City of Canberra Concert Band. On a side trip we took to Sydney, I had a chance to hear some players of the Australian Aborigine's native instrument, the dijeridu, perform on that most primitive of horns. I knew I must include one in my show and bought a dijeridu that is nicely decorated but was also short enough to fit in our suitcase.

"Lark in the Morning", the Ran Dung and the Herald Trumpet

San Francisco had a wonderful store in the Cannery building near Fisherman's Wharf called "Lark in the Morning." They sold an amazing variety of musical instruments from around the world. It was there that I first saw and then purchased a small Ran Dung, a Tibetan horn. Ran Dungs come in many sizes and they actually telescope to three times their original length. They are "drone" instruments that can't play melodies, but the Ran Dung made a great addition to the show. It's especially popular with kids as it makes a loud fart-like noise! Then a few years later while

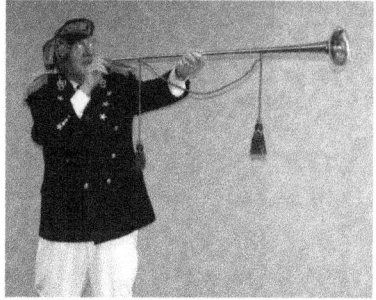

Herald Trumpet

visiting the small "Lark in the Morning" store in Mendocino, the charming village on the California coast, I spotted a handsome lacquered brass herald trumpet which claimed another spot in the show.

The Red Pocket Trumpet

My close friend and fellow musician, Sally Johnson of Concord, California owned a cute little red pocket trumpet that had been made in China. I was admiring it one evening at a brass quintet rehearsal when Sally surprised me by giving it to me as a gift. Audiences are always surprised and delighted when they see and hear it.

Hose-a-Phone

Anyone can make a Hose-a-phone, but actually playing it is a lot harder. It is made with about 12 feet of garden hose and a plastic funnel duct taped on at one end. The key component though, is a mouthpiece installed at the other end. I made my own Hose-a-phone and taught myself to play "The Farmer in the Dell" and "A Hunting We Will Go." It has served as the humorous ending to my shows almost from the very first one.

Hose-a-phone fun
Barb looking on

A Horn from the Sea

My 15th horn was also a gift. It was a "Kelp Horn" given to me by our friends Joe and Marcia Grossman for my 80th birthday. The kelp horn is made of a section of dried kelp, commonly called sea weed. It can play three notes and demonstrates how it's possible to make horns from natural materials.

The Hornman "Look"

Barbara is mostly responsible for the way the show looks. She designed, painted and sewed the banner/ table cloth we use at all of our programs. She also decorated my jacket with gold braid and epaulets. We bought my beautiful blue and

Barbara's handmade Hornman table banner

gold sombrero in Juarez, Mexico and other hats and a mask in various places. The program at the very beginning was a recital of some popular classical music, but it evolved over time into a complete entertainment with humor, audience participation, a "sing-a-long" and surprises.

Performances

We have performed the "Hornman" show hundreds of times in libraries, schools, retirement homes, veterans hospitals, in museums, campgrounds, in schools for the blind and for the developmentally disabled. I also wrote arrangements making it possible to perform with concert bands and symphony

The Hornman with the Castro Valley Orchestra

orchestras. The performances were in the San Francisco Bay Area, Northern California, Monterey County, Reno, Nevada, Scottsdale and Phoenix, Arizona, Naples, Florida and in Peninsula, Ohio.

The Horn*men*

These days as I am writing this story, because of a great deal of necessary dental work, I have temporarily lost some of my playing skills. I am determined to get them back in time, but for now I have been very fortunate to have my son Mark share the program with me and perform on most of the smaller horns. Mark is a superb professional trumpet player and has been the principal

Bill and Mark opening the show
at the San Jose Children's Discovery Museum

trumpet player in San Francisco's world famous Golden Gate Park for several years. So, we are now "The Horn*men*."

What We Don't Want to Talk About

For folks my age there is a very big elephant in the room that we don't want to talk about. But consciously or unconsciously we're always aware that it is there. Sometimes the elephant shrinks and becomes silent. Sometimes he expands enormously and trumpets loudly.

It's actually a matter of good genes, decent living, luck and simple arithmetic. In the beginning, each of us was given just so many years and now we're running out of them. The tricky part that seems to keep the elephant in check is that we don't know exactly when the last number will appear.

Let's lay it out plainly in plain language. It's not about "passing away," "coming to the end of our days," or "checking out." It's about dying—pure and certainly not so simple.

I picture the pattern of life as if it were a sturdy fabric, a heavy duty canvas. In the beginning, and for many years, it is strong and stable and durable. But time, the sun, and the cold gradually take their toll. You or someone close to you becomes seriously ill and the fabric starts to weaken. There is a death in the family and now there is a hole in the fabric. Time passes, the fabric weakens, there are more deaths, and more holes in the cloth.

We've been on this incredible journey called life for a long time now and find it hard to accept the idea that someday the world will go on without us. How do we have the courage to face the end of the journey? My upbringing has taught me not to expect to die and go to heaven if I'm good or to hell if I'm bad. Somehow I'm relieved about that. Although I've done pretty well by the "Commandments," I'm not carrying a 4.0 average.

No, I believe that when it's over, it's over, finished, completely completed—no heaven, no greetings at the "pearly gates" from the Angel Gabriel, no leering, pitchfork wielding Lucifer at the smoky, flaming fire pit.

But that doesn't mean that I think there is no way to achieve some kind of life after death. Judaism teaches that after we die we live on in the hearts and minds of those whose lives we touched. If we were kind, considerate, loving and a positive influence on their lives, they will always remember us that way. If we were mean, selfish, destructive and inconsiderate and a negative influence on others, we will be thought of in that way, and most likely, very soon be forgotten.

Such a way of viewing death can direct us to live richer fuller lives right now rather than directing us to focus on an afterlife, an afterlife that I personally believe does not exist. I realize that belief in an afterlife is a great comfort to most people and I certainly respect and understand the need for that belief. But while belief in an afterlife can be totally benign, it can also be extremely dangerous and harmful. Daily we see examples of people with bleak lives here on earth who become convinced by those who are filled with hate that they will be rewarded in the afterlife through their martyrdom. Most pathetic and tragic are the wasted lives of suicide bombers who destroy indiscriminately with the motivation that their reward is a place in paradise. How tragic and deluded!

Teachers and artists of all kinds have been able to achieve a special kind of immortality. If you are a teacher, you have no idea how far your influence reaches. It can impact generations to come in wonderful ways. Creative artists such as composers, writers and visual artists have given us works that have lived for centuries, and in so doing, they live on. And within the past century the audio and visual recordings of performance artists have afforded them immortality as well.

One of the most troubling things to think about is exactly how the end will come. Will it be long, drawn out and painful or will we merely grow weaker and die peacefully in our sleep? Personally I'm hoping my body will simply wear out and that my mind will be able to accept that fact.

I recently took stock of those who have touched my life and realized how much death I have had to confront over the years. It's probably fairly typical for a person eight-four years old. My grandparents died over fifty-five years ago and my parents, thirty-five years ago. My first wife died over twenty-five years ago and my step-brother who was ten years younger than I, ten years ago. At one time I had twenty first cousins and now I have ten. The last of my seven aunts died seven years ago at ninety-three. My seven uncles have been gone for many years.

While in Junior and Senior High School, I belonged to a club we called the "Zephyrs." Eugene, Herbie, Stan, Larry, Marv, Ernie and Art are gone. I've lost track of Bernie, but Eddy, and I carry on. Countless other friends, lovers, former colleagues and even many of my former students are gone as well.

My sheet of canvas in the pattern of life is now old, sun bleached, threadbare and riddled with gaping holes. It flaps limply in the breeze, but somehow it still holds together. It is held together by my family, my friends and my hopes for the future. So, for now, even though I know it cannot be, I go on wishing to live long enough to see how it will all come out.

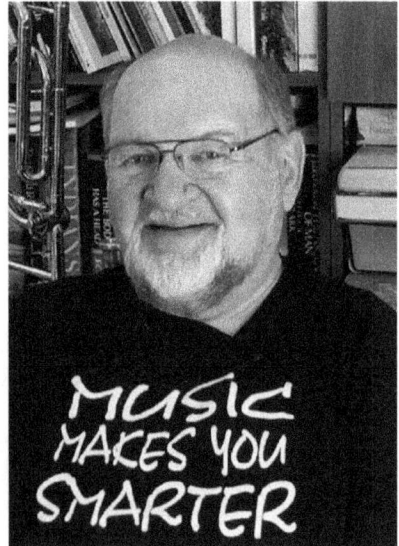

Bill in 2012

Taking Stock

On November 23, 2008, my children put on a great eightieth Birthday Party for me, so I must actually be eighty years old. I know I was born in 1928, but part of me, the part that is on the inside and getting further inside every year, is some place in my childhood, or my thirties or forties. But the part the world sees and that looks back at me in my mirror tells me a different story.

I'm taking stock to see where I am so I can reconcile the differences. Do I really own the baggage of an eighty-year-old man? I'll break it down into different categories and see what I discover. There is health, there is my physical appearance, my mental attitude and there are my activities.

The biggie is health. The first sixty or so years were pretty good. I didn't break any bones and only had a couple of minor surgeries. But then about fifteen years ago I had to deal with cellulitis. Following that by a few years, I developed an overly enthusiastic prostate thing and had a trans-urethral resection, also popularly known as a roto-rooter job—great fun! Next on the docket was cataract surgery in both eyes—no big deal. In 2004 I had a triple coronary bypass and replacement of my aortic heart valve with the valve of a cow. Heavy duty stuff! In 2007 they replaced my bum left knee.

During my lifetime I've had lots of X-Rays, a myelogram, several electro-cardiograms, some echograms and some CAT scans and other grams and scans I can't recall and certainly can't spell. I've had colonoscopies, sigmoidoscopies and countless blood tests and injections. I've also had my left lung drained with a four-inch needle while wide awake and wishing I were somewhere else. Today my heart is working fine and so is my knee. But each time they carved me up, they left another reminder on my body.

I have other reminders of infirmities that take time and energy to deal with each day. There are glasses to clean, batteries to be put into hearing aids and dental plates to deal with. There are the pill containers to fill and the pills to remember to take at the right time; Hytrin, Lovastatin, Lasix, Lisinopril, Aspirin, Iron, Melatonin, Glucosamin, Probiotic, a multi-vitamin and a fish oil capsule. There is also Beano, to deal with—well, beans! Then there is the Dairy Digestive for lactose intolerance, and Gas-ex and heart burn pills.

As to my appearance, I can think of only one positive thing. Today I weigh only about ten pounds more than I did in college days, when I was also overweight. My male pattern baldness began in my forties and by my early sixties I had, in desperation, resorted to a ridiculous "comb-over," finally giving way to my baldness in my seventies Somehow some of my hair is still brown but the gray is in full attack mode while the brown is in full retreat. My face is adorned with well-earned wrinkles on my forehead and around my eyes and my bald pate sports subtle blotches. I also own that puzzling paradox of older men; the hair on my head is gone, but my nose and ear hairs grow with reckless abandon. There is also the loose and flabby neck and arm skin and my limbs are now thinner than they have ever been.

As to my mental attitude, I have been blessed with an optimistic nature. Mostly, my cup is half full and occasionally it "runneth over." While I have tried to learn to live "in the moment," I am also always looking for something to look forward to; playing a concert, going on a trip, starting a new project or completing an old one. I enjoy good food, good conversation and good humor. As far as sex is concerned, there is still a lot going on upstairs, but not much going on downstairs. My memory for things long past often amazes me, but I have to work hard to recall what I had for dinner last night or to attach the right name to a photo of a person whose name came readily to mind a few years ago.

How do I spend my time? I haven't done any running in years and I haven't danced in a long time because I have no one to dance with, but I do walk someplace almost every day. I haven't held a full-time job for nearly sixteen years but lately I have been very busy as a "house-husband," doing things that Barbara can no longer do—washing the clothes and the dishes and preparing meals. Barbara spends a lot of time in bed these days and we stay at home more than we ever have in our lives. But occasionally we do go out to eat and often go to Home Town Buffet where the choices are good, the price is right and at lunch-time there are a lot of gray heads around. When we are up to it, we go to museums, plays and concerts.

We belong to a book and film discussion group and I get together with one group of old men for a walk every Friday morning and another old men's discussion group once a month. My Monday writer's group has become a very important part of my life. I keep closely in touch with our family and friends by phone and email and especially enjoy tracking the lives of our grandchildren. Music is still central in my life. I play in a concert band and an orchestra and do my Hornman Show from time to time. I also serve as chairman of the board of the Friends of the Golden Gate Park Band.

Now that I have taken stock, I'm a little sorry I took on this project. After reading what I have written here I can sense the child and young men in me rapidly retreating into the shadows and making room for that eighty-year-old who is crowding them out. And while all in all, I have a pretty good life, it's much more distressing to have to accept the octogenarian status with its primary message. The time is growing shorter. Make the most of it.

* 9 7 8 0 6 1 5 7 3 1 4 3 8 *